GURGAON

Veena Talwar Oldenburg is a professor of history at Baruch College and The Graduate Center of the City University of New York. She is the author of *Dowry Murder: The Imperial Origins of a Cultural Crime* and *The Making of Colonial Lucknow, 1856-1877*.

Praise for *Gurgaon*

'Gurgaon is a metaphor for the new India, rising maniacally from below through the efforts of its spirited people, almost despite the state. By artfully weaving together legend, history, and delightful stories of contemporary life, this highly readable book has captured Gurgaon's messy contradictions with energy and balance.'
—Gurcharan Das, author of *India Unbound*

'Veena Talwar Oldenburg writes with competence and in detail about the growth of modern Gurugram in its many facets—good and bad, beautiful and ugly. Its successes and failures carry urgent lessons for all of urban India.'
—T.N. Ninan, chairman, *Business Standard*

'*Gurgaon* describes India's third richest city as something beyond "Gurujam", a "concrete hiccup" or a "village on steroids". She gives it a history and thus an identity. She sees it through the eyes of the professional class who drifted south from south Delhi, ancestral property owners in the urbanizing villages bordering Delhi, migrant domestic workers who have hit a gold mine, BPO working women who are less keen on settling down than their male co-workers, and entrepreneurs who have taken wing in India's skies. It is a kaleidoscopic view that includes the exclusive floors of "Mongolia" (Magnolias) overlooking the Arnold Palmer–designed Golf Course, and the almost-clone of Khan Market, "Gil-lehria" (Galleria). I have lived in the Gurgaon she describes for thirty years, and her book helped fill out my own identity.'

—Aditya Sinha, co-author of *The Spy Chronicles* and
Kashmir: The Vajpayee Years

GURGAON

From Mythic Village to Millennium City

VEENA TALWAR OLDENBURG

HarperCollins *Publishers* India

First published in India by
HarperCollins *Publishers* in 2018
A-75, Sector 57, Noida, Uttar Pradesh 201301, India
www.harpercollins.co.in

2 4 6 8 10 9 7 5 3 1

P-ISBN: 978-93-5302-034-7
E-ISBN: 978-93-5302-035-4

Typeset in 11/14 Adobe Caslon Pro at
Manipal Digital Systems, Manipal

Printed and bound at
Thomson Press (India) Ltd.

For the wonderful team at I Am Gurgaon that works untiringly to make Gurgaon a city we shall all be proud of

Contents

Preface

From its obscure origins as a hamlet to its present-day status as India's Millennium City, the story of Gurgaon is a long and eventful one. In 2010, when a station of the Metro line connecting Gurgaon to Delhi was named 'Guru Dronacharya' after the resident sage in the Sanskrit epic Mahabharata, it was a reminder that this city, with its sleek malls, towering residential and corporate high-rises, and its Arnold Palmer–designed golf course, had several hoary incarnations before it became the microcosm of a rapidly urbanizing India.

Gurgaon's transformation covers the entire arc of Indian urbanization and yet, it has been ignored as a subject of history. This book is the first history of Gurgaon and will, it is hoped, become a fixture in every literate Gurgaon household and beyond to relate to adults and children the story of Gurgaon's making. The media notices Gurgaon mostly when an untoward event occurs—like the flooding of its streets after a heavy rainstorm, or the oft-told tale of its poor and unfinished infrastructure. Today one can find information on Gurgaon, piecemeal, in a few scholarly articles, or on the Internet where official and media websites have proliferated, and even Wikipedia has an unedited, patchy entry on the city. This volume goes beyond scattered snapshots of the present that periodically appear in newspapers worldwide, and gives a layered and thematic account that connects this new dot on the global map to the history, economy, society and ecology that produced it. I've traced its forgotten antecedents and tracked the sweep of change that ends in today's startling megalopolis with its hurriedly changing way of life, demographics, civil society, consumerism, architecture, and infrastructure.

Gurgaon's unprecedented growth has left city planners dazed and paralysed, and conflicts and collaborations have emerged between private developers, politicians, bureaucrats and middle-class residents. The lack of water and electricity, unfinished roads and incomplete infrastructure, and its exploding migrant population, all reflect the larger national trend of hard-pressed agricultural labour moving to cities that offer jobs and better living conditions. It many ways, it is modern India's apt metonym and the emerging model for how a partnership of corporations and government authorities might prove dynamic and fruitful.

Gurgaon has defiantly rejected its image as a suburb and is fashioning an urban identity of its own on an ambitious scale. Worldwide media reportage, fiction, films, and more than two dozen blogs share vignettes that dwell on its jarring contrasts—palatial houses of millionaires on leafy streets screen temporary shanty towns; cows meander on freshly painted zebra crossings; open drains, an inadequate sewerage system and ubiquitous litter exist side by side with the well-tended lawns of gated residential towers with round-the-clock power (some of it privately generated) and water supply.

In roughly two decades, its urban sprawl has engulfed some fifty-odd villages as Gurgaon has expanded and real estate prices have soared. The natives—Gujar herdsmen, Jat peasants, and Yadav traders and workers—are now a minority; they resent the flood of poor

Bengali, Bihari and Rajasthani migrants and the wealthy middle-class professionals. Yet, for the city to thrive, it is totally dependent on the services of these very natives and the migrants. These conflicts and convergences are creating a modern epic.

It is important to make clear, though, that this is but a layperson's history. In analysing the bewildering and interlinked themes, trends, issues, events and actors of these past three decades, I have tried to tell the intriguing story that conjured present-day Gurgaon in my own voice, and often inflected with my personal experiences and opinions in the decades that I have known it. I have not written this book for academics, so it has no review of the literature that exists on Gurgaon, just passing references of a few works I found relevant to my narrative. It is written in plain language for the people of Gurgaon, or at least its English-reading public, the majority of whom are strangers who migrated to Gurgaon in this period of its hectic development and might be curious about the city they find themselves in. It has no scholarly pretensions or jargon but it still is grounded in extensive research I did for about five years before I put pen to paper. It is especially for the young—the 'millennials'—people who were born here and have grown up in this strange yet familiar place, where they are exposed to its glamorous side and in their hurry, cannot explore their curiosity about what lurks in its shadows. I do not think this history can be comprehensive or even complete—it is impossible to keep up with a city that is still growing at so rapid a clip. Gurgaon changes everyday; its politicians and bureaucrats, builders and citizens are in a triangulated relationship, often a three-sided tug of war, to shape and control its future. Its landscape adds features even as I write, things I saw half-finished are now complete, but I couldn't return to update things. I have, therefore, chosen to focus on the main trends and grasp the forces that created it. So, there will always be events, places, and people who are clearly part of this history but time and space defined what could have been included. And isn't history a point of view of the facts, interpretive and opinionated? This is clearly my own interpretation of what I encountered and cobbled together. If it provokes arguments and further reading, part of my goal will have been accomplished.

There is plenty to admire in this brash, bold and young city and there are also huge missteps and omissions, planned and unplanned. Yet, overall, I am optimistic about Gurgaon's future as a premier city in India. My foray into its vibrant civil society has turned up a host of non-governmental and web-based organizations involved in a synergetic effort to improve what is patently wrong with Gurgaon. A new, burgeoning middle class of young professionals, retirees fleeing the congestion of Delhi for more spacious accommodation, Indians returning from abroad and looking for creature comforts to which they are accustomed, have flocked to Gurgaon. They demand, in organized and sporadic attempts, open spaces and parks, footpaths, running and cycling tracks, art galleries, performance spaces, fairs and public safety. Public vigils, protests and activism of all sorts have enlivened a formerly moribund space and given it the profile of a bustling city. Non-governmental organizations (NGOs) like I Am Gurgaon, SURGE, We the People, Greening Gurgaon, Keep Gurgaon Clean, Planting a Million Trees, and Running and Living are transforming Gurgaon, retrofitting it with pavements for pedestrians, creating the stunning 350-acre Aravalli Biodiversity Park, rescued from illegal miners, and, with luck, honing Gurgaon's civic pride.

Gurgaon is also a site for the profoundly changing relationship of gender and power. Social conflicts abound in India, and Gurgaon showcases every single variety. Through the stories of local and migrant women, we can index social change in a better way. Women, struggling with segregation and exclusion, inhabit the villages that survive as enclaves within the city limits. They stand in stark contrast to their affluent counterparts who live in the recently built city. Honour killings, illiteracy, the poorest female sex ratios in the world, sex segregation, and the scandalous khap panchayats (clan councils) that attempt to regulate social mores in these urban villages are still rampant.

Can we, in the chaotic blur of Gurgaon, discern a pattern or find features like that of the Hindu, Islamic, or colonial provincial towns that preceded it? Is it a new breed of 'instant cities' (just add water?) or is it merely a district headquarters or a suburb on steroids? Is it replacing the old vocabulary of colonial town planning with its own imperatives and aesthetics demanded by avid middle-class consumers to give us a qualitatively new city, a global city? And finally, is this blueprint of the future sustainable? Can the fragile ecology and scarce natural resources in the national capital region absorb this manic development, with its onslaught of migration, inordinate consumption and waste? The answers to these serious questions are sought in the following pages with rigour and energy.

Prologue

Gurugram ... Gurgaon: Myth, Metaphor and Metro Station?

The earliest alleged trace of Gurugram or Gurgaon, some 24 kilometres south-west of Indraprastha, the first of the seven cities of Delhi, is to be found in folklore and popular oral history passed down from its earliest inhabitants to those of the present day. They tell of the hamlet's hoary vintage from the Mahabharata, the longest, and most searing of all epics in the Indo-European tradition. It is recorded in the earliest *Gazetteer of British Punjab* of 1872 as Gurgaon, and situated in early maps at 28.5 degrees North latitude and 77 degrees East longitude, 10 kilometres south of Mehrauli and the Qutab Minar. A long spur of the Aravalli range broke up the flatlands where wildlife was plentiful in the forested ravines, where seasonal torrents carved the topography into a picturesque hunting ground. It was a popular venue for Mughal and Rajput nobility and finds an early mention in Babur's memoirs, circa 1530s. It was a time when forests were loud with the clucking of wild hens, quail and partridge, and the scamper of rabbits, foxes and porcupines. Deer, and nilgai, the large blue-grey antelope, roamed and foraged freely.

Folklore has it that in this village in an unremarkable homestead dwelt the ambitious teacher of martial arts, Acharya Drona Bharadwaj. What the Mahabharata indubitably asserts is that his mastery over the existing military technology was unsurpassed. In a lucky twist of fate, he became the esteemed military guru of the rival cousins of the kingdom of Kuru, the five Pandava princes, and their hundred rival cousins, the Kauravas. It is believed that Yudhishtir, the eldest of the five Pandava brothers, gave the hamlet to Dronacharya as guru dakshina, the customary fee tendered to a teacher by his students, and so it came to be known as Gurugram. This alleged link with the mythic past is deeply cherished by the natives of old Gurgaon whom I interviewed. The name 'Gurugram', one assumes, contracted over time into the more colloquial Gurgaon, or, as the native Haryanvis pronounce it, Gur-ganvaan. This pronunciation has generated an alternative agricultural explanation: that Gurgaon was named thus because it was a centre for making *gur*, or jaggery from sugar cane. The residents of old Gurgaon scoff at this theory, though. 'We have never made gur here, and the lack of water made it impossible to grow *ganna* [sugar cane] as a cash crop,' said a retired colonel who has inherited farmland that has been in his family for five generations.

The aura of a military expert, who taught the rival noble Kshatriya clansmen, who fought the most devastating fratricidal war in all epic literature in Kurukshetra, has proved more durable. It matches the self-image of the principal native inhabitants of the Haryana region—the Jats, the dominant peasant caste, and the Ahirs and the Gujars, both traditionally cattle-herders—as martial men. Hunting, doing battle and expanding the lands they controlled was part of their occupation. It is not surprising that they were recruited in large numbers as soldiers and endorsed collectively as a 'martial race' by the British, who thought more in racial terms than occupational.

What has reinvigorated this historic claim and made it official, is that the very first station of the Metro line in Gurgaon that connects it to Delhi is named Guru Dronacharya Metro Station, now painted a brilliant blue and sponsored by Indigo Airlines to mark its inception in the Corporate Park office nearby. This Metro station is the new welcoming point to the city and in popular perception settles the dispute about the origin of the name Gurgaon. Mythic cartographies are spatially impressionistic and do not correspond to actual physical locations. The Pandavas appear to have ranged widely on their hunts since we can find similar traces of their abodes in Himachal Pradesh, the Kumaon region in Uttarakhand, and elsewhere. This tells us more about how strongly beloved the Mahabharata is in north India, and how those who know it even partially and episodically fortify their geographical appropriation of it by associating a village, a hut, a dwelling, a well, anything, with one of the major figures in the Mahabharata. Gurgaon's fabled origins, reiterated in official, historical and media accounts, and the presence of the physical vestige of a tank on the western side of the road to the railway station, marked as the guru's well, have all contributed to it becoming an unimpeachable, historical factoid.

The original two square kilometres that constituted the 'gram' or 'gaon' have spread like a bloodstain in the arid heart of Gurgaon district. By 2010 it had engulfed some fifty-two villages within its official municipal boundary of 207 square kilometres. The small core of the Gurgaon district headquarters is still discernible as 'old Gurgaon'. The sprawl has transmogrified into a bustling city of two million and growing, but Haryana chief minister Manohar Lal Khattar bafflingly renamed the city Gurugram in 2016 to reassert the belief in its epic origin. Perhaps a spanking new name befitting its muscular urban avatar might have been more appropriate. A name like Vilayatpur (since many of its newly built neighbourhoods have English names) or Nayashahar might have been more suitable for a place so totally reinvented in modern times. I facetiously suggested InstaGram to give it a modern cybernetic ring, and others came up with sarcastic names—Garbagegram, Sookhapur, or Gandagaon. I have settled for Gurgaon because that is what it was officially called in the historical sources and for the duration of my research and writing.

As Guru Dronacharya gets rehabilitated as the putative 'founding father' of Gurugram, his intriguing story bears retelling in some detail. I decided to refresh my own hazy memory of this legendary guru and found that there was more to his story than meets the eye, especially in the way that it meshes with the charming tale of how Dronacharya began his own upward climb from obscurity. The parallels are fascinating.

One day, the story goes, the royal cousins—the five Pandavas and the hundred Kauravas—were gambolling near Drona's hermitage when the tip-wood they were hitting around with their sticks (perhaps the game known today as *gulli danda*) landed in the well of the sage (supposedly the well that is extant on the road to Gurgaon Railway Station). Drona skilfully retrieved the tip-wood by hitting it with a reed from his bow, followed rapidly by many more, to form a chain that enabled him to pull it up from the depths of the well to the utter amazement of the young princes. Drona told the Pandavas to return to their capital, Hastinapur, and report his incredible feat to their grand-uncle, Bhishma. This led to Drona becoming the guru of the royal cousins—the Pandavas and the Kauravas—to turn them into accomplished warriors with bows, swords, clubs and maces and all other forms of warfare known to him at the military academy he established.

Arjuna was his favourite pupil and the guru assured him that he would be the sole, invincible toxophilite in the land. However, another archer, indubitably superior in skill to the left-handed Arjuna, was perceived as a threat to this goal. This was the brilliant Eklavya, an Adivasi, one of the aboriginal Nishadas, who were disdained as low caste by the Brahmins and Kshatriyas. He had, as an aspiring young archer, been scorned and rejected as a pupil by Dronacharya. (B.R. Chopra's television version of the Mahabharata that riveted Indian audiences represented him as a Shudra and not an Adivasi, reinforcing upper-caste prejudice against Dalits). Undeterred, Eklavya taught himself archery, making a clay image of Dronacharya for inspiration, and eventually rose to be the chief of the Nishadas, whom the Kshatriyas of Hastinapur had been unable to vanquish.

One day, Eklavya, disturbed by the barking of a dog while on a hunt, deftly silenced it by sealing its mouth with arrows without causing it pain. Arjuna witnessed this remarkable feat and knew that he would never match Eklavya's prowess or be the best archer in the land. But Dronacharya assured the skulking Arjuna that he would take care of his rival. Without scruple or pause he summoned Eklavya and ordered him to reveal the name of his guru. Eklavya said that he considered Dronacharya to be his guru, even though the latter had harshly refused to accept him as a pupil. Dronacharya, with cruel cunning, demanded his guru dakshina—Eklavya's right thumb. Eklavya, in his unswerving devotion to his guru, promptly severed his indispensable digit and offered it to Dronacharya. With Eklavya permanently disabled as an archer, Arjuna could now consider himself as the best in the land. The ruthless Dronacharya then proceeded to conquer the valuable Nishada lands. Eklavya's sacrifice made Arjuna invincible in battle.

This unconscionable act showcases the injustice that marks the relationships of higher castes with those they deem inferior. Dronacharya lives on in infamy in a widely known text that is punctuated with many morally repugnant decisions made by gods and men. Does he uphold the dharma of a guru? Or was this one more pitiless act in the annals of the Brahmin–Kshatriya nexus against lower castes, a chauvinism we have not overcome in our day and age? Is naming a Metro station 'Guru Dronacharya Station' celebrating the guru or is it also an oblique reminder of his epic-sized dastardly act against an exceptional self-taught man? There are signs of the old caste and ethnic discrimination reappearing against Gurgaon's recent migrants.

However, according to a front-page story in *The Indian Express* on 4 May 2017, others revere Eklavya in Gurgaon. In Khandsa village, now a part of Gurgaon city, it is believed that a shrine to Eklavya was built on the very spot where his amputated thumb was allegedly buried. This shrine was very popular, but lost its sheen in the last two centuries and is about to get a makeover. The popularity of this one room 'temple' is to be revived, according to Priyavarth Bharadwaj, general secretary of the Gurugram Sanskritik Gaurav Committee (GSGC), an initiative that includes the BJP and its affiliates. A special puja is scheduled here annually on 14 January, according to the same report, 'when the rituals will be performed by a member of the same caste to which Eklavya belonged'. So the epic tale has a modern-day twist and it is a notable irony that the general secretary quoted is a Bharadwaj Brahmin, the same *gotra* or lineage as that of Acharya Drona Bharadwaj, perhaps in atonement for a putative ancestor's sin against an Adivasi.

As we know, nothing in the Mahabharata is simple or straightforward—heroes and gods do villainous acts and its lessons are found in convoluted ways. Patriarchy, for example, was the order of the day, and is fiercely adhered to in Haryana, but it would knock the Haryanvis off their string cots if they knew that it is subversively mocked in the great epic. Pandu's wife, Kunti, when she married him, had already had given birth to her firstborn son Karna, sired by the god Surya in a pre-marital liaison. None of the five famous Pandavas were the biological sons of Pandu, and Kunti found divine partners to father her three later sons: Yudhishtir, Bhima, and Arjuna. She then adopted the twins, Nakul and Sahadev, the sons of Pandu's other wife, Madri, by *her* celestial consort, when they were orphaned. Pandu never fathered a single Pandava, and for the thoughtful reader of the Mahabharata, that sets the belief in institutional patriarchy and dynasty rather on its head. Kunti, the mother, is the progenitor of all six of them and the undisputed matriarch. Will the revival of these mythic associations make Gurgaon a better place for women?

As some readers might remember from watching the Mahabharata as a television serial in the late 1980s, after a vengeful war, Guru Dronacharya accumulated holdings of half the Panchala kingdom that belonged to his childhood friend Drupada, the Crown prince of Panchala. As a young boy, Drupada had pledged that when he succeeded his father as king, he would share in all his wealth with Drona. So, years later, when Drupada ascended the throne of Panchala, Drona, by then an acharya, promptly appeared at the former's court to redeem his childhood pledge. However, King Drupada arrogantly repudiated his promise, slighted his poor friend and sent him away empty-handed. Enraged, Dronacharya plotted revenge. Drupada, fearing retribution, offered a yagna, a sacrifice to the gods, and prayed that he might sire a son who would kill Drona, and a daughter, Draupadi, who would marry Arjuna, the Pandava prince. Dronacharya retaliated by commanding the Pandavas in a war against Drupada and defeated him. Although he spared his life, he took half of the vast kingdom of Panchala as his private trophy. Vengeance and greed were simultaneously sated. Meanwhile, Drupada's two wishes were also fulfilled in the course of a very long and twisted storyline that culminates in the bloody confrontation at Kurukshetra. This war annihilated all but a handful of the Pandavas and Kauravas, and Guru Dronacharya met his end as Drupada had wished: at the hands of his son, Prince Dhrishtadyumna.

I first thought it was rather embarrassing for a modern city to be so closely identified with the wily Guru Dronacharya, but the better I got to know the reinvented 'Gurugram', the more the name seemed to fit. This is where Gurgaon's mythical fate and modern reality intersect. Dronacharya's insatiable craving was for technical superiority in the art of war and for landed wealth—real estate. His protégé, Arjun, could only become the best pupil by eliminating Eklavya as a rival. On another level we will see how Gurgaon bests Faridabad in its new-found quest to become a city. A dusty village was put on steroids to compete with the designated industrial city, as we will see in the following pages.

Dronacharya's desire for land and wealth seems to be replayed in our own times in the new Gurgaon where real estate barons jockey for land and their desire for wealth is hard to quench. The exponential growth of Gurgaon is enabled by alliances between the new castes of politicians, bureaucrats and builders. Together, they've acquired land owned by the alleged lesser castes—Jats, Gujars and Ahirs of Gurgaon—by fiat or at the lowest rural prices, and converted it into incalculable urban wealth by transforming the rural into the urban by simply changing the use of agricultural land into residential and commercial space as if by a sly sleight of hand.

Is a class war playing out in the exclusive practices in Gurgaon's residential areas? Is Eklavya a symbol for migrants who serve the city and have built it new colonies and yet are forced to live in ghettoes as second-class citizens? In renaming the new city, should the Haryana government not have chosen Vishvakarma, the legendary architect in the Mahabharata who built the fabulous Pandava capital of Indraprastha, as the person to be honoured in naming the first Metro station in Gurgaon? Other parallels and resonances will emerge as we recount the story of the making of Gurgaon city.

One

The Obscure Millennia

Almost two millennia have passed as Gurgaon lingered in forgettable rusticity as a hamlet, undocumented and ignored by chroniclers. It appears not to have a 'history', a record of important events or changes, as it lay in the shadow of the dynasties that ruled from Delhi. Even the punctilious gazetteers of Gurgaon district, who compiled the gazette periodically from 1872 onwards, dismiss it with a shrug: 'During the flourishing times of the Mughal Empire Gurgaon may be said to be without a history…' they repeatedly state.[1] I would strongly argue against such condescension because its fate was irrevocably bound to Delhi's fortunes, and was reckoned, to use an anachronistic term, as an integral part of the 'national capital region' under successive rulers from the earliest times. Gurgaon was an indirectly involved party at historic moments that often occurred in the region of Punjab where Haryanvi was spoken (the official state of Haryana came into being only in 1966), such as wars and regime changes, when its male inhabitants were recruited as fighters. In the sanguinary engagements of the Mughals (who introduced

1

deadly gunpowder) with firearms, matchlocks, and cannon that changed the nature of combat on the battlefields of the subcontinent, Gurgaonwallahs were chiefly cannon fodder. Those who returned from battle were welcomed as heroes and given the honorific of '*fauji*'.

Gurgaon lived, as it were, in the churn. Constituting the immediate southern verge of Delhi, beyond the Qutab Minar and Mehrauli outposts, some of the action for the coveted north Indian empire inevitably spilled into it. Major historic battles that decided the fate of the northern part of the subcontinent were fought not too far away, in Panipat, some 96 kilometres north of Delhi. It was where Babur founded the Mughal Empire after his triumph over the Delhi sultan, Ibrahim Lodi, in 1526, and Gurgaon was swept into its embrace. Babur's son and heir, Humayun the Hapless, added to the empire during 1530–40, and then lost it all to the intrepid Afghans, led by the soldier of fortune, Sher Shah of Sur, who ruled Delhi for fifteen years, strengthening and reorganizing its administration. Humayun fled from pillar to post, from Sindh to Punjab and on to Kabul, where even his brother, Kamran, refused him shelter. He eventually sought refuge in Safavid Persia (now Iran) in 1544. The Safavid emperor's crucial aid came at a price: Humayun, a Timurid Sunni, became a Shia convert and personalized Turk, when he returned to reclaim the thrones of Kabul and finally, in 1555, of Delhi, slaughtering all those who opposed him, including his own brothers. His triumph was short-lived because Humayun was accidentally killed in a fall from the steps of the library in the Purana Qila (built on a mound that may well be, in its lowest levels, Indraprastha) on a wintery morning in January 1556. Countless Haryanvis perished as soldiers and civilians under Afghan and Mughal rule; Gurgaon's sons made this history—but remained nameless outside the annals of the time—whose authors did not include the lowly but brave soldiers in their narratives.

It was in Akbar's reign in the second half of the sixteenth century that Gurgaon garnered some notice. Barely had Akbar and his regent, Bairam Khan, taken charge when they were attacked by a powerful Hindu foe, King Hemu, who hailed from Gurgaon pargana, born in the village of Rewari. By this time Hemu had become the dominant force in northern India and defeated the Mughal forces in Kannauj and in the Battle of Delhi in 1556, and came within a hair of wresting the Mughal Empire in the next battle. But, as luck would have it, he was stuck by an arrow in his eye, and was quickly taken prisoner and beheaded. The cream of his army, drafted from the plains of the Gurgaon region that formed a horseshoe around Delhi, was mercilessly decimated. Hemu was arguably Gurgaon's greatest native son and a memorial to him was built soon thereafter by his surviving followers at Shodapur village, where Akbar had camped near the battlefield in Panipat. The *samadhi sthal* was erected on the spot to commemorate Hemu's bravery. Its ten acres of grounds are now encroached upon; Gurgaon has not been able to save this.

The early Mughals perfected the tented, mobile city, more an elaborate camp, so that the capital would move with them. Besides, it was their presence that defined where the capital was. Their huge retinue of non-combatants, including musicians, dancers, boon companions, cooks, cleaners, barbers and coolies, all were camp followers and created a capital wherever they travelled. The exquisite walled citadels of Agra, Fatehpur Sikri, Lahore, and Shahjahanabad (today's Old Delhi) were the serial capital cities of the Mughal Empire. Emperors Akbar, Jahangir and Shahjahan built grandiose red sandstone and marble forts, the finest mosques, palaces, tombs and shrines with pierced marble screens, and gardens laid out in four squares on the template of Paradise, embellished with fountains and water channels. These cities, surrounded by the vast countryside, remained the few unrivalled built environments of the pre-modern world. City building was a celebrated art form—something that, some would say, eludes several private commercial builders who tried their hand at Gurgaon, for example.

*Subah*s, provinces, of the empire, like Awadh and Hyderabad, also had spectacular regional capital cities with a medley of places of worship, palaces, specialized markets, gardens and orchards.

Lucknow, with its special Persianate flavour and the wealth of a spectacularly fertile hinterland, epitomized the court city of its time. The common urban feature was a cluster of mohallas, neighbourhoods that were established by prominent nobles who built and lived in fine town houses. The mohalla was the pre-modern form of the gated community: quite self-contained, a gate and a chowkidar armed with a lathi, a long stick, guarded its entrance. He kept out the unfamiliar and the undesirable, especially at night, and kept crime rates low. Thousands of artisans, tradesmen and servicemen dwelt within in three-storeyed buildings along meandering streets in mixed-use neighbourhoods. Residential quarters occupied the floors above the shops, and the clutter of hawkers lining both sides of the street, making traffic, that comprised a variety of manual and animal-drawn vehicles, pedestrians and animals, move slowly. Streets were narrow and labyrinthine, often the destination rather than the route to it, where people went to shop at the hawkers by the roadside, or to mill around, meeting and greeting friends, or just enjoy the evening crowds. Many alleys ended in cul de sacs, the buildings on either side keeping them shaded and cool. *Kasbah*s, small towns, replicated these features on a modest scale. Throughout this period when trade grew and kasbahs speckled the map, Gurgaon village had too few inhabitants to qualify even as a kasbah, unlike Faridabad, Rajokri and Nuh. At best Gurgaon had a *piau*, where drinking water was available, where Emperor Akbar's entourage is supposed to have customarily stopped for refreshment en route to Amber, and a large grain and vegetable *mandi*, a wholesale market, for farmers from the hinterland to sell their produce. This small brick pavilion, with classic Mughal arches, existed until recently, when it was thoughtlessly demolished without trace in the construction of Guru Dronacharya Metro Station in 2009.

Although there were small traders and artisans who contributed to the economy of the area, agriculture was the chief occupation of Gurgaon's small farmers and co-sharers, who eked out a frugal living growing chiefly millets, such as jowar and bajra, oil seeds such as mustard and castor, during the rabi (winter) season and pulses, vegetables, and small amounts of sugar cane as their kharif (monsoon) crop. Nearby, Sohna supplied a brownish salt harvested from the briny water drawn from its wells and evaporated in large salt pans. The population comprised several village castes, the dominant being the Jats, followed by Gujars and Ahirs and a small sprinkling of Meos. The Jat men, tall and muscular on average (as the British were quick to recognize the 'martial races'), cleared the forests, ploughed the fields, dug the wells and maintained irrigation channels, while the women performed all the other tasks, from sowing, weeding, harvesting, garnering, grinding the grain and pulses, cooking three meals a day and reproducing the next generation of soldiers and peasants. They also managed their cattle for domestic consumption of milk, yogurt, butter, buttermilk and ghee, and turned the dung into cakes for fuel and for plastering their mud huts.

Animal husbandry was a common occupation for villagers, particularly the Ahirs and Gujars, who kept a spectacular species of large black goats, water buffaloes and large horned cows that supplied both milk and meat, not only to Gurgaon but also for the insatiable appetite of nearby Delhi. They also joined the armies of chieftains in the region and enlisted in large numbers in the regiments of the East India Company to have a steady cash income and gain land and become agriculturalists and soldiers. They used their brawn to decimate forests and were rewarded with the arable land they created and came within the fold of revenue-paying subjects. At the bottom of the pile were the once pastoral Meo, whom the British had dismissed as 'proverbially thriftless', 'slovenly,' and 'lazy'. They had arrived on the scene from Sindh after the Arab invasions, and settled mainly in Mewat, and in Ferozepur and Nuh tehsils of Gurgaon district.[2] They were once a ruling group, but were marginalized over time. They converted to Islam, and made their living herding animals and also making regular raids into Delhi and Punjab as feared bandits. Gurgaon tehsil was the poorest of the five in the district, where very few Meos lived, in small and poor hamlets, with dwellings of mud and thatch rather than of stone and brick, like those of the Jats.

The Ahirs spoke a dialect of Rajasthani, and the Jat and Gujar, Haryanvi, a dialect of Hindi that slowly gained wider acceptance, and is the language of what is now Haryana. There was not an urbanite among them except for a sprinkling of Khatris, Brahmins, Kayasths and Banias, who moved in to work as clerks in the administration or to create small businesses and better shops for a place with growing needs and brought with them a whiff of the small town. It can be safely assumed that a healthy diet of coarse grains, lentils, dairy and occasionally meat from goats and abundant wildfowl and fresh water fish produced lean and strong people that today's paunchy urbanites would envy. The quotidian rhythms of life were monotonous, but frequently a war would erupt and life would become tense, even dangerous.

In an economy of scarcity, the hard-working peasants with their 'martial' potential, the Ahirs and Jats, were quickly harnessed by the astute colonial regime as foot soldiers of the East India Company's army, with cash payments and land-related awards for loyal service. They raided for treasure, defended their lands from Afghan and Rajput invaders, and died heroically for causes that were often not their own. This obsession with warlike activities and engaging with enemies required ever-larger numbers of young men. Given the patriarchal framework for daily living, a preference for male children was an inevitable outcome.

The women themselves had internalized the need and dependence for protection by men against men; the sex ratios were dismal from the mid-nineteenth century, when such figures became available, but from the second half of the twentieth century, they have dipped to a shocking low of 84 women to 100 men. This gender imbalance is a real crisis and the only way that all Haryanvi men can get wives is to marry very young girls—barely five or six, or marry girls of migrant communities from Bihar, Bengal and the southern states. And this state of affairs was a disaster as a Gujar I spoke to put it convincingly: 'Without a wife there is no family and family is the most important thing in life; there can be no family, no pleasure, and no wealth. We are nothing without our women. A man without a wife is seen to be as a cursed and incomplete person; he is useless.'

The several scores of village men within Gurgaon, whom I interviewed during 1995–97, echoed this sentiment in varying degrees. Be that as it may, wives are treated without much overt respect and are certainly not conceived as equals; this is vivid when you observe gendered behaviour in the village even today. Not much appeared changed since Malcolm Darling of the Indian Civil Service (ICS) visited Gurgaon often in the 1920s and 1930s and wrote of it in his acclaimed memoir, *At Freedom's Door*, that women were treated no better than their cattle and, none of them seemed to think that daughters were as valuable as sons. Men seem to have found an infallible answer to the 'woman question'. 'Sons bring home wives who become part of our family, they run the household. Girls marry and go away, so how can they be useful to us?' argued one Gujar, exhaling hookah smoke, as he imparted this wisdom to me. 'Yet,' he admitted, along with his three male kin who shared this conversation, 'women are prized as wives, a price was paid for them to their parents, and they worked hard at home and in the fields; we cannot make our daughters work in our fields.' He seemed pleased that his circular logic had left me nonplussed. He did not know that I was thinking that more benighted specimens of humanity would be hard to find anywhere, underscored by the fact that Haryana has among the worst female sex ratios in the world.

In 1761, the third Battle of Panipat was waged between two doughty coalitions that had whittled away Mughal power over the past half-century. On the one side was the vigorous Maratha confederacy, assisted by European soldiers of fortune that ousted the Afghans from Punjab, took over Kashmir, and finally seized Delhi in 1760. On the opposing side were the Durrani Afghans, who, smarting at the loss of Lahore to the Marathas, managed to persuade their co-religionists, the Nawab of Awadh and the Rohillas of the Doab, and several French mercenaries to bolster their offence. Gurgaon was then under the sway of the fearsome Jat ruler Suraj Mal of Bharatpur who could have tipped the scales against the Afghans and would have created Gurgaon as an important seat of power. It was not to be. Suraj Mal, along with the Sikhs and Hindu Rajputs, failed to join forces with the Marathas, and this contributed largely to the Maratha defeat, leaving the space open to the expansionist East India Company.

While the Afghans apparently won, after the huge loss of blood and treasure on both sides, they were unable to sustain their hold on Delhi. The British appraised this internecine disaster that had weakened all the parties involved with gratitude and glee. The forces of the East India Company, the paramount power in India since the decisive Battle of Plassey in 1757, were continually on an expansionist prowl, waiting for the chance to pounce on Delhi to consolidate their hold on the heartland of Hindustan. It was their pragmatic policy of employing the toughest native mercenaries that made them the conquerors of Delhi and its environs in 1803. After many gruelling encounters, they defeated the resurgent Marathas when Company troops outgunned them. These decades were replete with examples where native soldiers on both sides fought and died in battles that, fatefully, subjugated their own lands for the Company.

In a colourful and romantic interlude during these sanguinary wars, Walter Reinhardt Sombre, a German Catholic mercenary and opportunist who fought on the winning side, inveigled the Mughal emperor to reward him with the small but very prosperous estate of Sardhana, near Meerut, about 85 kilometres north-east of Delhi. For other military services, he acquired Jharsa and Badshahpur, parts of Gurgaon pargana, where he built a cantonment for his private army.[3] After he died in 1778, his second wife, Farzana, of obscure lineage and possibly a courtesan, whose ambition and astute management of powerful men won her admirers, reinvented herself as Begum Sombre, colloquially the fabled Begum Samru. She converted to Catholicism, her husband's faith, and became a power to contend with. She was the quasi-independent sovereign of Sardhana and Jharsa-Badshahpur for sixty years, until she died at the age of eighty-five in 1839. Her innumerable political and amorous exploits are beyond the scope of this narrative; briefly, she managed her vast fortune and her subjects with admirable competence, adopted Reinhardt's grandson from his first marriage, Dyce Sombre, as her heir, married a French colonel, and was widowed again. Meanwhile she cajoled the Mughal emperor and the officers of the East India Company and extracted concessions from both, not without whiffs of scandals. She built Catholic churches and palaces in Sardhana, and a classically styled palace in Gurgaon where she often resided. This palace, the grandest building Gurgaon then possessed, was confiscated, like the rest of her estate, by the British after the Begum died, despite her adopted legal male heir, whom they conveniently refused to recognize.

Begum Samru's palace, once animated with feasts and entertainments for important noblemen, was converted into the office and residence of the deputy commissioner of Gurgaon district and became the East India Company's base to manage the new district. This building, which still stood when I made my first trip into the administration of Gurgaon in 1995, was encroached upon by small shops and makeshift residences, and its once palatial appearance was haggard and in need of restoration. More recently it had a fresh coat of paint and some tidying up, but none of its glamour is discernible now.

Gurgaon, however, remained resolutely rustic in temperament through the turmoil of the eighteenth and nineteenth centuries; it was a tramping ground for dacoits and armies on the move, from Delhi to Agra and Jaipur, where elephants, horses and the thousands of infantrymen had beaten out tracks that were, in the distant future, to be metalled, the first being the road that led through Mehrauli and Hauz Khas to the Red Fort of Shahjahanabad. This same route was chosen by the Metro, which began service in 2011, snaking underground and reappearing on its elevated tracks near the Qutab Minar, as a major conduit between Delhi and Gurgaon. Another dirt road running south and west had earlier transported the Mughal armies and diplomatic envoys from Delhi to Amer.

In 1727, when Mughal influence had waned, Amer's famous maharaja, Jai Singh the second, built the magnificent royal city of Jaipur based on ancient principles of Vastu Shastra. Its grandly planned environment and civic features could well have served as the model for the new city of Gurgaon but, unfortunately, its builders, discussed in Chapter Three, never conceived of a holistic city. In this new millennium, a parallel eight-lane road, the partially elevated National Highway 8 (NH-8), was built just east of this wonted path at the behest of Delhi Land and Finance (DLF), the major corporate builder who had bought the less attractive acreage on the other side of Gurgaon to construct its new residential colonies. NH-8 then proceeds southward on to Mumbai, linking Gurgaon to India's largest port city and to global commerce.

The Environmental Debacle of the Colonial Period: 1803–1947

The colonial era began after the 1803 blood bath between native forces on both sides. The British were harbingers of the earliest change of Gurgaon from a village to a basic, small town that would administer the freshly conquered district. They also understood that knowledge was power, and their in-depth study of the land, its people, and its potential was quickly under way. Within five years of British occupation, Gurgaon district had its boundaries marked and the villages in its five tehsils enumerated with their revenue settled for several decades at a time. With the Collectorate transferred to Gurgaon from Bharawas village in 1816, the core of a colonial provincial town, referred to as Gurgaon Station, came into existence, and it became the administrative headquarters of the district.

The British applied what I have grasped as their basic template for a colonial provincial town elsewhere.[4] Their formula, as I see it, can boil down to the five Cs: a Collectorate for taxes, a Courthouse for dealing with their inevitable injustices, a Cantonment for the army, a Civil Lines for administrative officers' residences, and a Church for its Christian inhabitants. And one may add a sixth: a Cricket ground for military and civil officers. Marked now as a dot, Gurgaon, the district headquarters made its appearance on the maps of the British Empire in India that connected it to the world. Geographers carefully calculated its precise location and marked it in the virtual global crosshairs: latitude at 28⁰ 27' 30" North, and longitude 77⁰ 4' East. It was some 32 kilometres from north Delhi and connected to it with a fine metalled avenue shaded by handsome jamun trees. It was also linked to Sohna and Rewari, two older towns with avenues of neem and sissu trees.

They built a cantonment for their cavalry units, bungalows for the European officers and separate barracks for its European and native troops, stables for the cavalry, a parade ground, and its *sadar bazaar* (main market). They also completed the British cantonment about a kilometre and a half away from Begum Samru's Jharsa cantonment, to keep an eye on her army and create their own power base. The Gurgaon cantonment was named Jacombpura, after Mr Jacomb, the deputy commissioner who laid it out. In addition, a sessions court, a church and bungalows for the officers along leafy streets constituted the 'civil lines' that abutted the cantonment. This was a fledgling step towards urbanization in Gurgaon.

The Collectorate at Gurgaon quickly became a hive of activity. The deputy commissioner was in charge of all district affairs. The district had changed its footprint several times as tehsils or components were added to or removed from it. It is bounded by Delhi to its north-east and Agra to its south-west, and Mewat, with its seat at Alwar, to its south while the Yamuna river forms its eastern border. Today the five tehsils or boroughs of Gurgaon district are Rewari, Palwal, Nuh, Firozpur, and Gurgaon, and each of these contains fifty or more villages. In Gurgaon town there was a dispensary, a police station, a jail, a sessions court, a dak bungalow (guest house for officers), a post office, a small market square, a school for boys (none for girls) and two serais, inns kept in good repair for native travellers and weddings. A public garden was planned and laid out in the centre of the station, and by 1908 a nursery, chiefly with tree saplings, was started by the government to plant some trees back in the district that had been denuded. This became a profitable enterprise and landowners from as far as Pataudi, some 30 kilometres away, became regular customers. Nearby townships, Rewari, Sohna and Palwal, were constituted as municipalities in 1885, but Gurgaon did not make the cut because its population had not reached 5,000, the threshold that distinguished a village from a town. Its municipal corporation made its elected appearance only in the second decade of the twenty-first century. Gurgaon became a patchwork quilt, as developed areas were interspersed among the fields of villages that it absorbed, such as Nathupur, Sikandarpur, and Chakarpur, with the rural and the urban shaded into each other.

The East India Company officers, who fancied themselves as officer-anthropologists, wasted no time in describing, categorizing and pigeonholing the vast swath of humanity they conquered in the subcontinent, and Gurgaon was no exception. Registers were filled with detailed ethnographic information, customary law, and the ways of life of what they perceived as distinct 'tribes' (rather than castes). The district population was never sparse by the standards of the early nineteenth century, and hovered around 127 people to the square kilometre, but Gurgaon tehsil with its fifty or so villages (the area subsumed by the modern Gurgaon city) was the most populous and averaged more than 154 people per square kilometre. Yet, it fell short of being reckoned officially as a town. It was not assigned a municipal authority, like neighbouring Rewari and Palwal, because its population had not reached the required threshold.

Colonial conquest brought about huge environmental changes in this area and devastated its natural fertility and forest cover. Why do I pin the blame on the colonization of this region from 1803? The evidence for the indictment comes from none other than the British accounts of the region upon their arrival. Early nineteenth-century British portrayals describe Gurgaon's scenic environment at the time of its conquest. It was indeed idyllic: its jhils, small lakes, gushing seasonal torrents, and vast central wetlands that supported spectacular bird life, deer, antelopes, and even cheetahs and leopards. After the British took over, they developed the hot springs into bricked baths at Sohna, a neighbouring small town with decaying Mughal structures, and built a sanatorium, by creating a colonial health resort where many of the British came to rest, rejuvenate or recuperate from their 'Delhi ulcers' in the nineteenth century. The Gazetteer of 1882 states that Gurgaon 'was well known for the excellence of its spring-water and the salubrity of its climate'.[5]

The ecological catastrophe that ensued has its roots in John Company's policy to obsessively expand its revenue base to underwrite its ceaseless wars and conquests. It looked hungrily upon their freshly acquired expanse of fields and forest and immediately calculated that the land would yield many million rupees in additional revenue if one could get the sturdy, hard-working yeomen to chop down the trees and cultivate the land; timber and fuel would be welcome by-products. The greed-fuelled frenzy of slashing forests for timber and create agricultural land in the first half of the nineteenth century was officially reported as progress and prosperity.[6] The natural corollary to having created more cultivable land was to find more water to grow the crops. Clive Dewey summarizes the problems that colonial meddling created with the natural rhythms of rainy and dry seasons.[7] For thousands of years, Gurgaon received few but ferocious rains but it benefitted from the annual flooding from the Yamuna river that brought rich silt to the Gurgaon plains and the seasonal torrents that drained into the centre of the district and created a huge internal basin with no outlet to the sea. The monsoon normally expanded the winter marshes into large jhils which shrank during the dry season, leaving the margins saturated enough to raise bumper crops without additional irrigation.

The British, believing that they would 'improve' matters by trying to exploit the torrents, built numerous small bunds, earthen check dams, to block their flow and create reservoirs from which water could be drawn in the dry season. Farmers closer to these reservoirs built their own bunds to divert the water to their own fields. However, the rate of extraction was soon high enough to reduce the torrents into trickles and to desiccate the once flourishing wetlands, causing huge losses to bird and animal life and to the production of food. This well-intentioned but hopelessly ill-advised building of dams left Gurgaon with a parched and barren centre—a veritable lake district had vanished along with its prosperity and beauty. The jhils were now shallow, stagnant marshes that became the perfect breeding grounds for mosquitoes, vectors of epidemics of malaria, filaria and typhoid. This problem looms large in Gurgaon even today, compounded with the lack of drainage more recently exacerbated by the paving over of many natural nullahs and torrent beds to create tarred roads and flyovers, and support the mindless development of residential colonies and high-rises.

The colonial plan for the 'development' of Gurgaon district in the long run was a failure for its residents. A canal and wells would water the newly arable lands. A channel of the West Yamuna Canal opened in 1841 to irrigate the western section of the district that was fertile and produced crops. At first these developments were welcomed and brought prosperity to the yeomen families who migrated to the new lands, but the ecological backlash was horrendous in the long run. Of the two tragic consequences of canal water, one rendered the once fertile and salubrious 'canal colonies' of Punjab into a waterlogged and briny wasteland; nothing could be cultivated here and poverty and undernourishment became widespread. The other was that in the dry season the small amounts of water retained in the canal became a prolific breeding ground for mosquitoes, with the result that Gurgaon district became one of the unhealthiest districts that lost more population than it gained in migrants. The extension of the Agra Canal, in 1874, passed through Gurgaon district on its way to the United Provinces. In a few years, its horrors became apparent. The spread of mosquitoes, viruses, bacteria and waterborne diseases led to outbreaks of malaria, filaria, typhoid, cholera, influenza, the plague, intestinal upsets and unrelenting fevers, and soon overwhelmed the population of this formerly 'salubrious' environment. Colonial rule envisaged it only as a rural headquarters, but Gurgaon's ravaged and infertile lands unwittingly paved the way for its future evolution into a city. These barren fields were close to Delhi, so it was inevitable, given the rapid rise in its population after 1947, and vast, cheap unproductive acreage of villages on its southern periphery, that it would become the sites of booming cities more than a century later.

In 1879, a district officer reported the splendid harvests irrigation had enabled in the United Provinces, but he also predicted a dire future ahead for Gurgaonites. He wrote that he hoped that 'the proximity of the canal does not permanently enervate them as seems to be the case with the Jat landholders on the Western Jamna [sic] Canal'. 'There seems to be some danger of the latter calamity, for this year [1879] in particular fever has literally devastated the tract through which the canal passes; some villages have in a few months lost one-sixth of their population,' he cautioned, 'and scarcely a man who has not been greatly reduced in strength by repeated attacks.'[8] These fears for Gurgaon were more than warranted. An estimated 90,000 people perished between 1881 and 1931 and the survivors of epidemics were often too debilitated to work in the fields. This invited immigrant labour to harvest the fields. The side effects of the fevers, mortality, and abject poverty were manifold. Children were stunted, the adults suffered from chronic fatigue and depression, and families lacked able-bodied men and women to tend to the business of living. Gurgaon saw its population dwindle.

The canal brought with it another devastating ecological consequence. Over time, the water level rose and the fields of this region became barren with saline deposits and brackish waterlogging. Gurgaon's landscape lapsed into brown desolation; its fields were rendered almost worthless for agriculture, for which its forests had also been ruthlessly slashed. Much of the land in and around Gurgaon was now *banjar*, salt encrusted wasteland. These were new dangers in the countryside where disease and financial insecurity became widespread and colonial rule created more poverty than this region had known under its former rulers.[9] These circumstances go a long way to explain why small peasants joined the rebellion against the British in 1857, which spread like wildfire from village to village far beyond the 'mutiny' that the British had claimed it was.[10]

These traumas of environmental debacle, widespread disease, wars and rebellion made Gurgaon a desperate place. Regular outbreaks of malaria, typhoid and filaria hit the population very hard. Gurgaon, as Dewey concluded, now combined the diseases of the wet tracts with the crop failures of a dry one. This situation persisted for decades without relief, and was aggravated once railway tracks were laid in the 1870s. The rail tracks ran counter to the logic and direction of the remaining torrents and cut across them, blocking the flow of water and any drainage. Gurgaon's headquarters and the district around it languished. Clearly, as agriculture failed and even animal husbandry became difficult, these lands became marked for future 'change in land use' and thus Gurgaon would be reborn as a city.

It was this land, so closely wrapped around south Delhi, that desperately needed an infusion of capital and industry to revive it. It would not take much cash to tempt a farmer to part with this unyielding land and become the area on which the future concrete towers would spring. In many ways, the only solution the area had to pull itself out of the depression it was in was to succumb to rapid urbanization when the opportunity arose, and providentially that is what happened. In the 1970s and '80s, the descendants of these peasants owned ever smaller, subdivided holdings of degraded land. They were persuaded by real estate companies to sell their fields for cash, and perhaps to change themselves into city dwellers or buy cheaper arable land farther away from Delhi. The original owners of those lands did not dream that a city would rise in the desolate fields and boulder-strewn landscape.

The other fundamental colonial policy debacle that outmatched the ecological one was the stupefying attempt to 'rationalize' the seasonal revenue collection after its takeover in 1849, after Punjab was conquered.[11] It privatized landownership, a revolutionary move in these parts, and imposed the assessment and collection of revenue, a devastating system that had been put in place with variations in all of British India and thrust upon the princely states as well. The new revenue demand was based on the ownership of land rather than the actual harvest taken from it, in keeping the idea of proprietorship created by Lord Cornwallis in his 'Permanent Settlement' in Bengal in 1793. Briefly, the system caused a major revolution in the relationship of people to the land they inhabited. It altered the essential meaning of land, from an asset that was controlled by and its produce shared among joint cultivators to the English idea of land as a commodity with a single, registered owner. Land could now be privately and individually owned and bought, sold or auctioned off. Former rulers had taken a percentage, often as high as 33 per cent, visually assessed annually after the crop was standing. They also believed in the remission of the amounts due if the harvest was poor. The native system of annual assessments was compassionate and kept farmers on their land but in the eyes of the colonial masters it was cumbersome and expensive and so done away with.

The colonial objective, in stark contrast, was to create a taxation regime that produced a fixed revenue stream every year regardless of the condition of the harvest. Dues were based on past averages on a plot of land at 25 per cent of the yield, for a settlement period of fifteen to thirty years. This amount was payable to the government on 31 March and 30 September of each year, presumed to be dates closest to the rabi (winter) and kharif (monsoon) harvests respectively.

This tax had to be rendered punctually and in cash, no matter if the years were of dearth or plenty, at the district Collectorate—for many this exercise was no less than a two-day journey in a bullock cart on a rutted road. A defaulter's holding could be confiscated and auctioned off if sickness, a death in the family, or a year of bad harvests made it impossible for him to render his dues. Distress sales and forced auctions of land for non-payment of dues became a common nightmare at the end of each due date. Landlessness, a feature unknown in the times of former rulers, was now the dread in every peasant's heart.

In good years and bad, the moneylender, who had played a rather benign role as someone who was approached for small, unsecured loans in times of trouble, now became a big player in the agrarian economy. He could anticipate, especially in years when the harvest was delayed, that many of the proprietors would be making a beeline for cash loans to pay their dues. The moneylending scenario was also transformed. Loans were now substantial with the title of the landholding as collateral and the interest rates climbed to an exorbitant 40 per cent to 60 per cent. If an erratic monsoon delayed or ruined a harvest, a farmer could get into lifelong debt by borrowing money to pay the revenue before he had cashed his crop or waited for the next one. Farmers were haunted by the sound of the decisive bang of the government auctioneer's gavel or the spectre of crippling debt that they could never pay off. Landlessness, dispossession, and migration became the new features in the countryside and poverty became their permanent 'fate'.[12]

In 1875, the same year the Agra Canal cut its way through Gurgaon to transport water to the fields of Agra, the East Indian Railway snaked into Gurgaon on its way from Delhi to Bikaner. With this, Gurgaon's centre was linked to Delhi by rail, as it was to Alwar and Jaipur in Rajasthan. Tourists, however, were not exactly queuing up to buy tickets to visit important sites in Jaipur. The Rajputana–Malwa Railway began chiefly as an adjunct to the military establishment to move troops and supplies briskly from the various cantonments to the battlegrounds or areas of conflict and to haul raw materials closer to the ports. A small railway station was built on the road that still has a tank, believed to be Guru Dronacharya's famous well. The station was constructed in what was the unadorned and unbeautiful Public Works Department (PWD) style of architecture, which is best described as a shoebox with windows.

While the railway did not make Gurgaon quite a sought-after destination yet, the temple dedicated to Sitla Mata drew more than

50,000 pilgrims annually. Smallpox, a European import from the New World, had taken hold in this region. It was a terrifying and highly contagious disease, often disfiguring and blinding and even killing its victims. It called into existence the new goddess Sitla, the cool one, to calm the hot and angry pustules of the disease; temples were dedicated to her in many parts of India, and the misguided hope was that a visit to the cool goddess would be an antidote to catching the disease.

Every Monday, a fair is held at the temple even to this day, and the temple precincts have devotees come in every day of the week. Throughout the nineteenth century, every year the temple received offerings of more than 20,000 rupees, and these 'were formerly appropriated by Begum Samru but were now a perquisite of the proprietary body of Gurgaon Village'.[13] Although smallpox was declared eradicated in 1980, this temple still sees thousands of pilgrims visit, but I speculate that the priests have probably repurposed the curative powers of Sitla Mata to other ailments to keep the offerings coming, over which they now have complete control. Perhaps she is now the antipyretic of the debilitating assaults of the dengue and chikungunya viruses carried by mosquitoes.

A Maverick's Idea: The Gurgaon Experiment

In 1920, a new and zealous evangelist, Deputy Commissioner Frank Lugard Brayne, who was an expert in rural reconstruction, took charge and became the newest occupant of Begum Samru's erstwhile palace. Brayne was outspoken, opinionated and came with an unshakeable sense that he could make Gurgaon a model village and district in the Indian empire. Mind you, he never thought of it as a model town; his goal was to make it a model village and his plan was called The Gurgaon Experiment. Unlike the ilk of evangelist Charles Grant in 1879, who had only condemned the 'Indian race' with disparaging phrases like 'a race of men lamentably degenerate and base ... and governed by malevolent and licentious passions ... sunk in misery by their vices', Brayne believed fervently in social and moral uplift as his bounden duty to redeem the Haryanvi-speaking peasantry.

For the next seven years he toiled at bringing about this 'uplift' through his blueprint of village reconstruction (latrines were a large part of his plan) that was greatly applauded then and is, to this day, duly acknowledged when a government scheme to improve the countryside rears its head. He introduced some useful innovations, like his 'bhoosa box', a wooden box insulated with hay that would keep food from spoiling overnight, and the iron-belted wooden wheels of bullock carts to make them go faster and last longer. Brayne's mission was practical, his philosophy simple, and his methods arbitrary. Using Gurgaon as his chief inspiration, he wrote several books about village reconstruction, of improving the ways and customs of villagers and townsfolk. He was inexhaustible in his ideas of 'betterment', he blamed the people's poverty not on colonial extraction of revenue, but on their 'thriftless' and 'improvident' ways, which he set about to change. Waste and improvidence were his watchwords: he was a terrible nag about women investing in gold and silver jewellery when they could put the same money to better their children's lives. He absolutely abhorred pierced ears studded with gold earrings; he was even provoked enough by one woman's ornaments to have violently ripped them out of her earlobes. But despite his crude exasperation with the 'benighted', he claimed that his heart was with the villagers and the years he spent in Gurgaon he claimed to be his happiest.

However, nothing sums up the essence of his evangelical fervour than his sternly stating, 'Let me ordain where the nation shall defecate [sic] and I care not who makes their laws.' When I first encountered a far longer version of this quote, it sounded both amusing and bigoted and I used it as an epigraph of a chapter in my book on Lucknow. Now, in 2018, when I dare to walk through the streets of Gurgaon that are woefully lacking in footpaths but endowed with ubiquitous piles of garbage and building materials, I carefully dodge traffic and sidestep rubble, potholes and, yes, human and animal waste, I can understand his anger and wish to endorse his wish. A clean city is a pleasure to live in. In New York, for instance, I have observed that its inhabitants, armed with plastic bags, pick up after their leashed dogs and toss their litter in the many bins dotting the cityscape, to leave the wide, well-maintained pavements spotless. The civic authority enforces the rules and levies hefty fines on those who infringe them. What made the pooper scooper law work was the fact that the law gave dog owners 'cover' to scoop up their dog's excrement, and knowing that everyone was going to be doing it made it a very acceptable practice. At the time of writing this, one can only dream that one day, in the not too distant future, the ordinary citizen's latent civic pride and good governance will combine effectively to bring ordered, well-marked, well-lit and well-swept streets, convenient and usable litter bins, efficient sewage disposal, treatment of waste water, and clean, clear pavements to Gurgaon. Brayne's experiment will finally be a reality.

While Brayne's writings reveal his frustration for those he wished to uplift, he was sincere about his mission and felt deeply about causes that are unwittingly close to the hearts of many non-governmental organizations (NGOs) operating in Gurgaon today. He wanted well-trained schoolteachers to involve themselves in the lives of their students for them to lead tidier, more hygienic and healthier lives. He insisted that the education of girls and women were the keystones of a better society, that farmers should use better implements and seeds, build drains and latrines, control mosquitoes, use quinine against malaria, save money and join cooperative banks, invest their savings in interest-bearing accounts of the cooperative banks that had sprung up, rather in silver and gold jewellery, and these small measures would make life much better. Lifestyle changes were at the heart of his intention, but his self-righteousness, reliance on authority from above, and the stark poverty of the villagers made his 'Gurgaon Experiment' fail. In fact, it collapsed as soon as he was transferred out of the district. It is shocking that a century later, when a huge city has emerged in that same region, we could still look upon Brayne's experiment, although not his attitude or his methods, as our own unfinished agenda. Mahatma Gandhi's attempts at creating a better world for Indians were aimed to promote self-sufficiency in its villages; cities were not part of the vision of India's future. He worked hard to make Indians realize that they must build toilets and clean them. His desire to get Indians to respect 'untouchables' and low-caste menials as the 'children of god' was equally wasted. Today, there are fifty villages in a city like Gurgaon, so Brayne and Gandhi were justified in their rural emphasis; if the villages within Gurgaon were endowed with civic amenities we would have a much better city. Prime Minister Narendra Modi's scheme of Swachh Bharat, 'clean India', remains an empty slogan because it has foundered on the same social and cultural rocks on which Brayne's and Gandhi's dreams of a hygienic India were dashed.

Gurgaon failed to become the model village of Brayne's vision for his scheme lacked any real commitment by the colonial government that deliberately failed to bring jobs in the manufacturing sphere. The only advance visualized for it was more agriculture and trivial 'improvements' of the misguided kind that proved environmentally disastrous. What was fundamentally wrong with colonial rule was the revolution it purposely withheld from India: a transfer of technologies that brought about the Industrial Revolution in England. That would have created jobs and prosperity for its many underemployed and desperate farmers, just as it did there. Urbanization would have replaced rural stagnation. Gurgaon, therefore, remained a small town with a few low-level administrative jobs, while a huge opportunity to develop industry was wilfully neglected, and postponed until the end of the twentieth century.

The British role in building cities or creating industry was severely limited given the scope and the funds available to them. They were content with their fortified port cities that were major gateways for trade, the hill stations for retreat in the unbearably hot summers, the small railway stations and district towns for the practical purposes of administration and revenue collection, and building civil lines and cantonments as the European quarters in the older captured regional capitals, like Delhi, Murshidabad and Lucknow—cities they had partially destroyed during the Rebellion of 1857. Even Delhi would languish for more than a century as a provincial town after its conquest in 1803 with the base of operations in Calcutta. It was not until 1911 that New Delhi, grandly conceived and built by Herbert Baker and Edwin Lutyens, would be proclaimed as the capital of Britain's Indian empire. And it was not until Delhi was overwhelmed with refugees in the Partition of 1947 with the movement of Punjabis into its Haryanvi-speaking area that its fortunes materially changed when industry came to Faridabad and eventually to Gurgaon, as we shall see later in the book.

The vital flaw in Gurgaon's make-up at the outset of the urban explosion was the lack of reliable and plentiful water, a chronic dearth that is part natural and part man-made, as we have seen. This condition is not peculiar to Gurgaon, it is shared by large parts of India and by many cities, most notably its neighbour, Delhi, where the population has burgeoned to bursting point and the Yamuna has contracted to a polluted trickle. Today, ecologists have figured out that the large-scale deforestation and the laying of railway tracks from east to west that bridged or blocked the north-south flowing torrents of the Gurgaon region have magnified the danger of the city dying of thirst. After the springs and torrents that drained into jhils that made up the avian-rich wetlands had dried up, the push was to tap groundwater, an alternative that was pursued with a vengeance, as it is the only source of potable water supply that exists for urban use. Construction companies have dug tube wells to exploit this resource freely. The turn of the present century has brought fresh warnings against the falling levels of groundwater, and boring tube wells have been banned. But huge exceptions exist: the city has permitted the biggest private consumers whose wells service high-rise apartments and office buildings. It also has no means to stop the urban villagers, as we shall see later, from extracting groundwater in unorganized residential colonies, called as *lal dora* areas. The village well owners pump water into small tankers that travel to homes in old and new

Gurgaon residential colonies, dispensing water for a price. The retail price in 2017 was Rs 700 per 5,000 litres in a tanker that would serve a family of four for a couple of days.

With new extractor technology and equipment, mechanical drills now bore through schist and quartzite, often going deeper than 300 metres, to find precious aquifers that are being sucked dry. Severe water shortages are experienced in most of Haryana, where there is no large river, even as its population explodes and the consumption of water grows exponentially. A place that did not have the 5,000 inhabitants it needed to be designated as a town in the late nineteenth century, today has an approximate population of two million and growing.

Two

A New Wind (God) Stirs the Town

Something had to powerfully spur the transformation of a small town into an urban behemoth, because there was no official plan and no private visionary who had dreamed up the enormous changes to come to Gurgaon. No one redirected the attention of the nation and its future developers to Gurgaon as much as Sanjay Gandhi, the younger son of the then prime minister Indira Gandhi, unwittingly did. In his quest to build an indigenous small car that would, he had vainly hoped, become the vehicle for the common man, he became the unintentional and unacknowledged catalyst for the first wave of modern industrialization in Gurgaon.

How did this transpire and why is it pertinent to our story about the making of Gurgaon? Contrary to accounts that make DLF the moving spirit of what created the city, I believe that after Sanjay Gandhi chose Gurgaon as the site for his presumed automobile factory in 1970, it abruptly changed the business climate of this sleepy little town. Originally intended to remain a small-scale industry and agricultural outpost, it came to be viewed as a potential site for big business and a future city. This was some years before DLF or its chairman, Kushal Pal Singh, decided to take his business, as a builder of residential colonies in Delhi, to Gurgaon.

The Sanjay Gandhi initiative—it soon came to be known as the 'Maruti saga'—is important to remind the old and to enlighten the young because its relevance is undiminished as a forerunner of the repeated collusions of private entrepreneurs, politicians and bureaucrats in the making of the city.[1] For all its plot twists and pig-headed characters, it showcases how the lead actors in the state and Central governments connived to bend the rules for personal gain. It was a murky augury for Gurgaon to come as deals were cut in the acquisition of land, the granting of licences, the allocation of scarce and valuable resources. This retelling will also clarify the dubious public–private partnerships that have so bedevilled the proper development of Gurgaon. To elucidate the complications that haunt the building or expansion of a city is the foremost aim of this book.

Sanjay Gandhi was, by all accounts, a man with an immense sense of entitlement, who unabashedly took full advantage of his family's political clout, quite unlike his elder brother, Rajiv. Sanjay was not afraid of the law or the consequences of his actions because he was Indira Gandhi's (favourite) son. An obstinate and self-willed recluse, he had scant respect for scholastic routine or his teachers, and made very few friends. The friends he did make were, as Vinod Mehta put it in his book *The Sanjay Story*, 'by and large, like him: rich, spoilt, academically dim, uninterested in sports'.[2] Among this tight group was one Kamal Nath, nicknamed 'Frog' by their Doon School cohorts, who was the leader—and who later led Sanjay into politics.

Sanjay's dream project was to build the 'people's car'. Inspired by Adolf Hitler's success with the Volkswagen in Germany, he began a chain of events that are breathtaking in their audacity. Sanjay disdained the idea of academic degrees and wanted to work 'in a car factory' to gain practical experience with car engines. The only 'professional credentials' Sanjay had to nurture his dream was as an apprentice at a Rolls Royce manufacturing plant at Crewe in England, a company that patently did not make small cars. He was supposed to move from shop floor to shop floor learning the ropes for three solid years, attend evening classes to get the necessary engineering background, but Sanjay was distracted by his rather more engaging social life. While he was there, he was arrested in December 1966 for driving without a licence, a bit surprising for one who loved driving cars.[3] Sanjay Gandhi abruptly abandoned this stint after two years.

The subject of manufacturing a small car in India had been debated off and on by the cabinet and in the print media since the early 1950s, when in 1962, V.K. Krishnamachari of the Planning Commission dismissed the idea on principled grounds. India's needs were not for a small car, the Commission had rightly argued, but for investment in public transport for the masses. Buses, trains, bicycles, scooters and trucks were the need of India's poor and swelling population—not the luxury of a small private car that only a few would ever be able to purchase and maintain. There were already three private motorcar manufacturers in India—the sturdy Birla Ambassador; the smaller Standard Herald, both British; and the sleeker Italian Fiat made in collaboration by Premier Motors. Fiat even had floated a proposal to make their 600D model, which would cost Rs 9,000 (ex-factory), but it did not find any traction. Other alternative proposals from notable manufacturers worldwide met the same fate.

While this debate was raging in the corridors of power, Sanjay was back in Delhi, and in 1967 made his desire to build his small car quite plain to his mother. He did not care that the Planning Commission had decided otherwise. He began toying with the alleged prototype of its engine in a primitive workshop he had set up at Gulabi Bagh in Delhi. In July 1968, not uninfluenced by the fact that Sanjay Gandhi was a major player, it was decided that the small car project would go ahead despite the priorities and objections of the Planning Commission and that it would be placed in the private sector. Indira Gandhi, indeed, overrode its strenuous objections ignoring her own 800 pound gorilla-sized conflict of interest in this case, and presided over the cabinet meeting in September 1970 where the decision was taken. A month later, Sanjay Gandhi submitted the blueprint of a two-door car fitted with a rear-mounted 14 horsepower engine, with wheels the size of those of a scooter rickshaw. It would be 80 per cent indigenously sourced, with a capacity to hold six persons and luggage, and would cost Rs 6,000 (ex-factory). Fifty thousand vehicles, he optimistically asserted, would hit the road annually.[4]

The irregular procedures allowed to Sanjay Gandhi were cringe producing; for a normal applicant the project report was to be the annex to the application for an industrial licence. In this special case, the project report was evaluated *before* Sanjay had even applied for an industrial licence. This plan was sent to the Directorate General of Technical Development (DGTD) for scrutiny. The DGTD raised many serious technical questions and its response politely but sternly averred, 'although the concept was laudable, nothing seemed viable about the project'. After much timorous hemming and hawing by many top bureaucrats, the project was conditionally cleared—it was agreed that a road test of 30,000 kilometres would be mandatory for the completed car. Indira Gandhi's looming personal concern in the matter did not elude those who were making these decisions.

Irregularities multiplied with many more meetings. Discussions, delays and concessions ensued, and the project evaded the maze of regulations. Unfazed, Sanjay Gandhi then demanded a letter of intent from the Licensing Committee even *before* the prototype of his car was ready. Bureaucratic compunctions were brushed aside, yet again; Indira Gandhi supported the project publicly in a speech and a week later, all official misgivings evaporated. A letter of intent was issued to the company registered as Maruti Limited, on 30 September 1970. It was valid for six months and permitted him to establish a factory in Faridabad, Haryana, for the manufacture of 50,000 cars annually—a figure greater than the total number of the cars produced by the three automobile companies that then existed. Sanjay Gandhi instantly began his war of attrition and managed to overturn every single stipulation of the letter of intent, including his rejection of Faridabad as the location for the factory and—and here we have it—choosing Gurgaon instead.

The tale of how he chose Gurgaon is a stark example of how nepotism, corruption and power combined to make a real-life national scandal. First, Sanjay tore up the letter of intent in spirit, and dug his heels in for the change of the venue for the proposed factory from Faridabad to Gurgaon. A shed was built, but as my informant, Vijay Mathur, who worked for the Suzuki Company from close to its outset in Gurgaon, informed me, its roof was unsupported by steel girders, it leaned ominously, and the 'factory' had no modern machinery to speak of to produce even half a dozen viable cars. The amazing black-and white-photos that illustrated Uma Vasudev's interview with Sanjay Gandhi in *Surge* in 1976 reveal this graphically and it is hard to capture in words the handmade ambience of the workshop.

Worse yet, as I read the summary of the evaluation team's interim verdict of 29 March 1974 on the Maruti prototype, I thought I was reading an amusing parody. After completing a test run of only 7,800 kilometres, rather than the required 30,000, the car's multiple defects were exposed. It exposed the 'cracking of the trailing link', the fact that the 'vehicle [was] pulling to the right', that its battery had leaked 'electrolyte', and there was 'brake failure', 'breakage of silencer', 'breakage of propeller shaft bush bearings' and 'the steering was stiff'. In addition, the car body and rear bonnet vibrated and rattled in fourth gear, the vehicle's 'self-centring' was poor, and during the waterproof test, water seeped into the passenger compartment, the engine, and the dickey.[5]

On 24 June 1974, the prototype car, while undergoing a reliability test—which followed its truncated and failed roadworthiness test—'had a major failure of the steering tie rod' and the prototype vehicle 'fell into a ditch' and was seriously damaged. Needless to say, this stillborn brainchild never did legitimately pass any tests, even though it actually had a smuggled German engine, and was never subjected to the full distance of 30,000 kilometres mandated for a licence. Instead, the manufacturer's staggering transgressions of regulations and the laughable end product were overlooked, the scrupulous objections of those who had tested it were totally disregarded, and an industrial licence was handed to Maruti Ltd that same year to build a factory that claimed it would produce 50,000 units annually. This unprecedented permit was as ironclad, as Sanjay's failure was spectacular. More on this later; first let's look at how the Maruti project was wedded to the state politics of Haryana.

Thanks to Bansi Lal, the then chief minister of Haryana, the art of the land deal was to become the biggest game in town. He saw his chance in Sanjay's refusal to accept any of his offers of three distinct sites, and a generous package of finance, electricity and water supply to build his factory in Faridabad, a developed industrial city. Sanjay demanded, without a written application, 75 acres of land for the purpose in Gurgaon and not the meagre 5 and 8 acre plots he was offered in Faridabad. His insistence on a rural outpost like Gurgaon, something that seemed foolhardy, was actually astute under the circumstances. Sanjay lived with his mother in the prime minister's house at 1 Safdarjung Road in Delhi, and regularly visited her farmhouse in Chhattarpur, less than 8 kilometres from Gurgaon. Faridabad was definitely going to be a long and inconvenient commute for him. Also, land in Gurgaon was far cheaper and more abundantly available than in Faridabad. Gurgaon was therefore the logical choice for Sanjay and he was not to be thwarted.

Bansi Lal had paid close attention to the journey of Sanjay's application, because he was desperately looking for access to the prime minister to further his own political ambitions. When asked by a senior bureaucrat why he was assiduously pursuing Sanjay Gandhi, he famously remarked in a Haryanvi agrarian aphorism: '*Jab bachhra apne haath mein hai to gai to chali aayegi.*' (When you have the calf in hand the cow will automatically seek you).[6] In an instant he became the sponsor of the Maruti project and wrote to Fakhruddin

Ali Ahmed, the then Union minister of industrial development and company affairs, urging that the licence be granted to Sanjay Gandhi without demur.

This brings us to the seminal matter that set an example for future deals in Gurgaon: the impropriety and illegality of acquiring land in Gurgaon district for Maruti Ltd. Long before Sanjay Gandhi applied for land for his factory, Bansi Lal had tactically acquired, in bold contravention of the Land Acquisition Act, nearly 600 acres for developing industry in Gurgaon. Of these he pre-emptively allotted 297.3 acres—Sanjay had asked for only 75 acres—to Maruti Ltd in Gurgaon when Sanjay turned down Faridabad as a possible location for his factory. Sanjay was delighted with this arrangement and their mutually advantageous friendship blossomed.

Bansi Lal's action, however, was hasty and the land was riddled with problems. Not only had he ignored the alternative of acquiring the hilly and fallow lands on the Mehrauli–Gurgaon road in Nathupur and Chakkarpur villages, he had chosen strictly prohibited lands for acquisition. About 157 acres of this land was under occupation of the Ministry of Defence and were part of the inviolate cordon sanitaire of an ammunition dump, which the Indian Air Force had created off the Delhi–Gurgaon Road, at a mandated safe distance from the airport. Normally, as we know, the defence of the nation takes precedence over all other considerations; but this was clearly not a normal case. Sanjay Gandhi and Bansi Lal were impervious even to the objections of Jagjivan Ram, the then defence minister, because of the lengthening shadow of Indira Gandhi looming over the proceedings.

There was, and still is, a statute in force that forbade 'haphazard and sub-standard development along scheduled roads and in controlled areas' and the construction of a building within 30 metres on either side of such a road. The Delhi–Gurgaon Road was indeed such a road and Sanjay Gandhi, undaunted, now planned to build his factory right off it. There were other stipulations in the Land Acquisition Act that would have made the construction of the factory on the chosen site illegal, but these too were ignored. The balance of

140 acres included in Sanjay's allotment was one of the most fertile and highly populated regions in the district, and being in the 'rural zone' could not be legitimately acquired for industrial use. Even as these serious constraints on the site were presented to the interested party, Jagjivan Ram was ordered by Indira Gandhi to immediately release the aforesaid 157 acres of air force land on 14 November 1970. And she was obeyed.

Realizing that he had not even formally applied for this land that was now his, Sanjay Gandhi hastily wrote to the director of industries in Haryana on the same day stating that he required 300 acres of land, which he had already selected. He proposed to pay for it in instalments; the first instalment, he stated, would be paid five years after its acquisition. The Haryana government under Bansi Lal footed the bill in the interim. Had a normal citizen of India the temerity to make such an outrageous and belated request he would have been pronounced a lunatic and his 'project' would have been consigned to the waste-paper basket without a moment's pause. Instead, Sanjay Gandhi's wishlist was met with accommodating nods and smiles. To comply with his demands, the Gurgaon Town and Country Planning Department speedily modified the land use from agriculture to industry. What is even more astounding is that in the application he had stated that his factory would require 75 acres, so the fourfold increase in allotment of encumbered land to Maruti Ltd remained unexplained. He also referred to his 'previous correspondence' on the subject of the land requirement—none of which, it turned out upon inquiry, was found to exist anywhere.[7]

The Indian government has been known to be a very arbitrary acquirer of farmland, but in this case it acted against its *own* legal stipulations. More than half the acreage allotted to Sanjay Gandhi in the capacity of a *private entrepreneur* belonged to the Ministry of Defence, and the rest was part of the government's own non-acquisition zone. Any corporate executive reading this would salivate at the prospect of acquiring even a fraction of this land on the terms extended to Sanjay Gandhi. The process of acquiring land expressly protected by law is an object lesson in how such things are possible to manipulate if highly connected entrepreneurs, the highest elected officials, and a pliant bureaucracy are hand in glove. Bansi Lal managed to subvert very strict laws for this project and the prime minister's son invited him to his mother's house for intimate discussions that would eventually lead him to a seat in her Central cabinet as minister of defence.

Unsurprisingly, then, there was more skulduggery and nothing either legal or humanitarian was allowed to stand in the way of Maruti Ltd in Gurgaon. The collector's report on land acquisition emphasized that the agricultural land Sanjay Gandhi sought was highly productive land, and therefore not eligible for acquisition. The owners of the land, the report confirmed, 'were uneducated small landowners and except 50 all the other interested parties numbering 1086 were entirely dependent on agriculture'.[8]

The farmers whose land was to be acquired challenged the notification because it was done under Section 17 of the Land Acquisition Act, which is strictly for emergencies, and in this case, it was certain there was no emergency. In response to that, the notification was quickly withdrawn and at confounding speed, a fresh notification issued to acquire the land the very next day, 24 March 1971, and promptly published in the Gazette.

Serious legal hurdles arose and fell quickly. The strictures of even the Ministry Defence, as we have seen, were upended. Sanjay Gandhi's omission of how this vast swathe of land would be used by his car factory was shocking enough; but even 'the project report he claimed to have sent earlier was not traceable'.[9] With S.K. Mishra, principal secretary to Bansi Lal and R.K. Dhawan, personal assistant to Indira Gandhi, available to do the bidding of their masters, these awkward anomalies, omissions and errors were papered over while Sanjay Gandhi expressed his annoyance at the delay in the allotment of the land. He had also omitted to apply for the sanction of electricity, just as he did not have a working indigenous prototype to manufacture, and certainly 'no moral or other justification for dispossessing the tiller of the land'.[10] Bansi Lal, who communicated only orally, by phone or in conversation, as chief ministers are wont to do, had his principal secretary, S.K. Mishra write all the letters and iron out the wrinkles of this procurement, which he dutifully did.

The assessment for this hastily and arbitrarily acquired land was achieved at an astounding speed. The farmers whose livelihood depended on the land were perceived as mere hindrances and their removal was expedited. The land acquisition collector, O.P. Yadav, claimed that he was able to hear and decide on the compensation of the cases of 118 petitioners with varying qualities of land, and various assets such as trees, wells and buildings on each plot, situated in four different villages, in a few hours on the same day. Equally astonishing is that the awards, running into seventy-four typed pages, were also produced in an hour, with only one stenographer and one typist working on a manual typewriter. Yadav and his stenographer must have acted like the frenzied characters in the Charlie Chaplin film, *Modern Times*. When interrogated as to how he had so quickly assessed so many plots of land, with trees, wells, houses, huts and barns, he claimed the same magical powers to be able to judge this instantly to beat the deadline. He later confessed that he had decided the cases en masse, based on the calculations for compensation he had already made for the various grades of land that existed and, in truth, many judgements had been typed up even before the cases were heard. This ungodly haste, with which the wheel of law seldom turned in India, was prompted by the deadline that Sanjay Gandhi had imposed on the officials to sort out the land deal. He was unmoved by the plight of the more than a thousand farmers rendered landless, while he had the land with no viable plan, even on paper, to use so vast an acreage.

Corporations that exist in Gurgaon today would reel in disbelief at the astonishing promptness with which the government acted. With Sanjay Gandhi's deadline of 10 July 1971 impending, the top brass of the Haryana government scurried to a meeting summoned by him in Chandigarh on 3 July 1971. The group included Bansi Lal and his top cabinet members, besides the director of industries, the chairman of the State Electricity Board, and the director of town and country planning. All this is astounding and reads like fiction, but the difference between fiction and reality is that fiction has to make sense, as Tom Clancy, the novelist, said. When we pause to consider that Sanjay Gandhi was a private citizen and wielded this clout to intimidate politicians and bureaucrats on the sole qualification of being the prime minister's son, we might say that it makes no sense at all in a democracy.

The minutes of that meeting state that all outstanding issues were summarily resolved. It's clear that a number of unlawful decisions were summarily taken. It was decided that Sanjay Gandhi would pay Rs 12,000 only per acre although the final award was not yet made; he would make a 10 per cent down payment and the rest in eighteen equal instalments two years after possession of the land. This was not all—the Haryana government 'would underwrite 25 per cent of the share capital, up to an aggregate sum of Rs 1.25 crore, in preference shares'.[11] All state and purchase taxes due on materials bought in Haryana would be treated as an interest-free loan for a period of five years after the date of production.

Sanjay demanded yet another concession: electricity had to be supplied to the Maruti plant on a priority basis and the cost of installing the transformer and the cost of the electricity would be totally borne by the state government.[12] No one blinked; they might even have pulled their blinkers on tighter. It is dumbfounding that such prompt and generous concessions were made by a government that was almost bankrupt, socialist in its appeal and where Indira Gandhi had launched her 'Garibi Hatao' slogan. This was rather ironic because the land acquired for Sanjay's factory left a thousand subsistence farmers landless.

To compound the egregious violations of getting the land allocated to Maruti Ltd, Sanjay Gandhi committed many more irregularities. For instance, when the draft agreement for the sale of the land was given to him to approve, he had it typed on stamp paper that was neither dated, nor named the vendor or the buyer, or the court from where it was bought. An omission as big as this would make any legal agreement in India null and void. Further, he gave a cheque for Rs 3.53 lakh dated 7 August 1971 to the Town and Country Planning Department of Haryana as the down payment for the land, but the balance in the bank account on which it was drawn was not sufficient to cover the cheque. Bansi Lal got a bureaucrat to catch it in mid-bounce and hold it until later. This cheque was finally cashed more than six weeks later on 25 September 1971.[13] In the entire saga, the chief minister's contempt for the law was equally amazing and this attitude unfortunately is echoed in another more recent private land deal that has made national headlines. It involves an alleged sweetheart deal between DLF and Robert Vadra, a private businessman and son-in-law of the late prime minister Rajiv Gandhi. The court case is still making its way through the legal system. Turning cheaply bought farmland into prime real estate is something an alchemist would envy.

Sanjay Gandhi's land was supposed to have only a Maruti factory on it, as per the agreement, but he proceeded to build several unauthorized structures on it. In addition to the factory, he built a research and development wing, two complexes near gates one and two of the compound that were rented to several commercial tenants, and a five-storeyed staff quarters which also broke the zoning law that explicitly stated that no building was to be higher than two storeys. No fines were levied, no penalties extracted; a great small car, it was believed, was in the making.

Then there was the small matter of money.[14] Just like everything else, it was easy to raise money if you are Sanjay Gandhi, because investors clamoured to invest in his company—perhaps they believed that he was too important to fail. Banks, meanwhile, did not demand collateral or glance at his project report; they simply, ingratiatingly, loaned him the money he sought. Maruti started with an authorized capital of Rs 2.5 crore in 1971 and it rose to Rs 10 crore in the following year with M.A. Chidambaram of Automobile Products of India as its chairman. Fifty-three shareholders had shares worth more than Rs 1 lakh each. There were numerous smaller holders, named either Mishra or Jha, and they were all relatives of S.K. Mishra and his wife. There was a huge rush to get the coveted dealerships to sell this wonder car.[15] In 1972, Sanjay appointed seventy-five dealers who deposited between one and three lakh rupees each and were promised cars for sale within six months. A sum of Rs 2.18 crore was collected from dealers by 1974–75. Many of these hopefuls, and many who were coerced to become dealers by industrialists who did not want to disclose their investments in Maruti Ltd, took loans to construct showrooms to display the cars they were never to see, nor did they receive the promised interest on their deposits. Potential customers booked their vehicles against deposits and these were lost too.[16]

A prototype was eventually unveiled at the end of 1972. The few who actually saw it shuddered politely, some giggled in disbelief, and the one who rode in it found the experience 'frightening'. Sanjay changed some components and raised the price of the future car by 90 per cent. This didn't improve the product, though, and in the four years of Maruti Ltd's existence, the factory produced nothing that worked or could be sold.[17] Inept management, inefficiency, a fundamentally flawed design, and a severe shortage of capital transformed the promised little people's car into a national hoax.

If Sanjay was not an engineer, he was also neither an astute economist nor an efficiency expert. Naturally, major fiscal bungling ensued. He had gravely miscalculated the capital required for such an enterprise; he needed ten times the capital and the wherewithal to buy proper machine tools to manufacture a proper car.[18] He tried to cover up the congenital defects of his four-wheel baby by launching yet another company in June 1975, by which time Maruti Technical Services (MTS), another company he had set up to contravene the original letter of intent, had extracted Rs 10 lakh from Maruti Ltd. Registered as a small-scale industry, Maruti Heavy Vehicles Private

Limited was a subsidiary of the family controlled MTS, which held 59 per cent of its paid-up capital of Rs 15 lakh. It was also bound by contract to pay 2 per cent commission on its net sales to its parent company MTS for technical assistance for ten years.[19] This enterprise was to manufacture roadrollers, in synch with Bansi Lal's plans to expand the road network in Haryana.

Experts had cast serious doubts on the possibility of a viable car emerging from the very primitive factory where car bodies were stitched by hand, and newspapers began to investigate and corroborated these misgivings. There were angry questions by the Opposition in Parliament over the land deal, the dispossessed farmers, unsecured bank loans and the misuse of public funds. Unheeding, Sanjay continued to borrow money 'frequently from banks and public institutions by a combination of bluff and blackmail'.[20] Eventually, with the car nowhere in sight to contradict the negative accounts, banks became wary and even the Reserve Bank of India cautioned banks against lending any more money to Maruti, and intimated nationalized banks that they should not either. The Central Bank of India, that had been regularly milked by Sanjay, now refused to oblige him. Sanjay was irate as things were spooling out of his control—and then his mother declared a national Emergency on 26 June 1975. Some media reports stated that it was not only prompted by her own legal problems, but also to conceal Sanjay's embarrassing and legally actionable mess. What lent this theory credence was that Sanjay and his coterie of friends, which included Bansi Lal and Kamal Nath, began a vengeful battle against all those who had crossed or criticized him. A slew of transfers, suspensions, incarcerations and resignations of the top men in the banks and others followed. His unforgettable reign of terror lasted until Indira Gandhi lifted the Emergency and the Congress party lost the parliamentary elections decisively in March 1977.

This, however, is not the end of the catalogue of the sins committed—it is only the end of my readers' patience and disbelief that something so culpable transpired with the active complicity of the prime minister and the chief minister. Sanjay's much-vaunted car failed completely, hopelessly and irretrievably. It took down with it all the money that agents had advanced to sell the car—many lives were ruined, fortunes lost, reputations sullied. The ill-conceived Maruti Ltd was liquidated in 1977. Sanjay entered politics in the 1977 elections riding on the coat tails of his mother and they were defeated, but not for long. In the 1980 elections, Sanjay won and became member of Parliament from Amethi in Uttar Pradesh. But the same reckless, law-bucking stunts that extinguished his Maruti Ltd ended his life on 23 June 1980 as he took off in a Pitts S-2A two-seater plane with his ill-fated instructor, Subhash Saxena, and crashed it near Safdarjung Airport, not far from his mother's official residence. A grief-stricken Indira Gandhi came to pick up the pieces of what she had wrought. Arun Shourie of *The Indian Express* in an editorial summed it up with words to the effect that Sanjay was leading the country in the way he piloted his plane, and it was fortunate it was the plane that crashed.

Paradoxically, Sanjay's dismal failure and Maruti's resurrection became the key to Gurgaon's burgeoning as a city. With its inauspicious start, Maruti had no inkling of its future. Out of this darkness, Suzuki, then an insignificant Japanese automobile manufacturer, emerged as the knight in shining armour to rescue the stranded maiden venture. In 1981, Suzuki purchased the name 'Maruti', its licence, the dilapidated shed, and an invaluable factory compound of 300 acres. It bought 26 per cent—the then permissible limit for foreign direct investment—of the company from its caretakers in government, who owned the rest of it. It imported cars for two years into India, and in 1983 launched the iconic Maruti 800, a variation of its successful Alto in Japan, that actually proved to be a game changer. Many components were still imported, but the car was a runaway success. Suzuki had bestowed the transforming kiss that Gurgaon had been waiting for; the frog emerged from under the rock in the shape of a prince. Phoenix-like, Maruti, the ill-wrought rattletrap rose from its own ashes in the form of the sleek and most ubiquitous little vehicle on Indian roads—the Maruti 800. And for the purposes of this narrative, this event happened in Gurgaon—its rude, rustic birthplace—and was the most notable in its history. Suddenly it was the city that had India's largest automobile company. The nation and the new city drove off into the future, honking audaciously.

This compact car was to revolutionize motor car manufacturing in India and begin the middle-class's love affair with their brilliant product. The Japanese modernized and humanized labour and factory practices in India, and Gurgaon, the place where it was made, was suddenly a household name nationally marked on the map with a strong black dot that connected it to the larger global economy. In the years that followed, there wasn't a road in the country where a Maruti 800, a Zen, a Baleno, a Swift, or a Gypsy, its off-road vehicle, was not wending its way. For affluent women, the Maruti 800 was a kind of liberation from their husbands and drivers; they could now afford to own a car and drive it too, with its very smooth gearbox and comfortably small size and the ease of air conditioning and heating in a climate of extremes. It left the bulky Ambassador and the Fiat gasping for their lives; the former was on life support for several years until the Birlas finally pulled the plug on their workhorse in 2016, while the latter has had radical surgery to survive but its market share is today a sliver of its former self. Rapidly, Maruti Suzuki India Ltd, now wholly owned by Suzuki, with more than a dozen models of cars, had wrested 50 per cent of the market share in the passenger vehicles segment in 2018. It brought an avalanche of ancillary industries; trade and commerce created hundreds of jobs and Gurgaon now throbbed with the lifeblood of an industrial township.

It also opened the floodgates for more Japanese and foreign car manufacturers to follow suit. Today, the best-known names in the world of automobiles—Mercedes Benz, BMW, Ford, Honda, Toyota, Hyundai have factories in India that assemble vehicles and manufacture most of their car parts here. Gurgaon is home to their many showrooms and dealerships, and is the Mecca for automobile lovers, since new highways and roads are slowly being laid. By 2015, Maruti had sold ten million units in India. Their longevity, fuel efficiency and affordable servicing and maintenance make them the most popular passenger vehicle manufacturer in the Indian subcontinent and these vehicles are exported to many foreign countries as well.

The story of Suzuki's role in rescuing Maruti would remain lopsided and incomplete without a summary of the tragic labour unrest that erupted at its plant in Manesar—about 18 kilometres from Gurgaon—on 18 July 2012 and the severe aftermath of that event. I followed the story avidly as the media began by supporting first the management and then switching sides in favour of the labour union. A full investigative account published in *The Wire* on 19 March 2017 gives us a balanced picture of what transpired.

The whole episode is a tale of escalating violence, with deep roots in the unfair hiring practices instituted by Maruti Suzuki's management at the Manesar factory to keep wages from rising. From 2011 the management hired temporary workers at half the wages paid to the 500-odd permanent employees, and this led to a demand by the latter to create an independent labour union to negotiate their grievances; this demand was turned down and an undercurrent of resentment pervaded the labour force.

On the fateful day in 2012 a manager and a worker, Jiya Lal, argued vehemently after the former insulted Lal with 'casteist slurs'. In the subsequent skirmish, Lal was joined many other workers and the general manager of human resources (HR), Awanish Kumar Dey, was killed and ninety others suffered minor injuries. Allegations and counter-allegations were hurled and in both sides of the story, truth and falsehood sparred with each other. However, the police came in and arrested ninety workers, including all the newly elected office-bearers of the labour union.

The Wire goes on to say that the police slapped conspiracy charges against the union leaders and workers and started a massive manhunt for other workers on charges of rioting, arson, and Dey's murder. In total, the police arrested and charged 148 workers for the incidents of 18 July 2012 and imprisoned them at Gurgaon's district jail in Bhondsi. All the injured persons were discharged in less than a week. The company locked the factory for a brief period and reopened it on 21 August 2012 after terminating nearly 500 permanent workers. With over 1,500 police officers deployed, the Manesar plant was temporarily converted into a veritable fortress.[21]

The management's allegations, however, were suspect as the witnesses they produced turned out to be a set of names in alphabetical order drawn from their registers, the statements recorded were often identical in nature, and bail was denied to workers for three years—surprising, since it's commonly granted for such offences, and as a result they remained in jail for five years before the trial ended. There was plausible evidence that the police tortured incarcerated workers.[22] Thereafter labour unrest took on very ominous tones for Maruti Suzuki and it spread to other automobile companies: first Honda, and then to Hero, the largest motorbike manufacturer in the world. Protests, shutdowns and lockouts make the news periodically, and tensions run very high. The state government has tried to water down the strong labour laws and sensing the difficult aftermath of the Manesar incident, Narendra Modi, then chief minister of Gujarat, seized a lucrative opportunity and offered Suzuki the best terms to open a factory in Gujarat, which it has since done.

The workers who were imprisoned have suffered enormously for five years. Most of them were young men in the early twenties who found their lives falling apart; many of them were the sole bread earners in their families. In consequence, broken marriages, poverty and sickness have overwhelmed many of their dependent kin. These men could not afford such a long stint without pay or the physical absence from their families. The long and the short of it is that the tensions and sporadic violence continued until the plant was closed down and reopened in the middle of August 2012 with immense losses to the company, mass dismissals and total ruin for the workers. It is fair to say that the Indian management of

Suzuki in Manesar upended the Japanese humane and filial work culture that Suzuki had brought here when they originally set up shop in Gurgaon.

There was also pressure from the government on the proceedings of the case. It claimed that the Manesar episode had been very harmful for India's image and reputation of its business climate for international investors. This smacked not of justice but of judicious manipulation and strong-arm tactics against the workers. In my opinion, the horrifically slow and corrupt judicial system in India is the nightmare that scares away more private investment in the country than anything else, and it remains untouched by reform even in this age of a liberalized and globalized economy.

The Wire goes on to say: 'On 10th March 2017 the Gurgaon sessions court acquitted 117 workers and convicted 31 workers in the sensational Maruti Suzuki riots case, including all the main office bearers of the Maruti Suzuki Workers Union. The quantum of punishment differs: 13 workers were sentenced to life imprisonment, 4 were given 5 years imprisonment and the remaining 14 were let off with what they had already served.'

There is a calm after the storm that ravaged industrial labour for five long years and the unrest has finally subsided, but the threat of another squall is now in as much on the factory floor as it is in corporate boardrooms and management teams. Suzuki, the global automobile manufacturer, has a record of no worker unrest in countries as varied as the Philippines, Pakistan, Brazil and Mexico. So its Indian managers have to take a good look at their own working culture to see why they failed their own company and their employees.

So the story of Maruti—the entire amazing saga from start to finish—stoutly belongs in the annals of Gurgaon's making. We may look back on Maruti's early, disastrous incarnation and its miraculous rescue by Suzuki and find a parallel not only in the land scams to come, but also in the hopes and dreams and the thousands of migrant workers from all over India who have laid the foundations of a manufacturing hub in an imperfect city with less than ideal working and living conditions. This unlikely city is on its way, albeit staggering along, with all the shortcomings of being ill-planned and incomplete like the first Maruti. Perhaps a brighter, better municipal government will set it on the right track. Yet, it must be said, Faridabad, the highly planned and government-managed industrial hub, has been eclipsed.

Three

Building Gurgaon: From Fallow Fields to Gold Mine

If the legendary Draupadi had five consorts and was coveted by a hundred more, Gurgaon was the foundling claimed by too many fathers who cast their sights beyond south Delhi.

By the early 1990s, Delhi had become overcrowded, its infrastructure creaked, its cars were parked on what were intended to be pavements, its taps and wells were running dry, and its air seriously polluted. The city had reached saturation point and was pushing its limits. Its vacant spaces were carpeted with what were euphemistically called 'unauthorized colonies' or 'informal housing'. These clusters of jhuggi-jhopris, as they are colloquially called, are where its burgeoning numbers of poor migrants dwelt, because affordable housing was non-existent. These stretches of lean-tos were summarily demolished, the inhabitants herded to remote sites when an international event was to occur—such as the Asian Games of 1982 and the Commonwealth Games of 2012—otherwise they would expose the tattered poverty of India to foreign eyes. Private builders envisaged living spaces only for the upper middle class, and the government only for its employees.

In a bid to ameliorate the plight of the 'lower income groups' (LIG) and 'middle income groups' (MIG), two pieces of legislation had been passed that decimated private builders in Delhi. The first created the Delhi Development Authority (DDA) by the Act of 1957 and the other was the passing of the Urban Land Ceiling Act (ULCA) of 1976. The alleged 'green belt' of Delhi, a slice of which began in Chhatarpur and extended southward to its border with Gurgaon, became a no-build zone—although the rich bought up swathes of it to build their farmhouses with swimming pools, and grow vegetables, fruit and flowers, and many even now (illegally) lease these out for fancy weddings.

If the first piece of legislation took away the power of private contractors to acquire land and build on it, giving the authority solely to the DDA, the second, the punitive ULCA, took away even already acquired vacant lands bought by private builders. This included the plots already sold by private builders but the titles for which had not yet been transferred to the potential owners. This sent the real estate market and the Delhi-based builders into a tailspin. Naturally, Gurgaon, outside the purview of Delhi's constraints, attracted thwarted builders to continue to replicate the Delhi colonies they had been building.

This was a cue for Gurgaon's meteoric rise from a humble hamlet to the fastest-growing city in India. It was decidedly different to how other cities had come into being. Its procreators were from the private sector that gave it the fillip to grow so big, so fast. It came to be called the 'Millennium City', which means that it came to be noticed in the new millennium, the twenty-first century, and is among its few neutral descriptors, and recently in a detailed scholarly article it has more appropriately been dubbed 'Private City'.[1]

The unflattering epithets are a plethora: 'dystopia', 'dysfunctional city' and even I have described its chaotic development, in one of my cynical moments, as 'a concrete hiccup' and 'a village on steroids'. Nothing quite defines the phenomenon that is Gurgaon because it is a work-in-progress, a changeling with rapidly altering vistas, a sprawl that gobbles up scores of square kilometres every passing year. It can be bipolar with its affluent and squalid aspects, shading from rustic conservatism to cybernetic modernity within a stone's throw of each other.

Demographically and spatially, Gurgaon underwent a sea change in three decades. The census of 1991 reports that Gurgaon district had an urban population of under 125,000; by 2001 this had multiplied sevenfold to 870,000 and by 2011 to 1.5 million and by 2017, by all accounts, it has surpassed 2.5 million. In terms of area, the expansion is even more impressive—from the original 2 sq. km village in the Delhi district of British Punjab, it had absorbed 22 sq. km within its bounds by 1996 at the slow and steady 'Hindu rate of growth'. Then came an explosive period and within the next two decades, by 2008, it had expanded to 185 sq. km, and by 2010 it had ballooned to a ginormous 207 sq. km, more than a hundred times what Guru Dronacharya surveyed as his own and almost as large as south Delhi. I am sure it will have expanded further by the time this statement meets a reader's eyeball.

From a perch on one of the residential towers that now are ubiquitous in the city you will find an amazing view—as I did from the architects Atal Kapur and Swanzal Kak Kapur's palatial apartment one afternoon in January 2014. The horizon seemed to pose no impediment to Gurgaon's sprawl. I gazed at the scene where I could watch the city being physically built—a scattering of metal cranes, their angular limbs a vivid red or yellow against a pale blue sky, poised over scaffolded structures of steel and concrete where precariously balanced workers went about their daily tasks. A power drill, with its ear-splitting staccato, was boring the earth for water some 250 metres below the surface. The vegetation was sparse—construction had taken a heavy toll—but there were plans to replant these vast stretches with indigenous trees. Atal pointed out the new gated communities coming up that resembled symmetrical Lego sets with thirty floors of apartment slots with balconies, while I stood there with my jaw dropped, trying to gauge the pull of the magnet that Gurgaon had become. I could see faint tracks of roads and interior streets and electric poles sticking out like toothpicks to be joined with the spools of thick, black wires lying nearby that would enable a modern life in this bleakness.

It seemed to illustrate the real estate agent's mantra: 'location, location, location'. A British real estate tycoon, Lord Harold Samuel, reputedly coined this, although it appears to have been used in an advertisement for real estate in the *Chicago Tribune* from 1926. It could be the slogan for Gurgaon, because its location proved to be its most valued asset. When we think of housing and industry as the twin engines that ploughed the fallow fields of Gurgaon and converted them, rather hastily, into a modern city, there is no denying the fact that its location was what attracted them to it. True, the Aravalli range makes for a scenic backdrop, if you can see it at all any more, and bits of forest and fields of wheat and mustard added some verdure to the rocky terrain, but that alone would not have snagged India's biggest construction companies and the global businesses to set up shop here. People ask rather incredulously of those who have come here: 'Why Gurgaon?' The invariable answer is: 'It's the location, silly.' Sanjay Gandhi knew that well too.

What makes Gurgaon's location so special? Proximity to Delhi is an obvious advantage; Delhi had sprawled southwards, so being contiguous to it meant that builders could make their clients believe that they were buying affordable plots or apartments in an extension of the hugely overpriced colonies of south Delhi. Furthermore, the solution for Delhi's housing crunch was sought in declaring the borderlands of Haryana on three sides and Uttar Pradesh in the east as the National Capital Region (NCR) in 1982. It was created to enable coordinated planning around the capital city, and although the Metro has linked Gurgaon and Noida (the acronym for its clunky bureaucratic appellation, New Okhla Industrial Development

Authority) to Delhi, other kinds of coordination has been found wanting. If the periodic iterations of the master plans of Delhi and Gurgaon were collected in a pamphlet it would make an interesting piece of graphic fiction.

So, proximity to Delhi was good, but not good enough; there were other places even closer to Delhi that were older, better planned, and with more elaborate infrastructure, heavy industry, and rail connections like Faridabad and Noida. But they did not achieve the global city aura that Gurgaon quickly acquired. Its ace up its sleeve was Gurgaon's easy access to what was then the only international airport in north India. Only 8 kilometres away from Palam Airport, Gurgaon left its urban rivals in the dust. The new global knowledge-based industries, multinational corporations, and Indians living and working abroad (non-resident Indians, or NRIs) jilted Faridabad. Even Noida, a tidily laid industrial township on the banks of the Yamuna, which suggests better water and power supply, was upstaged because it was in Uttar Pradesh, a state that is reputed for being both backward and in the grip of babudom, and with a long and horribly jammed commute to the airport. A new airport has been sanctioned for Noida, in neighbouring Jewar in 2018, but in the meantime Gurgaon has taken an unbeatable lead in the new urbanization race. Since 2010, National Highway 8 (NH-8) links Gurgaon directly to the airport and the more recent Terminal 3 of the Indira Gandhi International Airport brings it ever closer. The Metro also connects Gurgaon to the airport, New Delhi Railway Station and the Interstate Bus Terminal, making it accessible by public transport. All these factors helped Gurgaon mature from being merely a place close to Delhi to a highly desirable destination. It redefined the NCR.

It should be stated emphatically at the outset that *none* of the major construction companies that rushed to build Gurgaon envisioned a brand-new city—they all had the same unoriginal idea of creating a new batch of housing colonies on parcels of land, much like the ones they had developed in Delhi. DLF, the biggest of them, which already had twenty-two residential colonies in Delhi in its portfolio with

South Extension, Hauz Khas and Greater Kailash I and II among them, was to dust off those old plans and adapt them to their new locale. Gurgaon, therefore, was created in a piecemeal, ad hoc fashion without a unified vision or coordinated plan for a holistic city—of the type that Jamshedji Tata had implemented in Jamshedpur or Le Corbusier in Chandigarh.

The presumably equally unimaginative Town and Country Planning (TCP) Department and Haryana Urban Development Authority (HUDA), still wedded to colonial building codes, had taken a stab at bringing some housing and small industries to expand the old city and demarcated lands as 'sectors', but none of these cohered, even remotely, into a planned city. The lack of a clear-cut, comprehensive blueprint that incorporated elements that are essential to creating a notable city or even a serious assessment of sustainable resources or infrastructural requirements haunts the city that came sporadically and hastily to exist. Today, all efforts at retrofitting the omissions, gaps, and lacunae are fitfully in progress. So, the race to house the new well-to-do denizens and place corporate offices in spaciously conceived business parks in Gurgaon fell to different private companies, as the demand for one fuelled the other, as we shall see in this chapter and the next. The real estate companies arrived with refreshed zeal to build their residential 'colonies' and it is to them that we will first turn.

~

The year 1982 had already proved to be an eventful one for Gurgaon because of the advent of Suzuki. Its iconic car, the Maruti 800, rolling off the sleek and modern assembly line of the largest car factory in India—one that employed 20,000 workers—was a sensation. It bestowed on Gurgaon the legitimacy of an important manufacturing hub, open to business, and therefore to residential areas that many of the new prospering middle-class Indians would call home. Suzuki's move generated a wishful rumour—perhaps a real plan that perished on the drawing board—that helped real estate companies rejuvenate their businesses. It was touted that an immaculately planned 'Japan City' was in the offing in Gurgaon, with a network of light rail and public transport that would link it to the airport and to Delhi, and with amenities so modern and stylish that it would beat anything that existed in India. Many people, weary of Delhi's chronic water and power shortages and overpriced real estate, sought this future utopia. I confess that I was one of them, and in 1984 bought a plot in DLF's Qutab Enclave Phase III in anticipation of living in a place with Japanese aesthetics. That hope was utterly belied.

The quick-pulsing economy of Gurgaon grew around the district headquarters built in colonial times. This old and settled town was automatically designated 'Old Gurgaon', with its civil lines, cantonment and colourful Sadar Bazaar, and its narrow alleys jammed with small retail and repair shops that spilled on to the pavements. It had hawkers lining the streets crowded with pedestrians; and the rickshaws milling around gave it the unmistakeable feel of a crowded mofussil town, but without the energy or capital to reinvent itself. That initiative belonged to then chief minister Bansi Lal, whom we have observed in his dealings with Sanjay Gandhi's land requirements. This time also he was quick to acquire the relatively inexpensive agricultural land within a stone's throw from the old town, creating numbered 'sectors' to be used to build the new city.

Udyog Vihar with its mix of commercial, industrial and residential dwellings straddles Sectors 18 to 20 on the right flank of the old Delhi–Jaipur road. The two heavy hitters among private developers, DLF and Ansals, began a land-buying frenzy from farmers by purchasing hundreds of acres. They quickly set up shop to sell plots, and sell or rent town houses and apartments, commercial and office buildings by the square foot. They began to market Gurgaon as a place with unique possibilities. The Ansals, who sensed the potential of Gurgaon, were the first to break ground in the late 1970s to develop Palam Vihar, the first residential colony of Gurgaon, one with relatively spacious rooms compared to apartments in Delhi. Its name invokes the couplet that describes the Mughal emperor Shah Alam's shrunken empire as stretching from 'Dilli to Palam'. To give their new colony cache they used the name of the Delhi Airport rather than billing itself as a new neighbourhood in Gurgaon. DLF was not far behind in announcing its sprawling settlement called Qutab Enclave—after Delhi's iconic and beloved monument. These builders were extending Delhi, or the illusion of it, not building a new city in Gurgaon.

In an illuminating conversation with Vinayak and Rumjhum Chatterjee, the joint CEOs of Feedback Ventures, an international infrastructure company, I learnt the story of their migration to Gurgaon for living and working. Originally, the Chatterjees had their business in Delhi and lived in a small, rented place in Saket in south Delhi. They soon wanted a place of their own but their budget would only buy them a small apartment in Vasant Kunj, which they considered doing. However, happenstance took them to Gurgaon.

On Christmas Eve of 1990, in Aurobindo Place Market we chanced upon a real estate broker, owner of Amba Properties. He urged us to try Gurgaon, but the very idea of Gurgaon made us shudder. Our friends already thought we were nuts because we lived so far out in Saket—can you imagine what they would think if we dared to move to Gurgaon? The broker persuaded us 'to see the beautiful houses that the Ansals were building in Palam Vihar'. 'But that is not in Gurgaon,' we insisted, 'our aunt lives in Palam Vihar and we have visited her, we know it is in Delhi.' He smiled and shook his head and politely revealed to us that it was *his own family*, the Saini family, that had sold 400 acres of farmland to the Ansals who had developed the colony and it was indisputably in Gurgaon. The Ansals had wagered that the proposed new highway would come straight down from Palam Airport along the old road to Jaipur, so they had bought this large parcel on the right side of that road. This plan was scuttled, we were told, by DLF, with its hefty political clout, so that it prevailed with the government to move the NH-8 closer to its own holdings in the villages of Sikandarpur and Chakkarpur, where it was building a huge residential colony called Qutab Enclave.

Saini then drove the Chatterjees to Palam Vihar and that visit persuaded them to move to Gurgaon and find something well within their budget. Vinayak continued:

> Palam Vihar had some empty plots. Saini took us to E block, to the house we both fell in love with. We compared the cramped apartment in Saket and the tiny apartment we were planning to buy in Vasant Kunj to this lovely house and garden on 275 square yards, surrounded with greenery and winter wheat and mustard in bloom in fields. Really, there was no contest. So, this became our home and it proved to be a very lucky choice. As our business grew we bought three other adjacent houses, knocked them down, and have a beautiful, large house now. It was wonderful because the commute to our office in Panchsheel Park was still convenient and the airport was only a short drive away. But later when we saw the splendid office spaces in Gurgaon, we moved our office here to Cyber City. It is a rare luxury to live in a home we love and work in this great office space in Gurgaon, only a fifteen-minute drive away. What is there to not love about Gurgaon? We would not change this for anything.

Today, a new underpass that opened for the public in 2017 has clipped their home–office commute to less than ten minutes. 'Since we have no infrastructure projects in Gurgaon, we live half the month abroad, so having the airport nearby is a great blessing,' Vinayak said. The Chatterjees had captured the allure of Gurgaon real estate in another trio—space, space and space. 'Our office,' Rumjhum said with a sweeping gesture over the 10,000 square feet expanse, 'is where 350 staff work.' Their broker, Saini, was a close friend now and they 'bless him every day'. It was hard to believe that they managed their

global business empire from Gurgaon. Their projects are far-flung—in
Bengaluru, Chennai, the Far East, Africa and Australia. But Gurgaon
is the nerve centre that controls everything, particularly the banks of
computers that winked their blue lights as the staff beavered on. The
Chatterjees are still outsiders to Gurgaon, but that does not bother
them. 'It is a city of migrants. Bengalis were not common in these
parts then,' Vinayak recalled.

> The milkman delivered milk to our homes in aluminium
> cans that were marked with our names; he had several cans
> with Punjabi names like 'Kapur' and 'Talwar', ours was
> simply labelled 'Bengali'. We asked him why he didn't write
> 'Chatterjee' on our can. He indignantly said, 'Because you *are*
> Bengali.' Then he asked us: 'Why do you add "ji" to your name?
> You are not Chhattar from Chhatarpur, so why do you call
> yourselves Chhattar ji?' This left us laughing helplessly. We told
> him that we were not Chhattras [umbrellas], but Chatterjees
> from Kolkata.

The air traffic rapidly outgrew even the improved and expanded
facility at Palam Airport, and India's growth spurt, following the
liberalization of its long-shackled economy in the 1990s, relegated
the old Palam Airport as a terminal for domestic flights only. Indira
Gandhi International Airport opened its Terminal 3 in July 2010.
It is a sprawling glass and steel, prize-winning extravaganza, and is
a ten-minute drive on the multi-lane NH-8 to Gurgaon with bold
signage pointing the way.

Undoubtedly, the airport was crucial for Gurgaon's good
fortune. A new category of residents—the well heeled and the
NRIs—flocked to the newly rising city to fulfil their desire for an
upmarket apartment, a pied à terre, a second home or a permanent
residence, near Delhi and close to the international airport. Abroad,
particularly in the Middle East, the UK, the USA, Australia or
even Africa, they measure the distance from their homes to their

destinations not in miles but in the hours it takes to fly and drive between the two; so for them Gurgaon involves little mental effort. This is also true of the executives of global corporations that have nestled in Gurgaon. NRIs, expats, along with the swelling number of corporate employees, account for the occupancy of many upscale houses and flats and offices in Gurgaon and for a large proportion of the footfalls at the airport. Some speculatively invested in plots or apartments in Gurgaon and have waited, very profitably, for land prices to triple and quadruple every year. In the last thirty years they have gone up approximately sixtyfold. A more lucrative investment is hard to find.

The exponential growth story, however, belongs to the corporate real estate sector that set the ball rolling along the Mehrauli–Gurgaon road and beyond. There was a huge stone quarry that had been allowed to excavate the Aravallis and enormous stone crushers sent billows of fine dust into the atmosphere as the handsome blue-and-gold-toned rocks of the Aravallis were dressed into manageable blocks and trucked away for building walls and cladding the houses of the elite of south Delhi.

Even in Gurgaon, with its rather loose reputation of being a frontier town with few regulations, and despite HUDA's centralized control of permits, this process was more a steeplechase than a canter. There were many bureaucratic hurdles to leap over, tangles of red tape to cut through, and sheer conventional attitudes to change. Two laws, in particular, barricaded the road to development: one was the Punjab Scheduled Roads and Controlled Areas Restriction of Unregulated Development Act, 1963, that had been blithely overridden to procure land for Sanjay Gandhi's enterprise. The other was the Haryana Development and Regulation of Urban Areas Act of 1975. In 1976, Bansi Lal, the very man who had enabled its flouting, made the first Act more stringent by stipulating that no private builders were to be permitted to develop such areas, and allowed HUDA, answerable only to the CM, an exclusive right to interpret or enforce this.

This made HUDA an unusual and extralegal 'single window' for all clearances and permits, which was rare in bureaucratic establishments. Gurgaon had no municipal authority until 2008, and only a Town and Country Planning Department that had few teeth. This meant that anyone who wanted to acquire land or build anything at all in Gurgaon had only to make tracks to the HUDA office, climb four flights of chipped concrete stairs and meet its officers. Gurgaon district had thousands of indifferent acres abutting this area and HUDA and the Town and Country Planning Department made it simple to buy huge parcels of agricultural land and promptly apply for a change in land use from agricultural to residential, commercial or industrial purposes. A wheat field one day was demarcated as 250 and 500 square yard residential plots the next. Farmers with holdings in the villages of Nathupur, Sikandarpur and Chakkarpur were now willing to dispose of their land and move to Sohna, Badshahpur and beyond, where cheaper and more fertile fields were available for far less. The unyielding land had finally become a phenomenally productive asset that enriched its sellers and its buyers.

While DLF was getting its running shoes on, a new athlete entered the race in 1985 in Gurgaon and changed the game in the housing colony building market forever. This was a small unknown company called Gulmohar Estates that made a fateful entry creating a residential paradigm shift that profoundly differed from the way housing colonies were hitherto conceived of in India: it developed the very first Western-style gated condominium residential community in the country on a compact plot of 23 acres in Nathupur village in Gurgaon. This radical departure from the norm of the south Delhi–style colony created 'Garden Estate', which later became one of the most imitated models for bourgeois living in modern India. It introduced a fundamentally new concept in building, living and management that took the country by storm and all the builders in contention went flying to their drawing boards to replicate it. Today, new housing in every city follows this trend.

I was scratching around for information on Garden Estate, beyond rents and prices and a list of owners, when serendipitously on 1 June 2016, Tutu Sikand, a resident, suggested I meet Patricia Rau, an original player in the making of Garden Estate. Patricia, a tall and elegant American woman, moved to India in 1959. She is ebullient, hospitable and lucid at eighty-five, living in an elegant flat in Garden Estate. She had me both riveted and regaled as she unspooled her narrative, peppered with delightful digressions and reminiscences, and punctuated with tea and lemon cake. I present a condensed version of her account, mostly in her words, interpolating it with my research and observations.

It all began with Ajit Haksar, then CEO of Imperial Tobacco Company (ITC) whom Patricia Rau got to know because her husband, Bertie Rau, worked under him. Haksar, she said, had transformed a staid English tobacco company into this wonderful, diversified corporation that had hotels, food products and other lines of business. Delhi's acute water shortage began in the early 1980s and Haksar was anxious about what this would mean for ITC's five-star Maurya Hotel, and desperately sought to secure a reliable source of water for it. He visited a scientific agency from where he learnt of an aquifer in Nathupur in Gurgaon, where it was feasible to establish a couple of bore wells and pipe fresh water all the way to the hotel in Delhi's Diplomatic Enclave. Haksar lost no time in investigating this tip, found it a sound proposition, and very quickly persuaded the villagers who owned the land to part with 23 acres for a far larger sum than what DLF had offered them. Ironically, it was a search for water, rather than land, that led Haksar to Gurgaon, and this quest led to a very influential development.

'The deal done, Mr Haksar left for Canada, invited by his architect friend, Mr Ramesh Khosla, for a fun visit,' Patricia continued. 'Mr Khosla was a Canadian citizen, and had designed ITC's brilliant Mughal Hotel in Agra, that won the prestigious Aga Khan Prize for architecture. This was a very productive visit. As they drove around in the suburbs of Canada, Khosla pointed out the gated condominiums that dotted those landscapes, which aroused Mr Haksar's keen interest.' They visited a few homes in these gated communities and Haksar 'asked why there were no such residential communities in India. His enthusiasm for the concept led him to ask Mr Khosla whether he would be interested in designing one in India. He was, but wondered where the land to build such a project would come from, since he knew that urban land was very expensive in India. Mr Haksar said he already had the land in Gurgaon, in a village called Nathupur on the Mehrauli–Gurgaon road.'

The next step, 'was to get a partner with deep pockets. Neither of them had the money to fund the project,' Patricia said. 'So Mr Radhey Shyam Agarwal, the largest distributor of ITC's cigarettes in India, who had brimming coffers, decided to fund the project. The three created a company called Gulmohar Estates and engaged a local builder who would execute Khosla's wonderful design under their meticulous supervision.'

Gulmohar Estates promoted this yet-to-be-built project as one with 'condominiums' and 'gracious living'—brand new ideas in those days. But their time had really come by then. To market this rather unfamiliar concept, Haksar hired Patricia. She had experience in marketing and advertising, having written brochures for corporations, but it was still a tall order because there were no women in the real estate business—certainly none with any prominent role in the sector. Patricia was very modest in describing her credentials for this position, but her appearance and engaging manner testifies to the aplomb she brought to this challenge. Besides, she was perfectly suited for the job: articulate, knowledgeable, vivacious, elegant and very, very persuasive. She explained that it wasn't easy and 'involved plenty of grit and hard-sell'.

No one had heard of Gurgaon leave alone 'gracious living'; and the word 'condominiums' needed much explaining. *Nobody wanted to live in Gurgaon!* Besides we were selling at Rs 350 per square foot while DLF was selling their town houses for only Rs 200 [per square foot] but Mr Haksar and Mr Khosla offered a far better quality of life. There was no electricity there at the time and Mr Haksar decided that he would have to make that too. He bought huge generators and promised twenty-four-hour electricity to those who bought residences. The water was drawn from wells that tapped the bountiful aquifer. He brought in landscape specialists and the area had many thousands of saplings planted as construction was under way. The plans included a huge swimming pool, a clubhouse with catering, a central block with amenities for large parties, a gym—whoever heard of a gym in those days?—a library, tennis courts, a café. All these made the place a quiet, protected paradise. There is also a vegetable seller and a grocery store for our everyday needs. Then Kusum Dutta, who ran the beauty parlour at the Maurya, bought a town house in Garden Estate and soon opened her own beauty shop. This completed the picture of paradise for many men and women who came to live there.

The enormous challenge of getting people to move to Gurgaon in those early days is difficult to imagine. At the time, no such gated colony was built and Patricia had to try very hard persuading people on the phone and in person and Haksar too worked on his connections. A total of 474 residential units were built, and were sold off entirely by 1990. There were many styles of residences planned: villas, town houses, blocks of apartments of varying sizes with two, three and four bedrooms, with modern kitchens and tiled bathrooms, a rather skimpy servant's room, and a parking space for each of the residences. The apartments were in blocks according to style, with exotic names like Terrace Greens and Manhattan Apartments, all separated by gardens and trees and winding streets with generous pavements, signage for strict speed limits, and a prohibition on honking. The street lighting was also excellent, with lamps reminiscent of the gaslights of nineteenth-century London. And even though

Gulmohar Estates sold at a higher price than its competition, it was still a fraction of the price of housing in Delhi without the gracious features. Yet, the people of Delhi were frigid to the idea of moving to Gurgaon. But even glaciers melt and the trickle of buyers gradually turned into a stream.

All said and done, Gurgaon seemed far away from the centre of Delhi. 'It is out in the sticks,' said some, 'it will be dangerous to live among Haryanvis,' protested others. Haksar insisted on a walled compound and a single entry point with guarded access and round-the-clock security. All non-residents would have to enter their names, addresses, and purpose for visiting in a register and disclose the name of their hosts.

And so, the sales began. Haksar was quite sure he would handpick his clients and therefore get a selection of people who would understand the meaning of gracious living. So there were no public advertisements; the sales were achieved mainly by word of mouth. Haksar approached the Kashmiri Pandits to whom he was either related or well known, and they responded with keenness.

'Mr Wanchu was the first person to buy an apartment. They all wanted the "Kashmiri discount!"' Patricia said, laughing at the memory of that early struggle. 'The very next person was Swaroop Nehru, and Betu, her son [Sunil Nehru], lives here with his lovely wife, Nina from Kerala. Then Mr Haksar called on his military connections, and General Hazari, who is married to Meera Nehru, a cousin to Sunil, came next, followed by the Rainas and General Vohra and the air chief, and so on, and soon many prominent Punjabis and Sardars also bought [villas here]. He wanted only professionals and their families; he did not want the business class. He was a pukka professional himself and he permitted himself this snobbery. He wanted the educated class and the word was out, and many NRI types also came in soon to buy. We have a lot of them now. They had to be people who lived in a certain way and who could share a common compound in harmony. They all have freehold titles to their properties now, but they still have to pay the common charges for maintaining the public amenities, like lifts, street lighting, the club and pool, and the gardens.'

The place is kept spotlessly clean and manicured, garbage collection is done regularly, and, recently, in every building, resident volunteers make sure that the garbage is carefully sorted—the recyclables from the rubbish and the stuff that can go into the compost, an activity that, alarmingly, not many housing societies in NCR region have adopted. Arun Singh, the former minister of state for defence, together with his partner Romola Ranganathan have taken on this responsibility for their apartment building and are very conscientious in discharging it. A spirit of living graciously is indeed pervasive. Garden Estate is full of nannies watching children playing, dogs being walked, residents on their constitutionals, and domestic staff, such as cooks and cleaners moving from one home to another to fulfil their part-time duties.

I remarked on the human scale of Garden Estate and Patricia agreed emphatically, saying, 'I feel like an ant standing in front of those tall identical towers on Golf Course Road, all built bang along the main road too with hardly any place to move. The apartment buildings and the villas here are all only five storeys high because this was strictly regulated. There was no permission to build any higher. The airport authorities restricted the height because they claimed it as a danger to landing aircraft. I wonder what happened to that danger with the twenty-six floors that DLF has been allowed to construct closer to the airport?' she said. 'DLF got all the rules changed, zoning laws changed, land use changed, and wound up as a very wealthy company. They were small when they first came and had competition acquiring land; now they can outbid anyone. Gurgaon made it very, very rich.'

'What was remarkable about Mr Haksar and his management,' Patricia continued, 'was that he broke ground in 1986, promised the buyers that their turnkey contracts would be handed over in 1989, and he was true to his word. Every single one of them was completed on time and handed over as promised. If you look at what is now happening in Gurgaon, or even in Bengaluru, where people have paid up and waited for up to nine years to get their apartments from DLF, it is such a shame. They copied the concept of the gated condominium but they have not been able to mimic the sense of integrity that Mr Haksar and Mr Khosla brought to their pioneering project. And everyone who lives here is grateful,' Patricia said. 'People love living here, have made friends here. Our children and now our grandchildren are friends; there have been a couple of romances, and even marriages. And they feel safe, in their clean and well-maintained compound. Our plumbing or electrical complaints are dealt with promptly, and the food from the restaurant can even be delivered to our homes, and it is such good food too. The lemon cake from the patisserie next to the Beauty Shop in the main building is very nice,' she said, offering me another slice. 'I enjoy going to the wonderful Garrison Church in Old Gurgaon in the civil lines area where a small Christian community gathers on Sunday mornings. My friends from Sushant Lok pick me up and bring me home. It is indeed a wonderful place, even for an elderly single person to live in great comfort here. And my neighbours are very kind and helpful too.'

Garden Estate became the inspiration for gated communities that DLF then built with a vengeance in a multi-storeyed format, raising it to thirty floors that made it hugely profitable but robbed it of its intimate charm. The rise and rise of DLF from its moribund state in 1975 is inextricably entangled with the story of buying agricultural acreage in Gurgaon and changing it to urban uses. It marketed Qutab Enclave as a collage of residential colonies with a clubhouse for each of its three 'phases', with business towers, shopping malls and markets and expanded to a fourth to include a golf course and luxury apartment buildings. This cobbled township later took on the name of DLF City—still eschewing the mention of Gurgaon. DLF's salesmanship of each phase was masterly, and if it owed its rejuvenation to Gurgaon, the growing city could return the compliment. Undoubtedly, the corporation to make the biggest change in its fortunes by making Gurgaon the object of its desire was DLF and thereby hangs an intriguing tale.

DLF and Gurgaon: Qutab Enclave Morphing into DLF City

With DDA's enviable monopoly in Delhi, a despondent Chaudhry Raghavendra Singh came to the brink of liquidating the storied DLF United Ltd by persuading his two daughters, Prem and Indira, and the latter's husband, Kushal Pal Singh (KPS hereafter), to sell their majority shares for a sum of Rs 26 lakh to his brother.[2] DLF was decimated at this juncture, its vast unconstructed acreage in Delhi forfeited, and its coffers empty. It seemed wise to Chaudhry sahib, as he was called, to accept the money his brother was offering and bow out with dignity. But destiny had other plans. The family shareholders objected, and the agreement to sell was torn up. Instead, they concentrated their minds to rebuild the company with KPS firmly in charge. Gurgaon's siren call was audible in the tumult of those days, and this decisive volte-face entwined the fate of the company with that of Gurgaon.

KPS decided to pour the family's private resources into the company to breathe new life into it. He had a precise goal: to acquire 350 acres of land to build a decent-sized residential colony. He set his sights on Gurgaon because although Haryana came under purview of the Urban Land Ceiling Act, Gurgaon was outside its restrictive ambit as it had not yet met the criterion for 'urban', so the sky was the limit. Here small farmers, who barely eked out a living on their holdings of 3–5 acres, could be persuaded to sell and go elsewhere to improve their lives. KPS collected some capital by selling a stud farm and his property in Bulandshahr (in Uttar Pradesh) and promptly tipped it into the almost empty DLF till to gamble on Gurgaon.

By his own account, KPS tenaciously pursued all levels of authority that ranged from the patwari, or the village record keeper of land transactions, to the departmental heads and successive chief ministers in Chandigarh, and even cultivating warm relations with the prime minister to enable prompt clearances. He spent two decades tirelessly networking with politicians, officials and menials alike and his total landholding in Gurgaon peaked at 3,500 acres. He handpicked his employees, including the architect Hafeez Contractor later, to devote the next three decades to make the company the biggest in India. DLF's initial public offering (IPO) in 2007 took its value up to Rs 100 crore. In 2011 its market capitalization was worth Rs 32,273 crore, or $7 billion. The incredible results DLF achieved endorse his narrative. DLF grew to become the most vigorous construction company in India and KPS its wealthiest citizen.

Bansi Lal, the chief minister who had inaugurated Gurgaon's journey to becoming a big city, fell out with KPS for reasons of personal pique. We have only KPS's side of the story for what it is worth, for Bansi Lal is no more and he did not leave a paper trail. KPS also alleges in his book, *Whatever the Odds*, that Bansi Lal proceeded not only to obstruct his plans but also to legally accuse the company of paying immense bribes to his political rival, Bhajan Lal, who had been elected the next chief minister of Haryana. After a lengthy and expensive litigation, KPS managed to get these charges quashed. This court victory cleared the impediments in his path and enabled Gurgaon to become a private builder's paradise. Clearly, some vital pieces of the puzzle are missing and, perhaps, with luck, an insider in Bansi Lal's government can give us the full story of the Bansi Lal versus KPS and Bhajan Lal saga. What we can absolutely vouch for are the palpable results of their hostile engagement: KPS forged a public–private partnership that other construction companies were quick to replicate, and these licensed companies shaped the future of the city of Gurgaon. There is no doubt that these agreements were imperfectly conceptualized and players on both sides scuttled some important stipulations. In this impasse lay the root cause of the urban ills Gurgaon continues to experience even in 2017.

Briefly, KPS faithfully deployed the same shrewd strategy that his father-in-law, Chaudhry Raghavendra Singh, who founded DLF in 1946, had pioneered when dealing with the farmers in the long years of building his twenty-two residential colonies in Delhi. He had persuaded the farmers to plough the money that they received from DLF for their land in Delhi, back into the same company as an investment, on which he guaranteed a handsome 12 per cent return paid out monthly in cash, delivered by Jeep to their doors. KPS, now in charge of the family concern, followed this tested stratagem faithfully, and perhaps went a bit further. He personally visited those sellers whose holdings averaged 5 acres or more and those who were reluctant to sell their land. He convinced them that many more fertile and cheaper acres could be bought with the same money if they moved farther into the countryside between Sohna and Alwar.

KPS also acquired a reputation for being kind and helpful and this became very clear to me as I walked around in Chakkarpur and Nathupur talking to farmers in December–January 2012. Farmers who had sold some of their land to him were very satisfied with his dealings. Two brothers of a Jat family in Sikandarpur affirmed that they were grateful for the appointment KPS arranged for their mother with a busy doctor. He helped farmers in ways that touched them personally: he helped the parents get their children admitted to school, arranged legal or medical appointments and dispensed free investment and financial advice. Being a Haryana Jat himself, KPS could speak in Haryanvi to them and win over diffident sellers. Others who had dealt with KPS agreed that he acted like 'a caring brother'. He dressed like them, sat on their string cots eating the food and drink offered, even taking puffs from their hookahs.

It was no surprise then that the small landowners were lining up in the makeshift office set up in what was to become the Silver Oaks complex of Phase I, near its post office, to sell and reinvest their money with DLF. Even the farmers with small landholdings found this a life-changing experience. This permitted most of them to buy more land elsewhere than they sold, and invest the balance for a comfortable income to live on. Now they could even afford a small car, send their children to school and pay for medical expenses when needed. Some, I learnt, did not take this sound advice and proceeded to squander the large sums they received on cars, alcohol and conspicuous consumption, and wound up broke, angry and unemployable in a few years. It was amazing to meet both types on my visits to Nathupur and hear their contrasting stories. (More on this in Chapter Six.)

A deep mistrust of the state government also enabled DLF to buy vast stretches of land. There was fear, and not without some basis in fact, after more than a thousand farmers were bilked in the land deal for Sanjay Gandhi's factory by the chief minister, Bansi Lal. The state government had the power to acquire land to develop Gurgaon, and the government—as anyone who has ever owned land that was acquired knows—almost never pays the fair market price and ties up many deprived owners for decades of expensive and futile litigation against it. Clearly, KPS's offer to promptly pay market price for the land to farmers created a sense of trust in his dealings. The shady deals that involved transfers of leasehold properties by power of attorney in undeclared cash, then common in the Delhi real estate market, did not plague first-time buyers in Gurgaon. Freehold transactions paid for by cheque in instalments in exchange for ironclad registered title deeds demonstrated that property could be cleanly bought and sold in India; Haksar, Sushil Ansal and KPS were to prove that and make it the norm. Buyers flocked to populate the villages that were being rapidly transformed into urban residential localities around Gurgaon.

Official sentiment against private builders in the central government was still strong and the government was hesitant to give them the licence to create the townships that were needed. In an oft-repeated tale, KPS claims that he surmounted the reluctance after a fortuitous encounter on a blisteringly hot summer day in 1981. He recounts in his memoir that he was visiting his precious first tranche of land in Gurgaon and was seated beside a roadside well when a Jeep driven by a young man stopped by to get a bucket of water for the vehicle's overheated engine. KPS promptly obliged only to realize that the lad was none other than Rajiv Gandhi, the older son of Prime Minister Indira Gandhi. This coincidence, KPS claims, led to a lengthy conversation, which ended with Rajiv Gandhi's invitation to KPS to visit his office to discuss his Gurgaon plans with him and his trusted friend, Arun Singh.

In trying to verify this 'urban legend' from an unimpeachable source then close to Rajiv Gandhi, I was reliably informed that this was wishful exaggeration. Indira Gandhi had already entrusted Arun Singh to formulate the plans for the direction in which the overpopulated capital should expand. The invitation was extended not only to KPS but also to all the other prominent private builders. Each of them brought in very detailed plans to develop their parcels of land in Gurgaon. Sushil Ansal, for instance, was first off the bat with Palam Vihar. DLF's Qutab Enclave was only the second.

Bhajan Lal, the then chief minister of Haryana, was apprised of Rajiv Gandhi's and Arun Singh's enthusiasm for private developers. Arun Singh requested Khurshid Ahmed, the minister for finance and town planning in the Bhajan Lal government, to develop clear-cut policy guidelines which would ensure that, 'while granting approvals for private sector development in Haryana, adequate regulatory safeguards were provided so that a certain percentage of the homes would also be made available at government-prescribed prices'.[3]

The new policy opened the floodgates to private builders who politely ignored the inconvenient clause to also build affordable housing for the working class. The very migrants who physically laboured to build this city at the behest of the private corporations and sustain the lives of its wealthy denizens found themselves consigned to temporary shacks around building sites and then, if they could afford them, they would move to the tenement housing built by the natives who held on to their lands within the *lal dora* area of urban villages, which refers to the red boundary on the map of the village settlement area where people lived, separating it from the surrounding fields, and within which town planning rules and building codes apparently do not apply. These areas contain the new invisible slums tucked away from the main roads of the city. Gurgaon, which is built on the surrounding fields of fifty-odd villages, has been developed for an affluent clientele, with many of the villagers—the landowners who sold or leased their fields or invested in low-income housing on the *lal dora* lands—being extremely well-to-do too. Only those who squandered their new-found wealth and have no other qualification to get jobs in the city that came up around them are today in wretched straits. Some of these have taken to a life of crime.

The guidelines also clearly specified other rules that were broken: the stipulations that green belts and parks should be liberally interspersed in the areas that were developed happened in a purely minimal and grudging way; concrete overlaid vast expanses of land. Most critical was the agreement that the building and expense of providing the on-site and off-site infrastructure was to be shared between the private builders and HUDA. The private company would invest in the on-site infrastructure of its colony, like inner roads and lanes, street lighting, security and sewers leading up to the main line. It would collect a quarterly maintenance fee from homeowners, based on the size of the plot or the area of the apartment, in the colony. The same bill would have 'external development charges' that it would pass on to HUDA to cover the latter's cost of building off-site infrastructure such as the main roads, drains and sewerage mains. The private and the public halves of infrastructure would connect seamlessly, like Lego pieces, to create a comprehensive system to serve the colony and the city. The same formula would be executed by the duo in electricity generation and distribution and maintenance. DLF, for instance, would maintain substations to distribute electricity in its colonies, while the state electricity board would generate it, sanction wattage for each individual owner, get the approved and sealed meters read and issue bills according to usage, and collect the payments.

This was a great formula, but both sides needed to be conscientious about doing their part. DLF was to hand over the maintenance of the colony to the municipal corporation once all the construction on privately owned plots was complete. This was also a ridiculous idea because to this day, DLF colonies remain incomplete. What they had not calculated was that many plot owners are speculators waiting for land prices to escalate to match their greed, and would be happy to pay the fine when they sold the plots. The empty lots are often treated as dumping grounds for rubbish and rubble. Until 2018, this formula had not worked and infrastructural and maintenance problems persist because the two parties blame each other for not keeping their side of the bargain while residents endure the fallout.

The blame belongs to both sides of this unconsummated partnership to the annoyance and inconvenience of the residents of Gurgaon. On the private side, Bhajan Lal's nod reversed the earlier regulation and permitted the private builders to develop residential and commercial areas in Haryana's urban spaces without the obligation to build any affordable housing. On the public side, it allowed that the government would receive the 'external development charges' without constructing the off-site infrastructural development. Gurgaon, the foundling, now grew day and night like a hormone-riddled adolescent with all the problems that that stage in life brings.

DLF was now free to build Qutab Enclave, poetically named after possibly the most elegantly carved and engineered stone tower in the world, which made it a very prestigious address that sounded like it was a part of Delhi, even though the closest DLF building in it was 10 kilometres away from it. Phase I was built on the first parcel of 39.4 acres in Sikandarpur and Chakkarpur villages purchased by KPS in 1979 at better than market rates—Rs 30,000–40,000 an acre. In the next five years, land prices soared and DLF paid Rs 5 lakh per acre to farmers for their indifferent farmland; it sold developed plots of varying sizes in 1984–85 at around Rs 30 lakh an acre, so their profit margin was still sixfold or 600 per cent. The pace of acquisition quickened as more farmers were willing to sell at the enhanced rate and Phase II followed with about 550 acres of land now under the DLF flag. What is sobering is that in 2018, when the market is not as hot as it was in 2013–14, three- to four-bedroom condominiums in the tonier buildings sell for ten to twenty crores of rupees.

Awash in capital and landholdings, KPS embarked on the most ambitious building plans that filled these vast aces with town houses, luxury apartment buildings, corporate office buildings, gigantic market squares, and malls, all at breakneck speed. Cyber City in Phase III, where many multinational corporations are headquartered, is perhaps architecturally the most exciting business hub in the country. Qutab Enclave promised a quality of life, albeit on smaller plots, that only Lutyens' Delhi residents enjoyed: twenty-four-hour back-up of electricity (produced by their own diesel-powered generators), water supply from their own deep tube wells, daily garbage collection. Promising shade in the day and good lighting at night, the residential streets are named after trees that were planted along them, like Gul Mohar, Siris, Jacaranda, Neem, and Amaltas, and lined with the ubiquitous electrical poles looped with thick black wires; uniformed guards patrolled and secured a new and opulent way of life for the upwardly mobile and those who had reached the top.

The Public Works Department that set the low-cost, no-frills style and taste of small-town colonial India is in irreversible decay. DLF was now leading the pack of private colonizers with fiscal muscle and political clout to become the eclectic designers and architects of the new neighbourhoods. Cupolas, flying buttresses, pillars, curves, balconies and plenty of steel and glass abound in the sea of new housing in Gurgaon. Even as Delhi nationalistically expunges the names of colonial officials from its streets, Gurgaon, contrarily, is embracing names like The Belvedere, Regency Park, Windsor Place and Hamilton Court, Beverly Park and Towers, and exclusive colonial-style clubs to trumpet its confident occidentalism. KPS, land-rich and a keen golfer, crowned this by inviting Arnold Palmer, one of the world's greatest professional golfers, to design a world-class golf course for his wealthy clients, views of which could be had from his new luxury condominiums along a four-lane road named Golf Course Road. With capitation and membership dues topping seven figures, it is a major haunt of the corporate executives and professionals, for whom it is a valued perquisite. Indubitably, it adds to Gurgaon's fame as a glamorous business destination.

No residential colony is complete without its own market square and one or more exist in every neighbourhood. The ones built early, like those in Qutab Enclave Phase I, are compact and double-storeyed, with small shops that supply the daily needs of a comfortable life. A lone office tower with British Airways headquarters in India stands in one corner; its swimming pool on the thirteenth floor created quite a buzz for being the first in Gurgaon at that elevation. Qutab Plaza is a poured concrete hexagonal building with a central courtyard which has small shops tightly packed around it, in the connecting radials and on the outer periphery; even the verandas have goods being produced, repaired or sold. The verandas are lined with tailors set up with their sewing machines clattering away, and tables heaped with seconds from the garment factories, and small dry goods. Besides retail, there are banks and coffee shops, and a chaat and halwai shop, Sunny Sweets, in the veranda where a small crowd is ever present relishng golgappas, pakoras, and samosas while slurping cups of sweet tea. It also has a fine Mughlai food restaurant, Dana Choga, with its sweltering cooks pulling out roasted chickens, kababs and crisp rotis from a blazing tandoor with aromas that make the average shopper salivate. Stalls of property dealers are ubiquitous because real estate is big game and the successful ones have moved from these humble quarters to formal offices with backlit displays of fancy properties for sale. The first floor is reserved for services—Dr Malkit Law's Clinic was in great demand for her amazing diagnostic and healing powers, and there were offices of lawyers, small companies, advertising and real estate and such like. Underground parking exists but it seems to be reserved for the traders and shopkeepers; customers' cars crowd the circular road around it or the small paid parking area within its gates.

On the other side of the colony, built around a large inner courtyard, is the thriving Arjun Marg shopping mall, a little more user-friendly than its counterpart, and serves as the base of operations for DLF with two floors of utilitarian offices upstairs. Neither of them is quite as tony as Delhi's Khan Market, although that too has its own challenges of hawkers in verandas, very tight parking, and some very small shops. They are like the markets in Hauz Khas or Greater Kailash in Delhi, that bear the hallmarks of DLF, their common builder. A very adequate book store, stationery stores, many dry cleaners, grocery stores, florists, kitchen and housewares shops, shoe shops, pharmacies, opticians and eye glass shops, clothing and hairdressing salons for men and several beauty parlours, many tailoring and bespoke clothing stores, the paan kiosks at the corners, chaat and mithai shops (the best one, Sweet Corner, formerly from Sundar Nagar, has moved to Arjun Marg), restaurants, cafes, fast food chains, music and movies stores with DVDs for rent or sale, fancy bakers and confectioners, electronics, including a well-stocked Apple Store with two 'geniuses' to help and repair crashed hardware discs, foreign wine and liquor shops, glaziers, a picture framer and carpentry shop, many banks, private brokers, couriers and photographers. Clearly, the modern markets sacrifice aesthetics and even tidiness, because space is precious and rents are high and builders' greed is insurmountable; they appear to have been designed on the principle of the sardine can, where sardines are tightly packed because the oil they are packed in is more expensive than the fish.

By the time Phase IV was being constructed, where the gated condominiums are clustered, it became clear that an upmarket square was needed, and the Galleria was built with many boutiques and fancy retail chains. Coloured tiles and a central fountain— although it seldom functions—soften its appearance and bigger showrooms with glass fronts make it a more attractive place; it would compare favourably with Khan Market if its restaurants are of the same calibre. However, in building to the very edges of their plots and streets of niggardly width, DLF failed to make provision for adequate parking and circulation of traffic. The square seems to be set in the midst of a permanent traffic jam, much to the disgust of those who live in the expensive condominiums that surround the market and have to negotiate the chaos on a daily basis. Suzuki's small car has been overtaken by bulky and ostentatious SUVs, many driven by bullies who seem to be oblivious of rules of the road and even common courtesy. In the malls, where there is provision for underground parking, the fees discourage shoppers and they park in the street. So the parking problem, a chronic national disease, is here to stay.

Whether such an orgy of construction and the deluge of well-heeled residents could be sustained by the finite groundwater and limited supply of electricity is a thought that seems to have barely crossed the corporate builders' minds. If this meant digging deeper and deeper wells and sucking up the aquifers and deploying mammoth diesel generators for power that belch polluting fumes, so be it. Its clients would live in airtight, centrally air-conditioned apartments, where filtered air and purified water are piped into their living quarters. They would step out and move directly into their chauffeur-driven, air-conditioned cars, never to face the danger of walking along a road without a footpath, breathing the air thick with particulate matter, or having to worry about where their sewage is deposited.

This new urban DNA, which is not the peculiar characteristic of Gurgaon but endemic to contemporary urbanization in India, is a nightmare for those who must walk or travel by autorickshaw to work and live in the village tenements or huts in insanitary conditions. Even within the gated communities where they come to work they cannot use the normal lifts nor sit on the park benches (even as they mind children playing in the parks), nor use the apartment toilets; apart from a few members who are exceptions these communities are not egalitarian, although they see themselves as enlightened and modern. They may not be caste-based or ethnically segregated, but they certainly enforce rigid class lines.

Gurgaon's growth astounded academics and administrators alike, and buyers matched the frenzy of the seller. Concrete towers were erupting along Golf Course Road despite the awareness of the mindless degradation of the environment. DLF found enough affluent corporate executives, NRIs and wealthy émigrés from Delhi as eager buyers. Other builders were riding in tandem, erecting equally fancy complexes. If the Laburnum complex, built by ITC, was the gold standard at the end of the millennium, then DLF topped that with its luxury towers, generously landscaped grounds and every amenity that ITC could offer.

However, the killing belonged to DLF; it had branded Gurgaon. The 304 acres of land designated as DLF Phase I Qutab Enclave was followed by the 245-acre Phase II; it also built Silver Oaks, the first group of multi-storeyed apartment buildings that offered security and healthy community dwelling for its owners. DLF maximized the take from every square inch of land by stretching their luxury towers on Golf Course Road from ten floors to thirty—watering down their exclusivity. Awash in profits, KPS found himself with a private fortune so large that it put him on top of the billionaires' list in India and he made it to the Forbes list of the richest people in the world.

The symbiotic relationship between 'land' and 'finance' with registered freehold titles paid for by cheque (white money) proved to be the invincible weapons that conjured the powerhouse DLF became. Interested in buying a flat in Delhi, I personally discovered that it was impossible to buy a property in Delhi in the 1980s without producing the entire sum in a single tranche, with 40 per cent of the purchase price in 'black' money (undeclared cash) only to get a dubious 'power-of-attorney' on leasehold in lieu of a title to the place. In Gurgaon, on the other hand, builders happily accepted personal cheques, had instalment schemes and loans ready at hand, at the end of which they gave the buyer an ironclad, registered, permanent freehold title to the property. NRIs like me were thrilled to find these transparent and hassle-free deals and came in droves to build or buy homes in Gurgaon. And while the deals were not cheap at the time they certainly multiplied a hundredfold in fifteen years.

The shopping malls in Gurgaon created a sensation in the media and among residents of Delhi NCR where this phenomenon had not yet appeared. Malls had only just begun to appear in big cities in India, and Gurgaon stole the show with the opening in 1997 of a mirage of glass and steel called the Metropolitan Mall on the Mehrauli–Gurgaon road in DLF Phase II, with two dozen more to follow and counting, which may have been an overenthusiastic response of what the traffic would bear. A medley of architectural styles is on display even though there is sameness in the glass and steel construction that these edifices have used. They glitter and sparkle at night when the lights come on. The two stylish malls that stand out in the crowd are Ambience Mall in Phase III and Galaxy Mall in Sector 15. All the other major players bought blocks of land on or near the Mehrauli–Gurgaon road, on a section of it referred to as 'Mall Road', where these huge buildings with neon-lit advertisements added a splash of colour to the emerging cityscape in 2000. Many of these were built by DLF, like City Centre and Mega Mall, but other builders, like Sahara, Unitech and Raheja built their own. These gleaming new emporia proved to be a huge draw even for people living in Delhi, particularly on weekends; the rest of NCR had not caught up with it yet.

By the 1990s Gurgaon was transformed into the most sought-after clinic for 'retail therapy' in the NCR with addicted shoppers coming from Faridabad, Delhi and Noida to buy and eat or simply to gawk at the novelty of merchandise so richly and profusely displayed while being wafted upwards on escalators. I asked a group of local women who were seated in the soaring air-conditioned atrium without shopping bags in sight about their reason for coming. They came regularly, they informed me, not to shop or to eat—they could do that cheaply in the village market in Chakkarpur. 'Sitting, watching the tamasha of the shoppers in the cool breeze is free; we don't waste fifty rupees on a small plastic cup of tea, like these rich people do, we come here for our amusement; then we return to the heat and flies of Sikandarpur,' one of them said. 'We also check out the latest fashion in salwar suits. I had one stitched exactly like one I had seen upstairs. I saved five thousand rupees.' They had come to beat the heat and to find some privacy in this most public of places, to gossip about their affairs, perhaps even romantic ones. The design of most malls imitates that of their American and British suburban forbears, but the spirit, sounds, spicy smells and sensibility of these temples of commerce is unmistakeably Indian. To add strongly to their attraction are the 'cineplexes' on the top floors in several of them, with at least half a dozen screens showing the latest English and Hindi films; a movie-mad public comes for their fix. Food courts provide a range of snacks and quick meals during the day and the bars and nightclubs make Gurgaon a wicked city at night.

Delhiites became avid buyers of real estate after they shed their attitude about Gurgaon being in the sticks, where, they believed, India's rudest rustics dwelt. The Punjabis, restless for a better life, cashed in their old dingy homes in Delhi's 'refugee colonies' for multiples of the price they would pay in Gurgaon, for spacious, modern houses and flats. There would be enough money left over not only to trade in their two-wheelers for four-wheelers but also have a sizeable interest-bearing bank balance that made this a very shrewd and stylish upgrade. On 17 May 2014, speaking to Ashwin and Rohini Chopra, indubitable members of Delhi's elite, was a revelation about the 'exchange rate' for old houses for new.[4] In place of the four-storeyed house in one of the toniest colonies in Delhi they wound up not only with their grandly appointed flat in ITC's The Laburnum complex, with sizeable reception rooms, four bedrooms with attached marble baths and quarters for their staff, but also with apartments for their two children in Heritage City, another coveted gated community for their kids, and a summer residence in an exclusive township, near Shimla in Himachal Pradesh. It was a coup to say the least. 'I missed Delhi only briefly because our children, Arvind and Aradhana, and their families were already in rented apartments in Gurgaon. Our grandchildren, whom we seldom saw before, are now a close part of our lives. The move makes the quality of life very special. And Gurgaon is a lovely place to live in—so much is happening here, from theatre to art exhibitions, good restaurants, clubs and the wonderful malls—and we live our lives in clean, green surroundings without the hassles of maintaining a house, getting diesel for the generator or getting the lift fixed. We are really just fine here,' Rohini said, smiling. She made the lure of Gurgaon so palpable and comprehensible.

Many similar accounts from Delhi's high society and literally thousands of well-paid managers and professionals seeking homes near their new workplaces set off the boom in real estate that has few equals in a new city in India. The builders had created a consciously Western lifestyle in their residential buildings. These complexes are even christened with classy English names such as Regency Park, Windsor Court, Beverly Park, The Icon, The Summit, Malibu City, Central Park and the super luxurious Aralias and Magnolias—all reachable by the old Pahari Road that has been renamed 'Sunset Boulevard'. We can appreciate the builders' propensity for unintended humour. Prices tripled in as many years, and then again, with more room overhead; it is no accident that the private builders reaped a building bonanza.

KPS had bought thousands of barren acres that were now a gold mine. He became the undisputed king of the concrete jungle he had partially created. The determined shift to building high-rises to imitate Dubai and Singapore (that mimicked New York) only multiplied the company's profits and the family's private wealth was reckoned in hundreds of millions. Phases IV and V became a collage of condominiums, each with three or four towers, with several apartments on each of the thirty or so floors, and the bare patch in Phase III became the impressive Cyber City, a business park, with scores of the biggest international information technology (IT) and computer firms making it their chief outpost in India (more on this in Chapter Four). The idea, again, was borrowed from major international cities that had made the best use of their land except that there the infrastructure, roads and electricity were secured first. DLF employed Hafeez Contractor, the Columbia University–trained architect who founded the Mumbai firm that bears his name, to design some of the modern high-rise buildings in Gurgaon. An impressive cluster of them, of bluish-hued glass and steel, are located in Cyber City, and he has sketched the forest of towers on Golf Course Road. His style is generic postmodern, and he is not known for ecologically sensitive construction. The Aralias and the Magnolias have vast and opulent interiors, even though the dun-coloured exteriors give them the uniformity of cookie-cutter products.

While KPS has remained chairman of DLF, he has entrusted the business to his children and senior executives. The transition to high-rise condominiums may have produced even greater profits but it has stained the company's reputation as an honest builder by its flagrant disregard of the promises it made to its wealthy clientele. Today, DLF stands accused of unspeakable delays, false advertising and unbridled greed, and many of these irate buyers, two of whom gave me this information on condition of anonymity, found themselves in a (high) class action suit.[5] They had paid crores of rupees in advance for luxury residences that were to be built in towers of no more than ten floors, but sheer avarice drove the builders to build nearly thirty floors instead. What was rather galling about this was that it was done in the dark, without discussion, warning or a reduction in price, or even an apology from the builder. To this were added woes of delays in the building schedule, and I heard strings of invective against the company issuing from very genteel owners. It is no surprise that the owners took DLF to court. The suit was settled by DLF in 2016.

The only decent consequence of this is that the lack of probity in the business of selling condominiums and shoddy service to the colonies operated by the builders has been exposed and buyers are now far more sceptical of the seductive spiel that builders and real estate agents give them. DLF was also berated for the lapses in the maintenance of the three phases of Qutab Enclave and resident welfare associations (RWAs) were busily filing complaints. I visited the DLF office on Arjun Marg several times, meeting the managers in charge to complain that one section of my street in Phase III was so ragged as to be barely usable (it still is that way in 2018). No repairs have ever been made in twenty years and it remains an eyesore in an allegedly posh area of the colony.

⁓

The dishonouring of contracts is a major hurdle in the making of a city. The public–private partnership (PPP), explained above, was entirely feasible but it needed good faith on both sides and this was patently absent. The most shocking lapse on the part of the private builders, who wrung many tax concessions out of the Haryana state government, was their failure to construct affordable housing for lower-income people or any housing at all for migrants, who were indispensable in building and sustaining the quality of life of the rich in Gurgaon. Even in the most spacious apartments, the servant's room is a careless afterthought: small, windowless, and stuffy, and certainly a place where the servant in question would have no temptation to retire to during the day. The age-old habit to treat the underclass with disdain is palpable even in the design of luxury apartments in the most modern of cities in India, and these shameful attitudes are deeply entrenched in our middle and upper classes.

In the encircling gloom, I also found some bright spots. While interviewing residents of various localities in Gurgaon, I discovered some who were socially aware, allowed those who work for them a day off a week and a two-hour break amid a fourteen-hour day, and were humane to their servants; and many paid for the schooling of their children. In one of the dozens of homes I visited, that of Latika and Mohit Thukral, I found a touching example of human decency: their servant's child sharing the desk with their masters' child and the latter was helping the former to do his homework on the computer. The atmosphere was one of sincere affection and commitment. The boy's family lived in the family house; he and his sibling attended the same prestigious (and expensive) Sri Ram School, thanks to the generosity of the Thukrals. I discovered a retired IBM executive, Santosh (Mintu) Pande, dedicating an hour of his time every evening giving private tuition for mathematics and English to a servant's child and paying for his educational expenses. Is this a trend of the future or is it just a few families like that of the Thukrals and Pandes taking this enlightened step?

In this inordinately wealthy city, will there ever be enough compassion to erase the need for vile tenements where the underclass is condemned to live in the villages that Gurgaon swallowed? Will the builders show any sense of social responsibility to improve the living conditions of those who enabled them to build this city and enrich them beyond any reasonable expectation? This matter is more deeply discussed in Chapter Seven where the focus is on Nathupur village. These are questions that hang like a pall above the luxury towers.

Four

Glimpses of Grungy Gurgaon

The paradox of unbridled 'growth' in Gurgaon is that while it is a measure of unprecedented economic progress, it is also the measure of the progress of stealthy cardiac problems. The side effects of pollution, scarcity of water, electricity and therefore clean air, and horrific traffic jams raises the imponderable question about the limits of urban growth. Should Gurgaon be allowed to grow boundlessly and should its residents hope that a miracle will save them from the menacing effects of overbuilding? Are the politicians and the real estate companies mindful of what they have wrought? One might anxiously wonder: is Gurgaon going to die of sclerotic arteries or dehydration? Will it wither away? Will its residents be forced to abandon it? Will its factories and offices shut down and move away? The single short answer to all these questions is a resounding 'no'. The long answer, however, is complicated and needs explication.

The fundamental flaw that emerged in Gurgaon's rapidly expanding circumference was the lack of perennial sources of water that would keep its deep aquifers recharged, such as lakes, ponds or even seasonal torrents, which dried up over time. The dearth felt today is to some degree natural but it is largely man-made. Certainly, Gurgaon is not alone: this condition is visible in large parts of India and in many cities, most notably its neighbour, Delhi, where the population has burgeoned beyond the wildest estimates, and the Yamuna contracts to a greasy trickle for eight months of the year. These problems have occurred gradually, first, as we saw in Chapter Two, under the colonial regime and then over three decades when an unsustainable population explosion forced rapid and uncontrolled urbanization.

Even as a small township, Gurgaon had a barely adequate power supply; and until 2011 the huge new demand brought about the plague of partial and total blackouts. The electricity supply remained somewhat erratic, although it is steadier since 2016 in areas where the generation of electricity is not entirely privatized. The logical push for alternative sources of energy seem to get stalled in the stacks of paper in the state-owned Dakshin Haryana Bijli Vitran Nigam (DHBVN) offices. Good, autonomous civic governance has not stepped into the breach, so the problems are needlessly perpetuated. And when you add up these three deficits—of water, power and good governance—the total becomes a frightening number that discourages a unified and sensible way out of it. Analytically, we can tackle them serially.

The scarcity of water is the gravest matter. Today, ecologists point to the large-scale deforestation and the laying of railway tracks from east to west that bridged or blocked the north–south–flowing torrents in the colonial period that created the arid landscape to replace the jhils that made up the avian-rich wetlands. Then came the modern collective push to tap the next available resource: groundwater. This has been done with a vengeance. With the improvement in techniques and equipment, mechanical drills now bore through schist and quartite, often exceeding 350 metres. The depths of precious aquifers are being sucked dry for the use of thousands of condo dwellers and office workers. The turn of the present millennium brought fresh warnings against the falling levels of groundwater, and boring of new tube wells has been banned. But the city has made exceptions for the biggest private builders, and it has no way to stop the urban villagers from extracting groundwater in the *lal dora* areas. The village well owners supply their tenement tenants and pump water into small tankers that travel to homes in Old Gurgaon and the newly developed residential colonies, dispensing water for a price to house owners who do not have tube wells. The retail price charged in DLF Phase III by suppliers in Nathupur in 2018 was Rs 900 per tanker of 4,000 litres that would barely serve a family of four for a couple of days. What is truly regrettable is that very little provision exists to conserve or utilize existing resources efficiently. Inadequate recycling and treatment of water and sewage (under the public–private regime of the last thirty years) warrants that a huge proportion of available water is simply wasted.

The falling groundwater levels are clearly etched in my memory. In 1996, when our house was being built in S Block of Qutab Enclave in DLF Phase III, we struck water at 25 metres at the site. It gushed wildly with perfectly potable water and we did not need anything more than a small jet pump to get it piped to the roof of our three-storeyed home to fill our storage tanks and to water the grove we had planted around it. Then this happy state ended and we had to dig a new well, now 130 metres deep and with a submersible pump; it gurgled and gagged and its distress told us that it was going to run dry in a few years. A third one, at 250 metres, lasted only a year before developing a dry cough and then becoming defunct. Of our neighbours, the doctors Mukta and Ram Dhariwal on Nathupur Road had a well of similar depth and water to maintain a luxuriant garden of ornamental trees. Other houses around us, unfortunately, have lawns (a deathless colonial idea) that need to be watered daily and fertilized to keep the grass green.

Every summer, the situation becomes more fraught as the water table plummets under duress from the huge pumps that belch water for construction and industrial needs. The public and private sectors have excelled each other in bringing about this sorry pass. Had

HUDA done its due diligence on sustainability and acted responsibly to conserve the finite resources of water and electricity, we might have had a more sensible and sustainable city. Sadly they foolishly handed out permits to dig wells like lollipops at a child's birthday party. So, the poor citizens seethe and scramble to fill a bucket or two while the rich have water pumps and immense storage tanks underground and overhead for their daily needs.

Had the real estate companies and their irresponsible greed been restrained with strict building limits, or had they been charged for boring their own wells and extracting unlimited 'free' water on per gallon basis, they might have been more mindful of the immense strain these soaring extravaganzas and lush green golf courses would put on the fragile ecosystem. Although DLF now has its own water treatment plant and uses only recycled water for its luxuriant golf courses, it is hard to dispute the fact that the recycled water originally comes from the strained underground water supply. The extraction rate—for their super luxurious condominium towers for which zoning regulations were shamelessly flouted—has not diminished. It was only in 2015, when the crisis loomed ominously and irreversibly, that the construction industry was ordered to use only treated water, but they continue to draw groundwater for the consumption of the occupants of residential and business towers.

Meanwhile, in the villages that Gurgaon absorbed, the landowners dug tube wells to profit from the needs of thousands of migrants who now live there as tenants. They do not have adequate bathrooms or toilets (if they have any at all), and very economically use the water that comes from a single pipe for a few hours a day for a cluster of shanties. Their use of electricity is similarly minimal; they live dimly in the glow of a single light bulb, for which they pay heavily. Some jhuggis and tenement apartments have formal connections with which some can run their fans and television sets, but this too points to a lack of calculation about residents' needs. Neither the builders nor the government made any arrangements to house the migrants that were coming into the new city from all corners of the country.

I visited the latter's offices looking for anything that would suggest that a 'sustainability' study had been undertaken but was met with hostile glares—because the needs of neither town nor country had been planned. The thick pall of sooty grey winter skies are also partly the unhappy products of uncontrolled growth in this city. Additional stress to the water situation in Gurgaon is added by the pervasive 'construction mafia', as the *Hindustan Times* of 31 May 2016 called it, who steal the drinking water supply to build their humongous construction projects, when they should really be tapping the treated water supply from the Dhanwapur sewage treatment plant. DLF appears to be the only private company that has responded to citizen outrage and built its own water treatment plant near its Arnold Palmer golf course that services the greens and the residents of its luxury residential towers, although it continues to siphon off groundwater from its deep bore wells for its older residential towers in Phase IV.

Bleak as this may sound, it is, fortunately, the darker side of dawn. Serious remedial plans, I was assured by an MCG (Municipal Corporation Gurgaon) official in 2014, are on the anvil and Gurgaon will have, within a few years' time, hammered out some of its grimmest problems. *The Times of India* on 29 January 2017 reported that the construction of the NCR water channel intended to bring water to Gurgaon that began in September 2008 was finally completed in 2017, and the relief for the residents of Gurgaon, as I can personally testify, is palpable. The report goes on to say:

> [T]he government officials say the new facility will increase the availability of the resource up to four times in the city. The NCR channel worth Rs 322 crore originates from Kakroi village of Sonepat district and culminates at Chandu Budhera in Gurgaon. It has the capacity to carry up to 800 cusecs of water. According to irrigation department officials, about 30 cusecs of water is being released in the 71-km channel from the Western Yamuna canal in Sonepat. The flow of water can be

enhanced later on. The NCR channel would help in supplying adequate quantity of water for the growing population of the Millennium City, a government spokesperson said … [T]hree quarters of this supply will serve Gurgaon and Manesar and the balance will go to new townships planned in Bahadurgarh, Sampla, Badli and Kharkhoda. There is also a plan to construct a large water works [sic] in Chandu Budhera village, with a capacity of 162 million gallons a day.

Other positive developments are also reported in that article. The government has finally built two water treatment plants: the first one in Sector 100, in Basai Village, to diminish waste and recycle water. The report goes on to say that additional improvements are also on the drawing board: 'HUDA will build a new water pumping station at the cost of 3.5 crores at its Basai water treatment plant … with a capacity of boosting 10 MGD [million gallons a day] of water.' Unfortunately, 'of the 170 cusecs of water that the Basai treatment plant gets from the Gurgaon Water Channel, only about 100 cusecs are used and the rest is wasted'. Clearly, the problem of wastage also needs to be seriously addressed.

The Basai water treatment plant has a maximum capacity of 60 MGD while another, smaller plant now in operation since 2015 in Chandu Budhera has a capacity of 22 MGD. Groundwater is drawn for 10 per cent of Gurgaon's requirement, and the three together constitute Gurgaon's entire supply of drinking water, catering to most of the residents' need for water, conservatively calculated at 26.4 MGD.[1] The city's management claims that this supply is sufficient, and it might well be, but the plant at Basai has acute problems with the supply of electric power—it is plagued with low voltage, tripping generators and frequent power cuts, which account for its inadequate performance. The blame was laid on a high-velocity gale that allegedly snapped the wires and the electric outage led to a drastic shortage of water in the summer of 2016.

An urgent short-term cure would be to generate sufficient electricity for the Basai plant, but in the long run—Gurgaon is expected to double its present population in ten years—more water and sewage treatment plants are desperately needed. HUDA had a plan to build a 66 kV substation on the premises of the Basai plant, but this project was languishing. Its erratic behaviour wad solved in a dramatic new development. To the rescue came the global electrical firm, Isolux Corsan, which, through its subsidiary Isolux Ingenieria, energized a new 66 kV GIS (gas-insulated switchgear) electric substation to serve Gurgaon. The new facility, the company's press release of 5 December 2015 stated, 'is part of a larger project to develop a total of three substations, commissioned by the State of Haryana, with a €14 million budget. The new Gurgaon substation will contribute to Government's plans to provide 24 hours power supply to cities, 16 hours to villages and 22 hours to district headquarters.' I verified this release by talking to friends and neighbours living in various parts of Gurgaon who feel the distinct upgrade in our electric supply. The power cuts now are rare and last a few minutes rather than a few hours and the voltage comes in at a steady 220 volts with no fluctuations. It has made all the voltage regulators attached to home appliances redundant. A brighter day has clearly dawned.

However, there are also political disruptions. The Jats went on a rampage against the government in February 2016, in their bid for 'other backward castes' (OBC) status, and unconscionably vandalized the water channels that lead to Gurgaon and the rest of NCR. Distressed citizens, who were deprived of water for ten days while the damage was being repaired, also rallied to march against HUDA. Little has been done about the malfunctioning infrastructure of the Daulatabad substation (in Delhi), on which it depends for its electricity. These chronic defects in turn prevent the water supply at the water treatment plant from being efficiently pumped to other parts of Gurgaon, and the worst affected by this are Phases I, II and IV and the scores of residential towers on Golf Course Road.

The good news is that there is enough water in north India to sustain its huge population and its teeming cities. The bad news is that water is poorly managed, improperly used, or carelessly wasted. A long-term measure that would be effective and make the land of Punjab and Haryana awash in that rare fluid is a change of crops in their vast agricultural hinterland. A return to its native drought resistant millets (or other crops and pulses) instead of the water-guzzling rice crops would stop the inevitable drought in its tracks. This will release a huge volume of canal water for other forms of consumption rather than the constant irrigation of paddy fields. Luckily, Punjab chief minister Captain Amarinder Singh, who spoke at length at journalist Shekhar Gupta's 'Off the Cuff' programme on 15 April 2017, addressed the water management concerns in his state. He is fully cognizant of the problem and promised to change the crops that the region can sustainably grow. This is an encouraging sign, and Haryana and western Uttar Pradesh need to return to this sensible path. It can only be hoped that this solution dawns on the governments of these contiguous states and the needed change can be wrought. Unfortunately, Singh is just as adamant that the Yamuna Link Canal will *not* be built (as the Supreme Court had decreed decades ago) to shift 'Punjab's' water to Haryana. One can only hope that he will see the bigger picture and change his stance.

Bore wells were already banned in 2011 but the laxity in enforcing this ban imperils the water table that will hit rock bottom in another decade or less. Other remedies are well known but need to be relentlessly monitored: rainwater harvesting and domestic grey water recycling done regularly can make a difference and create a culture of conservation among the wealthier residents. They are the primary consumers and wastefulness is a part of the affluent lifestyle.

Polluted air has become another major concern in Gurgaon, although it is not entirely of its own making; it is a rural and urban problem. The diesel generators in high-rises that belch smoke are not the only culprits. The burning of stubble in the fields is an even more harmful practice that fogs up the atmosphere in the winter months and shoots up pollution levels. The farmers' lobby is strong and they will resist such crop changes or polluting practices because the alternatives cost them money. A better deal for the farmers would solve this issue. If the governments of Punjab and Haryana were to increase the procurement price of wheat so that it would cover such costs, it is likely that the farmers would cooperate; after all they and their children have to breathe the same air. Passing court orders and banning harmful practices are ineffective particularly when they would mean further financial misery to the already beleaguered farmers of these regions. Urging home and factory owners to switch to solar power is an imperative that the country cannot delay for long. It should be a national priority to enable this transformation to occur as soon as possible.

By 2017, this frenzy of erecting tower after tower of residential apartments and business offices slowed down considerably because 40 per cent of office and housing stock is lying unsold or vacant. The slowdown in the real estate sector coupled with the demonetization of the 1,000 and 500 rupee notes seems to have taken the wind out of the sails of construction companies despite a sizeable drop in prices. 'The market is very much depressed even though prices are down and some good deals can be had,' said Pradip Bansal (not his real name), who looked rather gloomy himself when I visited him at his small office in the Qutab Plaza market on 12 May 2017. 'Builders have built too much and now Gurgaon is saturated. I have had no inquiry for anything this month. I feel I am sitting here killing flies. But I have many apartments for sale at less than 40 per cent of their price in 2010. Demonetization too has driven away many buyers, because deals were mostly 60:40.' The last refers to the fact that 60 per cent of the money to be paid for a property would be by cheque (white money) and the rest would be from a hidden stash of undeclared funds (black money) acceptable only as cash. A great deal of black money finds itself converted into real estate, which has been growing exponentially in value.

Although Gurgaon still has large swathes of open land that HUDA acquired and are eyed by builders, it might be wise for them to acknowledge that growth has plateaued and has probably reached its logical limit; these vacant lands should be made into parks or reforested to give the city the greenery and beauty it desperately needs. Further construction will only imperil what can possibly be sustained and made environmentally friendly. A drive through the city's countless sectors reveals many idle cranes hovering over skeletal apartment towers that dot the cityscape. There is news of a general slowdown but in Gurgaon it means that there are still 200 projects under various stages of construction in 2018. Urbanization has spread like an unstoppable contagion; Manesar is growing rapidly as are Sohna and Badshahpur, all as satellite cities of Gurgaon, with their own 'faulty towers'.

If the builders have been overzealous, HUDA has been in a state of awed paralysis in executing an admittedly unwieldy job. It occasionally startles itself to pay heed to the quotidian crises of Gurgaon, such as its effort to deal with the drinking water crisis, but mostly it sits on its perch far away in Chandigarh. It has all the towns of Haryana under its wing and refuses to delegate responsibility and serious funds to the fully elected Municipal Corporation of Gurgaon (MCG), and the officials were forced to twiddle their thumbs during their first term in utter frustration because they were given neither the authority nor the capital to tackle the problems at hand. Clearly, the state government and HUDA must loosen their hold on the enormous revenue that Gurgaon generates and deploy it urgently and honestly to erase the crisis of their own making.

The MCG, formed only in 2008, held its first election in 2013, and another in 2017, but is still struggling to establish itself on its own turf. Of the thirty-five councillors elected in the first round, one for each of the city's thirty-five wards, only one was a woman. I met her on 10 May 2013. Fortunately, Nisha Singh turned out to be articulate and thoughtful, and constructively critical of the general predicament the MCG finds itself in. She explained that the MCG is ineffective because it has neither the budget nor the power to function independently and solve the problems with which the city is besieged. 'It is handcuffed by the state and Central governments under which it is supposed to function,' Singh said. I visited her at her home from where she works, only because the MCG lacked an office, not to mention the funds to complete a road on which her house stood and get its signage painted. This new body will remain a wailing, helpless infant with thirty-five mothering figures but no one with the power to change its napkins. Gurgaon is the third largest contributor of revenue to the Central government in direct taxes in the country, but it hasn't been given the funds even to complete the roads or remove the piles of debris accumulated along the sides of such pathways. So it seems unlikely that the major work that needs to be done to ensure an uninterrupted supply of water and electricity will be taken up unless a true change of heart is experienced in Chandigarh, and Gurgaon gets its fair share to speed up its development. The city's aspiration to be world-class seems unrealistic by the mere fact that there is no elected mayor *with real power* and a clear vision to realize it. Instead, the mayor is a figurehead, often a prominent citizen or a routinely appointed bureaucrat who serves as a functionary who hears complaints but is powerless to deal with them.

'Have you seen Malibu Towne?' Nisha Singh asked me, and I nodded as I had fleetingly passed it in Sector 47 in Gurgaon when I was hopelessly lost trying to keep an appointment. Malibu Towne, built on 180 acres, is a private township, much like 'DLF City' or other gated communities. It sees itself as an exclusive enclave, unconcerned with its lack of integration into the larger city. It was built by Sudarshan Kohli, a US-trained mechanical engineer based in California, and K.S. Dhingra of Rajdoot-Berger Paints. 'Well, in the city's sanctioned plans there was a large piece of land that was to be a public park, something that Gurgaon sorely lacks. But, the builders slyly had the land use changed and a huge building now stands in the middle of that space. The homeowners around it put up boards saying "Shame On You" but do you think the builder was ever ashamed? They did nothing about it,' Singh said. I told her, not exaggerating all that much, that the former mayor of New York, Michael Bloomberg, would have promptly had it demolished and fined the offending party and probably put him on a fat and gluten-free diet for life. Public health and hygiene was very much part of his brief in New York and he took it very seriously. 'We need a mayor like that, who would hold the state and Central governments' feet to the fire and Gurgaon would be a world-class city because it has the potential,' Singh said.

Traditionally, most mayors of Indian cites have ceremonial functions but no real power; it is the chief minister and the state bureaucrats that wield executive power and pull the purse strings. Singh emphatically believes that the entire structure of the MCG is flawed, and she hoped that the entire system could be reformed and the citizens allowed to play a major role in the functioning of their city.

But lest one mistakenly think that HUDA is incapable of decisive action against illegal housing, it proved itself otherwise. On 15 May 2017, HUDA ordered a demolition drive that included the razing of 350 informal homes that had been built on 17 acres of land in Fatehpur Jharsa village in Gurgaon's Sector 47. The event was reported in *The Times or India* and *The News Minute*, among others, and this is a composite version, and the number of policemen deployed that day varies from 100 to 500.[2] The demolition was well planned with bulldozers and earthmovers to do the job and at least a hundred policemen, armed with lathis and teargas shells and some ordnance were present to keep in check the dwellers of these homes. When their homes were being razed to the ground, the occupants retaliated by throwing stones at the police. The police immediately attacked them with lathis, even though most of them were women and small children. Nisha Singh arrived at the scene after the violence had begun and stood well behind the phalanx of policemen and began to make a video of the police action on her mobile phone. They were beating the occupants of the jhuggis, manhandling women, and pushing and kicking the people to evict them. Although all the evidence on film and by witnesses point to the fact that she did nothing to instigate the riot, she was charged by the police for doing so. She was then beaten, dragged by her hair, and remanded to judicial custody—simply put, she was falsely charged, brutalized and imprisoned. News of her wrongful arrest as an elected official of the MCG was not just horrifying but extremely reckless on the part of the police. None of their charges or statements about her role at that 'riot' held water. The irrefutable video footage that covered Nisha Singh's actions from start to finish ended up exposing the police and put an egg on the face of the commissioner. The matter was politically motivated because the Congress members who were there were not arrested. Nine other women were also arrested after being subjected to unruly behaviour from the cops. Nisha Singh was refused bail and this caused a huge uproar among the citizens of Gurgaon. A petition for her release garnered 6,000 signatures within a few hours, but she was not released for three days. The other women arrested along with her were not released until much later.

In this entire episode, the infamous culture of Haryana police's brutality and misogyny seemed to be heavily underscored by beating up innocent women and children. HUDA, that has done little to provide legal and affordable housing for poor migrants, looks worse than ever in trying to occupy more land for high-end housing and business towers, when the city is already saturated and many apartments and business towers are empty with no buyers in sight. The Gurgaon police come under the jurisdiction of the city government, and the city government should be empowered to build adequate housing for Gurgaon's houseless poor, an area where HUDA has failed spectacularly. It is not clear from the reportage on the incident whether the 350 displaced families were ever compensated or given alternative places to live; such actions would have made tasty fodder for the talking heads on television news channels but I did not see any.

More recently, in June 2018, seven acres in the Biodiversity Park were cleared of squatters; these were migrants who have little money and no affordable housing to live in. The MCG came with 500 policemen and the job was done after a warning, so no one was brutalised. True, this was better than the last time but the root cause of squatters is patent to the meanest intellect: build housing where the migrants can dwell and then clear the illegal occupation of the few hundred acres in Gurgaon that have become 'slums'. I also wonder what these policemen do when they are not tearing down jhuggis; one hardly sees a man in uniform keeping the disorderly traffic under control where drivers of cars and motorcycles routinely break the law. We need a relentless crackdown and heavy fines on traffic offenders; it would enrich the MCG to repair all the roads and even pay for signage!

Nisha Singh's assault and incarceration finally made national news when she complained to the National Human Rights Commission and the National Commission for Women. With unassailable evidence on her side, she came out like a true hero, valiant, honest and a model for her colleagues. This shameful incident may well make the state government heed the demand for autonomy by the MCG. Ironically, this incident demonstrates that HUDA can act with planned intensity and get a job done when it wants to. Its tardy response to the larger problems of scarce water and electricity facing Gurgaon are, therefore, matters it wilfully ignores. What was even more discouraging to residents was that in the 2017 MCG election, Nisha Singh was no longer a councillor. Gurgaon dwellers will for long rue this loss of a strong clear voice.

Even more disheartening events have started to occur in Gurgaon. Since the beef ban implemented by the BJP government, vigilantism, that plagues Uttar Pradesh and other states under saffron rule, is making a spotty appearance in this modern city. In an article dated 23 March 2016 titled 'Gau Rakshaks in Gurgaon hold Muslim Migrants to Ransom over Beef', it was reported that a few days earlier, political vigilantes had struck. 'I was assaulted by "gau rakshaks" [cow protectors] on Sohna Road while I was supplying buffalo meat for a marriage party ... Since that incident I have stopped visiting Mewat [from where buffalo meat is sourced],' said Muhammad Noor Hasan, who runs a meat shop in Ghata, a south Gurgaon locality. Besides Mewat, most of the buffalo meat for Gurgaon comes from Faridabad.

'We will not only oppose cow slaughter but also cruelty meted out to other animals such as buffaloes because they are treated in an inhumane manner,' said Kuldeep Janghu, a member of Gurgaon's volunteer Gau Rakshak Dal. However, supermarkets and high-end restaurants continue to sell buffalo meat sourced from Mangaluru at Rs 390 per kg. The movement is tinged with an anti-Muslim stance that the BJP and Rashtriya Swayamsevak Sangh (RSS) have avowedly adopted; the love for cows is vivid in not stopping them from eating plastic waste as they forage in the garbage heaps in the city that causes them to come to tortured ends. Cows also roam the streets as soon as they cease to give milk and Hindu owners butcher male offspring ruthlessly because it is expensive to feed them. A similar group that calls itself the Sanyukt Hindu Sangharsh Samiti, that represents the worst elements of Hindus who are wrecking the religion and India's Constitution by their hateful actions against minorities, has taken to violently disrupting the Friday afternoon namaz held peacefully in public spaces since there are not enough mosques to accommodate the growing Muslim migrant population from Bihar and Bengal. They go on sprees wrecking the bicycles and motor bikes of the people at prayer and damage any personal belongings they can lay their hands on; they have flung prayer mats into ditches and made it impossible for the namaz to be read. The controversy had come to a head and CM Khattar issued orders for specially designated public spaces for the Friday prayers. The tension simmers as the unruly vigilantes have interpreted the presence of a BJP government to be the signal for causing communal disharmony at every opportunity. For a city that boasts of modernity and internationalism, such miscreants have to be severely punished and their activities nipped in the bud.

This has disturbed the general business-like air of Gurgaon; this behaviour has made national news and the Millennium City appears to have been embarrassed in many ways. When I thought we had now settled into a unbearable communal phase, something really heart-warming happened. In a move that reflects the very opposite sentiments and proves that that not all citizens totally approve of this ugly vigilantism, was the interfaith iftar held on the 10 June 2018. The Sanjha Iftaar sponsored by Gurgaon Nagrik Ekta Manch in the DLF Phase IV Community Centre was helped by many concerned individuals who spent their time and money to arrange this. I received two reminders to attend the iftar from Radha Khan, one of the organizers whose name signifies Hindu-Muslim fusion, and others like Saba blanketed her list with messages through social media and her efforts. There were volunteer donations at the door. Many Hindus showed up and shared the breaking of the fast on the last Sunday of Ramzaan, the holy month of fasting, and the spirit of unity and cordiality was evident throughout the event. I was there and my ballpark estimate is that more than 200 people came for this event. Some might have done it symbolically, others with a sincere wish to stamp out the embers of communal hatred that are old and hard to suppress, but all came with goodwill in their hearts and the message it sent to Gurgaon at large is important. The Commissioner made an appearance and that showed that officialdom was on the side of communal harmony—that is something to applaud. It might even deter the politicians who covertly support the vigilantism or encourage it with their rather aggressive Hindutva stance to sip from a communal cup of human kindness.

What brought tears to our eyes was the appearance of Yashpal Saksena of Delhi, whose twenty-three year old son, Ankit, was murdered by the family of his Muslim girlfriend. He had, the previous week, held an interfaith iftar in his own home in the sincere hope that this communal hatred, which has seen a new peak in the last few years, will come to a rational end. He spoke movingly and his words stirred the congregation. He had held a mirror up to the *nagriks* of Gurgaon and it was up to them to follow the path of forgiveness and love; religion and caste should not be the cause for killing lovers. If a man whose grown child was killed can be so large-hearted then nobody has an excuse to breed hatred. Fortunately the national media picked up the story and on the 11 June 2018, it could be read in the *Hindustan Times* and *Times of India* along with news of another interfaith iftar held by Muslim women for their Hindu friends and neighbours, who turned up to help put the dinner together. The media controls perceptions, and therefore reality; I hope their positive notice of this event and the spirit behind it affects many of its readers.

As a teacher of Indian civilization, I can certifiably assert that this ban on beef is a rather incongruous idea in a place that has just been named Gurugram. Beef was never proscribed in the Vedas or in the epics; Brahmins and Kshatriyas ate beef as a privilege and prasad after cows had been sacrificed at the Vedic altars and offered to the gods, making beef an auspicious food. Their diet included venison, pork, mutton, buffalo meat, and all manner of fowl. The Pandavas and Kauravas were avid hunters, as were brothers Ram and Lakshman. The philosophical loathing of violence of any kind was a Jain and Buddhist ideal, but even the Buddha ate meat when offered, and certainly did not proscribe the eating of meat of any kind. Hindus had been eating beef when available—think of the slaughter of the males born to cows—what purpose do they now have since their value as oxen has declined precipitously? The coming of tractors, water pumps, threshing machines and trucks made them redundant and male cattle began to disappear. Only a few survived to serve as stud bulls; the remainder became food. The proscription against beef gained traction in a much later epoch as a social rather than a religious measure. Such narrow-mindedness was not a part of ancient wisdom; the wise ones realized that human diets are not the concern of gods. And today, in the secular democratic republic of India, there is no place for such a ban or for the disruption of Friday prayers; they are an assault on the Constitution and the civil liberties of all citizens. The only creatures that really suffer under this ban are the cows themselves; older cows that no longer give milk are abandoned and they perish to horrible diseases or starve slowly to death.

What about women? Inhuman actions must also cease against that half of humanity that has borne its indignities and violence with enormous endurance. If one could divert the ferocity of the young

volunteers who call themselves 'gau rakshaks' against the endemic
violence against women, they might even become socially useful
instead of engendering hate and violence. Haryana, as I have written
extensively on elsewhere, has the world's worst sex ratios for women;
apart from the female sex-selective abortions, girls and women can be
killed or raped or beaten with relative impunity in their natal or their
marital homes. Crimes of passion, particularly between members of
different religions, castes and ethnicities, frequently go unreported, as
with the case in Nathupur I report in Chapter Six. Tensions created
by the influx of thousands of strangers and the stark contrasts in
wealth and the strict rules concerning contact between the sexes have
occasionally provoked murderous rage.

Instead of consolidating and governing effectively what already
exists in Gurgaon, and allowing new, independent townships to come
up after proper feasibility studies, the administration in Chandigarh
has added Manesar to form Greater Gurgaon that now shares the
same leaky pot of water and electricity. This has given the media
another opportunity to write yet more (premature) obituaries of
Gurgaon, which its residents, myself included, are weary of reading.
What gives credence to the indifference of Chief Minister Manohar
Lal Khattar's government to Gurgaon is its latest monetary sleight
of hand: the BJP state government dipped into Gurgaon's treasury
to 'loan' Rs 100 crore to the stagnating industrial town of Faridabad,
designated as one of the Central government's 100 'Smart Cities' of
the future. Oddly, Gurgaon never made the cut for this list. Without
proper funds the MCG pleads the inability to deal with the city's
waste. Thus empty lots in its residential colonies are habitually used
to dump rubbish, and both sides of Sunset Boulevard that sliced
through an Aravalli spur were, until very recently, used to dispose of
carcasses of dead animals and mounds of rubble from construction
sites. The MCG and the citizens of Gurgaon are justifiably irate for
having been ignored when the decision to divert the money was taken.

Streamlining governance is an imperative that Gurgaon has not
been allowed to grasp. The conflicting jurisdictions of builders and
government agencies have led to a disastrous neglect of residential

colonies and poorly maintained roads. HUDA has been regularly paid huge amounts of money as the cess the private builders collected from residents and agreed to pay as the External Development Fund (EDF). Clearly HUDA has been unable to keep its side of the bargain to build and maintain roads, implant the main sewerage lines and waste disposal systems, or even provide security beyond the private property lines where privately employed watchmen keep guard twenty-four hours a day, seven days a week. The police force is distressingly inadequate and politically partisan; and traffic policemen are rarely found when needed. The streets lack pavements; pedestrians walk long spells just to cross the roads as speeding cars ignore them; car drivers do not comprehend the meaning of white stripes on the few marked pedestrian crossings. Some traffic manager has substituted long loopy U-turns to replace traffic lights as four-way crossings disappear. Bad ideas pop up frequently to compound the disorder.

In an enlightening interview with Jyoti Sagar, an eminent advocate and general secretary of SURGE (Society for the Regeneration of Gurgaon and its Environs) of whom there's more in Chapter Eight, I gleaned that, to compound its sins HUDA has shown an utter lack of transparency in disclosing how the EDF, estimated in 2010 to be more than Rs 35,000 crore plus the interest that accrues on it, has been spent. HUDA was to preserve this corpus and use the interest (more than 8 per cent in a simple fixed deposit in a bank) on it to discharge its responsibility for providing the civic amenities it is legally obliged to provide. Patently this money was not used for the purpose it was intended and HUDA owes the taxpayers an accounting of this vast fund.

The technology exists, the money is there, and soon with protests and public interest litigation (PIL) from demanding and enlightened 'consumer citizens'[3] as John Harris has called them in his path-breaking essay, 'Antinomies of Empowerment' and of which there are many, we can see Gurgaon rapidly convalesce from the 'dystopia' from which it appears to be suffering. NGOs like SURGE and I Am Gurgaon are continually battling the inertia that grips the government, the corruption that allows designated parkland to become private buildings, and the lack of governance that allows a city to languish with insufficient water and frequent power outages, and forces pedestrians to walk on dangerous roads. The growing vocal section of Gurgaon's 1.5 million inhabitants is furious at the state of affairs. These serious breaches of faith by the succession of chief ministers, HUDA and DHBVN (Dakshin Haryana Bijli Vitran Nigam) reinforce the common view that only the private corporations or the active NGOs can save the city. This was expressed by many of the attendees who had joined a protest march on 24 April 2016 at the appropriately named Kachra Chowk (Rubbish Square), against the dumping of garbage along Sunset Boulevard and bordering on the Aravalli ridge. The citizens need to become more deeply engaged in the management of the city and MCG must assert its right as the principal manager of the city and wrest its share of funds from the somnolent HUDA.

National Highway 8 (NH-8), proposed on the old Delhi–Gurgaon route past the airport, was arbitrarily relocated at the behest of DLF.[4] Hailed as an engineering marvel, it was constructed as a partially elevated roadway that would bring Jaipur under four hours from Gurgaon, and would be extended to India's financial capital, Mumbai. It will eventually extend for 1,428 kilometres, all the way to Ahmedabad and Surat in a grand 'golden quadrilateral'. The Gurgaon–Delhi section of this artery, that became functional in 2010, showcases the congenital defects of Indian highway building. Its eight lanes, for example, narrow down to four without warning and expand again to six, creating a daily crawl of cars through the bottleneck. Honking, shouting and other expressions of road rage occur while the more aggressive wiggle-to-get-ahead game is in progress. There was also a horribly mismanaged, fury-inducing toll plaza that caused so many traffic snarls that it was finally dismantled, but not before one toll collector was murdered by an enraged motorist. Some clever administrator made the toll Rs 21, instead of a round number, and this caused each driver to stop and collect change, making it a complicated transaction. But that is not all.

The traffic jams are insignificant compared to the permanent disruption NH-8 caused to the spatial integrity of the city and carved it into two disjointed lobes. Two senior officers of the National Highway Authority of India (NHAI), who did not wish to be named, and an eminent citizen who lives in Udyog Vihar verified that the original plan for the highway was to widen and modernize the old Delhi–Jaipur road, a move that would not have left the old city internally disconnected to the new one. This route was forcibly altered after pressure from DLF, they said. The present route runs eastward privileging the three phases of its Qutab Enclave and Cyber City better, and rudely cleaves more than it connects the localities it traverses. Its presence in the middle of the city as a wide, elevated, three-dimensional structure on elephantine concrete pillars is as ungainly as it is inconvenient for those who live on either side of it, or should ever have to cross it on foot. There is neither provision for pavements nor pedestrian crossings, and cyclists and pedestrians have a very perilous time making their way along it. This kind of hasty and mindless development has given the city a permanent handicap; clearly those who claim they 'envisioned' a city had their blinkers on.

Even as I privately swear at the inadequacies of the roads and traffic management in Gurgaon, I found all the myths of regulating traffic in the city succinctly in a trenchant article by Anil Bhatt, director, integrated transport of World Resources Institute, India in *Hindustan Times* of 6 June 2018. It ought to be required reading for the newly created Gurugram Metropolitan Development Authority (GMDA), HUDA, MCG and the entire staff of the commissioner's office to realize that they are making things worse with their 'innovative' plans for wider eighteen-lane roads and signal-free driving. It is making the city traffic utterly ugly and dangerous because they have done away with intersections and made provision for nothing but cars, and more cars.

On one hand, it is known as Millennium City, but on the other, it is also branded in the news as 'Gurujam' because of its notorious traffic, he writes. He then sets out his impeccably lucid analysis of the chaos. I cite him extensively because every citizen should be aware of what is conceptually wrong with the 'improvements' made by the

authorities based on wrong-headed thinking. He says that there are
numerous reasons for the chaotic mobility in Gurgaon, but the three
major traffic myths are probably the root of it. The first myth he cites
is that everybody in Gurgaon moves by car. This is laughable, as Bhatt
points out:

A study by the Gurugram Metropolitan Development
Authority (GMDA) in 2018 on its city bus services points
out that within the Municipal Corporation area, the largest
mode of travel is walking (27 per cent), followed by motorised
two-wheelers (26 per cent), car users (10 per cent) and cyclists
(4 per cent). The remaining 33 per cent comprises people using
both formal and informal modes of public transport systems,
such as autos, taxis, buses, Metro and trains.

The results from this study are not surprising at all because
even the decade-old Integrated Mobility Plan for Gurugram
also estimated that one-third of the population was walking
and cycling, one third using formal and informal public
transport and the rest third was using cars and two-wheelers.
Therefore, it's a myth that everyone in Gurugram moves by
car and the 2008 and 2018 data points that only 10 percent of
the people do that.

The second myth is that more and wider roads will prevent jams.
Bhatt writes, rather amusingly:

The man who created the famous Say's law, Jean-Baptiste Say,
states 'supply creates its own demand' and what it explains
can be applicable for transport planning as well, i.e., if more
roads are built, there will be more motor vehicles. And while
the law may have been formulated more than a century and
half back, yet transport planners/engineers in Gurugram fail to
understand this fundamental concept and the city is obsessed
with building more flyovers, underpasses and widening roads,
as a result of which there is increasing traffic.

Gurugram's Golf Course Road is a classic example of how not to design an urban road. The signal-free road that was meant to provide signal-free connectivity to people living around the Golf Course to NH-8 is now frequently in the news for traffic jams. Therefore, if the sixteen lanes of road could not remove jams on the Golf Course Road, surely eighteen lanes won't do it either.

The third patent and widely subscribed myth is that removing intersections eases traffic flow. Bhatt's analysis is spot on:

Of late there is a trend in the city to replace intersections with 'U-turns', which is neither a clever form of planning nor traffic engineering. From the planning perspective, traffic signals are an important part of a city's transport system, as it helps various modes of transport, including pedestrians and cyclists, in crossing the road. They provide access to people on either side of roads that have continuous development such as Sohna Road, Old Gurgaon Road or any other road inside the city. Removal of these intersections forces cyclists and pedestrians to violate traffic rules, as detours are often lengthy and impractical, leading to accidents and often deaths. From an engineering perspective, it is well documented that an intersection with a traffic signal has much more throughput than if the same is replaced by 'U turns'. A simple stroll in the morning or evening hours on Sohna Road, HUDA City Metro Station, etc., will reveal the true picture of this experimentation.

It's time that the city moves towards prioritizing, planning for walking, cycling and public transport and a starting point of this is planning multi-modal streets, rather than streets only for cars. Else, it will be locked in, with no escape.

There is no better way to put this or explain it to the traffic managers that their ideas belong in the dustbin (which the MCG should provide) because they create the jams rather than reduce them.

They might consider the police force to play a constructive role in issuing challans to the violators of traffic rules and collecting fines. The current plan simply does not work.

Had the planners looked for a model for their street layout and traffic management they ought to have looked at New York, a city of eight million inhabitants and ten times as many cars that has far less traffic chaos than Gurgaon and honking is an offence that is punished. Most streets in Manhattan are on a grid, with timed lights for pedestrians and wheeled traffic at each intersection, have only two lanes and are one-way only, with footpaths wider than the motorable road width, and cycle paths and bus lanes clearly marked. Millions use the very extensive network of the subway system daily and it runs for twenty-four hours a day in a city that never sleeps. The highways run along the outer edges of the island and do not intrude into the city and bisect it. When there is the occasional traffic jam, traffic police get there immediately and the well-trained personnel and drivers cooperate to unclog the traffic to restore its normal flow. There are lessons there to be learnt.

In 2012, a picturesque six-lane highway linked Gurgaon to Faridabad, via Manesar. The dim memory of Gurgaon as a pit stop for Emperor Akbar's lumbering pachyderm cavalcade from Fatehpur Sikri en route to Delhi on a dirt road has finally been supplanted by this well-made road that snakes it way through the Aravallis and has become the destination for those seeking scenic locales for picnics and prenuptial photo shoots.

There are also bypasses being constructed to avoid the congested arteries of cities, and to make roads our preferred method of moving goods and people. The Dwarka Expressway, the North and South Peripheral Roads, the PMK [Palwal–Manesar–Kandili] Western Bypass to divert truck traffic around Delhi are some of these new instances of civic surgery. These may prove to be a fatal mistake we will repent at leisure when we cannot breathe the air, because we should be increasing our railway and metro networks to keep more cars, trucks and lorries from clogging the roads and adding to the pollution.

New and better roads connect Gurgaon to other cities but, alas, they do not breed good drivers. With more than a thousand new cars being added to the roads of NCR *every day*, the jams, the pollution and fatalities on the roads will only increase. Most drivers, some without even a driver's licence, travel these new highways with great abandon and are selfishly unheeding or even ignorant of simple traffic rules—like minding speed limits, driving on the left side of the road, obeying traffic lights, staying in a lane or indicating when changing lanes, not squeezing five cars abreast on two-lane roads, overtaking only from the right, using the headlamp dimmers at night, not taking a short cut against the traffic on a one-way street, allowing those with the right-of-way to pass, or even understanding what 'right of way' means. Add to this litany a simple 'me first' attitude and rude honking and you have the masters of creating traffic jams even on this broad new conduit. Gurgaon needs a platoon of well-trained traffic policemen who would enforce some of these rules honestly and regularly. Nothing will end the traffic jams until those who drive the millions of cars learn to obey the rules, or are punished with impounded vehicles, hefty fines and suspended licences.

It is easy to blame the lack of infrastructure in Gurgaon for all its ills; the human factor is seldom commented upon. A memorable and horrific traffic snarl, caused by a combination of a downpour on 28 July 2016, roads with large potholes and no drainage, stalled cars, and drivers with ugly roadside manners brought Gurgaon to a dead halt for as long as eight hours. The same rainstorm caused similar or worse flooding in Delhi but Gurgaon bore the brunt of the media's scathing coverage. The print media put it on their front pages with astonishing pictures of drowned and abandoned cars, and TV news channels had brilliant footage on the disaster. Perhaps the government was finally shamed into action. The *Hindustan Times* of 13 September 2016 reported that Haryana CM Manohar Lal Khattar sternly announced that all damaged and potholed roads in Gurgaon should be repaired by 1 November 2016. He ordered the Public Works Department (PWD) to do the job with help in manpower and equipment from

HUDA and the Town and Country Planning Department. The commissioner of the MCG instantly pledged his support to send engineers and equipment to the PWD to meet this deadline. While inner roads in the residential colonies, whose maintenance and upkeep are the responsibility of the private builders, continue to deteriorate, the public thoroughfares and main streets have received a thick coat of macadam. Much of this, I noticed upon my return from New York in February 2017, had indeed been done, which proved the point that we need an interactive management to set things right.

In August 2016, a special drive to change driving habits in Gurgaon and enforce the existing rules of the road had been bravely initiated across the city. Enforcement was also strict and traffic policemen collected over a crore (ten million) of rupees in fines from 29,752 vehicle owners over that period. This included 1,800 vehicles that were towed away and 3,600 fined for being wrongly parked, and as many as 2,020 vehicles were fined for driving in the wrong direction. The assistant commissioner of police, Hawa Singh, rattled off more of these alarming figures to the *Hindustan Times* reporter: '3,000 vehicles—including 2,500 auto-rickshaws, 374 taxis and 126 other vehicles—were impounded during the drives. Also, 3,500 persons were fined for not wearing seat belts and some others for drink [sic] driving … These [enforcement] drives would continue in future as well to ensure that traffic moves smoothly on Gurgaon roads.'

Puran Kumar was put in charge of traffic as joint commissioner of police in Gurgaon immediately after the big snarl-up, and he instituted these enforcement drives with stunning impact. Such drives and publicity of the fines imposed will produce results and revenue, and perhaps one day even the feral drivers in Gurgaon will be tamed characters. But the drive cannot be for a single random day; it has to be enforced regularly until there is a discernible change in driving habits. Alas, as we well know, this is not a malaise that afflicts only Gurgaon drivers—throughout the entire country, with few exceptions, the skills and manners of the drivers on Indian roads worsen as the cars get bigger and more numerous. Traffic jams during rush hours—that seem to have lengthened to incorporate most of the day—are now taken in stride, 'like mosquito bites', said a friend in Delhi where congestion on roads is a routine matter. I reminded him that mosquito bites are not trivial; they cause diseases like dengue fever, malaria and chikungunya, much like the deaths and disabilities caused by vehicular traffic.

Khattar's decisiveness has been selective and fitful, much like the previous chief ministers of Haryana. Any of them could have immediately ordered HUDA to implement the decades-old agreement of the public–private partnership (PPP) and complete the sewerage infrastructure and spare the residents of the Millennium City the indignity of having human waste flow into open cesspools at various locations in its stylish expanse. The well-known lawyer Jyoti Sagar has waged a persistent legal battle against this official lack of fiscal transparency and inertia. He is still engaged in a PIL to force HUDA to render accounts for revenue and complete its contractual obligations; his efforts have met with delays and high-handed obfuscation. The same lack of cooperation with the MCG from HUDA has rendered the councillors as mere figureheads; they were not even allotted an office building where they could all meet, and most of them worked out of their own homes in 2013, so inconsequential was its creation as a civic authority. The three new councillors I met then each wagged a frustrated finger at the HUDA regime under the former chief minister, Bhupinder Singh Hooda, calling him the puppeteer who kept all the strings in his fist. All expectant eyes are now on Khattar and a strong and able deputy commissioner (DC) and MCG, like T.L. Satyaprakash, who was promoted to special secretary of Town and Country Planning Department in Chandigarh on 19 May 2018. The *Hindustan Times* of 19 May reported that the reshuffle had brought Hardeep Singh, who administered HUDA in Panchkula, to replace him as DC Gurgaon. V. Umashankar, the officer on special duty to head the recently created civic body, the Gurugram Metropolitan Development Authority (GMDA), will also head the MCG as commissioner. The upgrade in the rank of the chief of the MCG, it is hoped, brings about an upgrade in its authority and funding. The overlapping civic authorities with a singular head that will sport three hats will give juggling new meaning and, it is devoutly hoped, bring some forceful action to the unfinished projects in Gurgaon and the proper maintenance of those already completed.

With due diligence the new commissioner, who has extensive experience with HUDA, might even demand an accounting of HUDA's ineptitude or indifference to matters such as solid waste disposal and water treatment plants. In July 2017, HUDA was still unconscionably squatting on the humongous accumulation of EDF (unless the money has been used elsewhere and there is no way of knowing that until it publicly discloses this) while the sewage spilled into large unlined pits that are an unsightly health hazard. This scandalous neglect has brought about condemnation from citizens and media alike: newspaper reportage on this subject, some quite graphic, is summed up in this succinct headline 'Gurgaon Drowning in Its Own Sewage'. Umashankar's work is cut out for him and he could save Gurgaon from this fate.

As a resident for more than two decades who has lived with many of the flaws which are our millennium city's wont, I have observed two opposing trends. One, in the absence of a coherent waste management and garbage disposal scheme, Gurgaon has gradually become insanitary and insalubrious where the groundwater is being contaminated, as the sewage remains untreated. And it is not just HUDA that needs to mind its manners; there are many neighbours and private contractors too who make life unpleasant. There is more garbage strewn in the plotted residential areas, particularly in the many vacant lots whose owners have delayed construction, perhaps never intending to build, but speculating that they can flog their plots when land prices escalate further.

I remember once when a plume of black smoke with a dreadful smell issued from Block T in Phase III of DLF City. Upon investigation, I found a smouldering heap of old rubber tyres that had been disposed of by a garbage collector and burnt, creating toxic fumes. The neighbours were distressed but there was no recourse, and the police did not apprehend the mischief maker.

Some residents refuse to pay to get the debris removed after the construction on their plots is completed; it lies in dusty mounds on the adjacent empty plot or by the roadside. For many years, we could not sit in our own back veranda because of the ramshackle diesel generator belonging to our immediate neighbour that erupted with ear splitting noise and thick fumes as soon as the electricity went off. This happened more than half a dozen times a day and it would send us coughing and choking inside. My complaints only brought a torrent of verbal abuse from the owner, a man even more noxious than his generator. Electrical surges were also frequent and during writing this book my PC and its UPS burned out, as did many kitchen appliances. DHBVN was indifferent to our loss, ignored our complaints, and did nothing to check the electrical problems so common in our neighbourhood until the new substation was built in 2016.

After many years of enduring this, things finally changed in 2016. The electricity now comes at a steady voltage and has only very short breaks, which eliminated the torture to which our neighbour was mindlessly subjecting us. The goal of twenty-four-hour electricity and water, available in the high-rises, is no longer a distant hope for private houses—it is now 95 per cent achieved in the plotted area and matches what Lutyens' Delhi gives its residents. What is next on the wishlist in this department is to get the looping, sagging transmission wires strung between ugly electric poles and the mess of black spaghetti that connects them to substations on the edges of roads to be dealt with. If somehow these could all be buried underground, Gurgaon would take a big step towards an aesthetic future. An announcement to this effect was made in June, 2018; Gurgaon would have a 'smart grid' managed by computers and all electrical wires would be buried to stop pilferage and disruptions in service by 2022. We will watch this with keen anticipation.

With a steady stream of public criticism, bad press, court cases, and continual complaints from residents, things began to move quickly in 2015. Many roads and two underpasses were completed. The two major laments against erratic electricity and water supply have been mostly quieted. It doesn't take rocket science or billions of rupees to fix what ails Gurgaon; it takes instead a large dose of common sense, a firm resolve to use the existing pile of money to tackle the problems that have known solutions with ironclad integrity. But when it comes to the challenge of managing sewage, rubble, domestic garbage and carcasses of animals, rocket science may indeed be simpler. Perhaps a strong mayor might shake off the constraints that HUDA puts on civic improvements and governance.[5] The technology exists, there are plans to build more water treatment plants, and soon, with protests and PILs from demanding and enlightened 'consumer citizens' as John Harris has called them,[6] we can see Gurgaon rapidly convalesce from the 'dystopia' from which it appears to be suffering.

While the media rightly castigates Gurgaon for its mismanagement, it is necessary to remind readers that the capital city itself (not to mention scores of older cities) sets a poor example. The approximately twenty million people now crammed into Delhi, where dry taps, frequent power cuts, potholed roads and litter are ubiquitous, except in the beautifully maintained colonial New Delhi where officialdom and old wealth dwell, diligently served by the richly endowed New Delhi Municipal Council. Delhi rapidly demolishes huge bastis or slums and clears its streets of beggars when some big international sporting meet is imminent in the city; its governance is as flawed as the next city's and is definitely contributing to the national urban crisis. It has arbitrarily taken away from Haryana a large share of the water allocated to it and the skirmish to get it back is occasionally waged in the media.

Even fictional and cinematic representations of Gurgaon have only underscored a dark and dangerous aspect. They have subliminally given the city the reputation of being more 'gruesome' than all its civic travails would warrant. The Man Booker Prize-winning novel *The White Tiger* by Aravind Adiga in 2008 set a trend, although the crime it showcases is clearly a class-based crime, of a male employee against his male master. It is a novel in which Bihar is starkly painted as the 'darkness' and Gurgaon as the 'light'. The protagonist, Balram Halwai, is a minimally educated Bihari migrant who works as a driver for a rich businessman Ashok and his sexy American-born wife Ms Pinky, who live in an apartment in one of Gurgaon's luxury high-rises. The driver lives in the warren of rooms in the basement that the scores of household servants inhabit. Balram is prepared to take the rap for Ms Pinky's drunken driving after she runs over a child from a basti, but nothing happens because the victim's family files no suit; instead the wife decamps for America. One day when Ashok has withdrawn a large sum of money from his bank and wishes to be driven home, Balram bludgeons him to death with a Johnnie Walker Black Label Scotch whisky bottle—the choice of the murder weapon speaks volumes—and dumps his body on the edge of the road and absconds to Bengaluru with the stash to begin a new life. The plot is hardly startling, since it is a variation on the real-life newspaper accounts of elderly couples being looted and murdered in their homes in the posh colonies of Delhi and other big cities, but the novel portrays corruption, greed and immorality as the pervasive trait that the rich and poor share equally. There is no hero or heroine in the novel. Adiga, a resident of Gurgaon, has spun a murky yarn that found many sympathetic readers in the UK and the US, while most Indian readers have greeted it with a polite shrug, perhaps because it describes master–servant relations in Gurgaon or Delhi quite convincingly.

Gurgaon supplies a convenient backdrop to tales of lust, greed and anger, its reputation for a savage peasantry, whether migrant or local, getting great publicity. The film *NH 10* (National Highway 10), set in an urban village in Gurgaon, showcases the lethal clash between cosmopolitan urban versus conservative Haryanvi values that grippingly plays out with a triumphal feminist flourish in its denouement. The contrast between Gurgaon's villagers and the city's Westernized urbanites as they get entangled in a culturally charged plot is underscored as a fight between a brutal tradition and enlightened modernity. Featuring black and white SUVs with Gurgaon licence plates as grunting, roaring, chasing characters symbolizing the bad and good characters who own them, it is a graphically violent and harrowing tale. The film depicts the brutality of a khap panchayat's decision to beat a girl and her lover to death. Just then a passing modern couple on a picnic in their white SUV get unwittingly embroiled and are forced to try and save the girl from her brother—the villain—in his black SUV. What added a touch of realism to my viewing of this film was the audience in the cinema hall. In the screen fight between the villain and the female protagonist, one heard the audience taking audible sides and it dawned on me that this was not a Bollywood morality tale—there are vociferous adherents on both sides, with the villain more popular than the brave woman. Native Gurgaonwallahs have a long way to go in accepting the social mores that modern urbanization has created. It has taken so much of its material prosperity in recent decades by importing foreign capital and industry, yet its xenophobia erupts more frequently even as Hindutva, a BJP-ideology that has repackaged Hinduism, increases its sway over the entire state. Religion is a purely private matter in a secular democracy; democratic governments cannot (and should not) legislate social control, as I have pointed out in the matter of an increasing anti-Muslim trend.

Bad as all this sounds, I, who have explored this underbelly more realistically, want to emphasize that on the whole Gurgaon is gradually getting much that was omitted or deliberately withheld. Gurgaon's ailments are curable and the medication is known and affordable—only the patient must be permitted to take it. It must take away the key to the lock where it is kept before its condition becomes fatal. A ray of hope for all these new towns is that the private sector pays a mandated 2 per cent cess on their profits as their gesture to show Corporate Social Responsibility (CSR); they choose the projects they wish to support and often channel funds through the NGOs that are proven to be working for the betterment of the city, such as I Am Gurgaon and SURGE. A fraction of what this amounts to annually could be designated to deal with the water, air and electricity issues by subsidising solar energy, resuscitating old torrents, creating more green areas and parks and planting trees. I Am Gurgaon has taken up that cause in the Aravalli Biodiversity Park, as we shall see in Chapter

Eight; ten more parks like that may make Gurgaon a city that will outlive its problems and even restore the natural beauty in the gaps of its built environment.

We know that things have improved at the Phase III substation that was continually breaking down, because this happens only a few times a month now and for brief stints and some of the old equipment, that had burned out a few times, has finally been replaced. Other substations are also receiving replacements for their crusty equipment. An electrical engineer should be checking on generators and completely forbidding the use of diesel for domestic generators; although the high-rise apartment dwellers would be totally out of luck and immediate alternatives if such a rule is indeed implemented. For water a huge concrete reservoir has been constructed in our vicinity that can hold (I am told by the mechanic who services its large pump and generator) a million litres of canal water for the use of residents in S Block. Others are also going to be built, he assured me; we only just started from this end of DLF City.

The sceptics should take note of this and, perhaps, change their negative stance acknowledging that urbanization in India is not a smooth and seamless process. There are fumbles and stumbles as the city grows. There is also no denying that inspite of the glitches Gurgaon has transformed from a reclusive backwater to a 'happening place'. The media thrives on the glitches, but it would only be fair to say that it too is acknowledging the good more often. *Hindustan Times*, sensibly, has started a column 'I Love Gurgaon' that publishes stories of residents who speak of their experiences that make them love their city; it may sound somewhat lame, but it is a change from the acidic reportage done in the past. Clearly, there is a lot of hope and optimism for Gurgaon to become that enviable city. Perhaps in another decade.

Five

The Cradle of Corporations

Like a pebble dropped into the stillness of a small pond, the advent of modern industry generated ever-expanding ripples in Gurgaon district, starting with the small fry and later netting some very large fish. This was fortuitous because Faridabad district had already developed into a robust manufacturing and residential centre. The florescence of industry was almost immediate—in the 1950s, the district's largest town, Faridabad, made a mark on the industrial map, because it was considered at a safe distance from the Pakistan border, unlike other eligible towns in Punjab. It had more than 122 large and 1,800 small and mid-scale industries producing an amazing miscellany of goods. The gazetted list (1983 Gazetteer: 271), boring to read, could be set to rap music or sung as a Punjabi tappa with the arrangement below:

> from ceramics to buttons,
> tractor-motor parts
> to little syringes,

bicycles to little pins.
Scooters and refrigerators
Tin boxes and bulbs

There were also hand tools, electric goods, machine tools and agricultural implements. Dozens of these industrial units had foreign collaborators.

In November 1966, Haryana became a state—it earlier was part of East Punjab—and this added fuel to the fire of growth. Some very big players entered the fray: the Escorts Group's pale grey Ferguson tractors became an ubiquitous sight in the fields of Punjab and beyond. International brands like Goodyear, Kelvinator, Metal Box, Bata and Eicher, among others, soon had offices and factories making their world-famous products here. Escorts grew in the 1970s and '80s to become one of India's largest engineering goods producing conglomerates that exported farm mechanization equipment and construction and railways' automotive parts to sixty other countries. A host of ancillary industries came with these to give Faridabad what appeared an insurmountable lead so that no town in Haryana could overtake it as the industrial nerve centre of the new state. Apart from manufacturing goods for the domestic market, Faridabad accounted for half the exports of India; it earned valuable foreign exchange as goods made there were shipped to the Middle East, Australia, eastern Europe, and some parts of Africa.

In the decades before the 1980s, Gurgaon held the dubious distinction of becoming nationally famous for making the largest number of hot water bottles than anywhere else in the country, for domestic use and export by Enkay Rubber Goods with a turnover of Rs 1.5 crore in 1963. Another factory manufactured seamless rubber basketballs for export. Optical lens grinding workshops proliferated and some sixty active units were registered in the early 1960s, and the largest of them employed more than 350 workers. Continental Paints produced high-quality paints and varnishes, and several small readymade garments concerns turned out clothes that were sold both in India and abroad. Two early foreign collaborations in Gurgaon in the 1970s were the Indo-Nippon Food Corporation that annually produced more than Rs 50 lakh worth of sausage casings (yes, sausage casings for which the principal raw material was indeed bovine and porcine stomach linings), and the large-scale Indo Swiss Watch Company that had a target of assembling six lakh watches every year with both imported and indigenous parts.

The policy of the new state government of Haryana welcomed and enabled young industries with cheap land with brisk, uncomplicated change of land use, and loans and tax breaks, and with Faridabad as its poster child. Combining hard work and ambition, Punjabi refugees had by now established themselves as the cutting edge of industrial north India. Very quickly they shed the adjective 'refugee' to describe one of India's most vibrant and prosperous communities. Rows of Ambassador and Fiat cars made their journey from Delhi to Faridabad (until the advent of Maruti Suzuki cars, of course) and it became a mildly clogged artery that serviced the bureaucratic heart of Delhi. So great was its success that in 1979, Faridabad was shorn from Gurgaon district to become a district in its own right. It also had the advantage of being an important stop on the main-line broad-gauge railway route to western and southern India. But Faridabad had been developed by the state government and land prices had already climbed, so private developers made a beeline for Gurgaon. It was still classified as rural and therefore its land was much cheaper, with land use change rules that were not as complicated as those established for urban areas, and protests from farmers who pleaded that grazing lands not be sold to builders were rudely ignored.

Gurgaon captured the imagination of the world's largest multinational corporations. Within two decades of spectacular growth, it became a major automobile manufacturing hub with Maruti Suzuki leading the way, as we have already seen. It is also the birthplace of Indigo, India's largest domestic airline, and the new genre of service industry based on information technology (IT) that needed large office spaces and an educated workforce that it had in ample supply. Even some traditional export manufacturers, like the garment industry, found the proximity to the international airport as something not requiring any mental effort for moving to Gurgaon. Faridabad stagnated, as it shaded more into a blue-collar city while Gurgaon grew exponentially as a young, vibrant, white-collar, middle-class redoubt.[1]

One symbol of its prosperity is the Arnold Palmer–designed eighteen-hole golf course with its DLF Golf and Country Club that made the news among golfing circles internationally when it debuted in 2006. Featureless agricultural acreage was contoured and landscaped with massive earthworks and water bodies shaped like jigsaw puzzle pieces, and large grassy greens and deep sand bunkers that line the chartreuse fairways. Tiger Woods played a much publicized round here, and international championship matches, like the Johnnie Walker Classic, and others have been hosted here. Its membership list is an accurate measure of the gravitas Gurgaon now projects as a business destination. The top management of many of the big-ticket corporations and established professionals, including lawyers, doctors, accountants, engineers, bureaucrats, academics, cultural aficionados, and young professionals looking for a leg-up, are members who make time to play a leisurely round of golf while they network, make deals, discuss projects or simply socialize in this exclusive place, a world away from the jagged concrete edges of the Gurgaon that surrounds it. It might easily rank as the golfing capital of India.

Six other golf courses have since come up in different parts of the city, a measure of its well-shod residents, but this is *the* club to which the residents aspire to belong, signalling their seven-digit incomes even though their handicap is still in double digits. For the latter, there's the DLF Golf Academy, the first of its kind in India, that 'offers a dual-level floodlit driving range', a chipping green, practice sand traps and a putting green for those who are working on their strokes or perfecting the putt that will put a rasgulla-sized, dimpled sphere into a small hole. On different occasions I found notable women residents like Malkit Law, managing director and chief administrator of Sadhu Vaswani Mission Medical Centre in Shanti Niketan in Delhi and Latika Thukral, co-founder of I Am Gurgaon, rise at dawn, appropriately attired in slacks, tee shirts and cleats, caddies trailing them with the elaborate equipment, as they whacked balls and raised a few divots. Dr Law said there was a reduced membership fee available for those who played on weekdays only—and she was one of them. DLF has marked with its brand the city that made it into the powerhouse it became.

I spoke to an impressively uniformed and moustachioed Nepali valet, Gopal, who parks cars and has a smile and manner that elicits a nice tip. He confided to me that Bentleys were easier to park than Jaguars, even though the former were heftier; but his favourites are Mercedes Benz and BMW—both had the best 'turning ratio'. I assured him that I would definitely eschew a Jaguar when my eight-year-old Suzuki Swift needed to be replaced. He added cold comfort: 'The Swift is also very easy to park, madam,' as I walked away to meet my host, Latika Thukral, for lunch. We chatted about the horror of the garbage in the city in the ersatz colonial-style dining room, with a view of the immaculate and verdant links; the menu included steak and potatoes, which I relished. The nonsensical beef ban and the accompanying savage vigilantism had not materialized yet. Wouldn't it be far more meaningful if the government, I mused later, substituted the beef ban with a ban on litter?

The DLF Company, which built, owns and maintains the golf course and club, seized a rich opportunity to situate their top-of-the-line gated communities, like the aforementioned Aralias and the Magnolias, with views of the luxuriant expanse, for its wealthiest clients. I went to a residents' meeting with a friend who owns an apartment at the Magnolia and then repaired to the upscale market, The Galleria, in Phase IV for a haircut at a favourite salon. The taxi driver, puzzled at the addresses I gave him, politely corrected me —'*Aap ko* Mongolia *jana hai na? Phir Ghileriya mar-kit?*' (You wish to go to Mongolia and then to the squirrel market?) It does bring one down to earth—the DLF management surely did not anticipate how Gurgaon locals would pronounce these foreign names. Wouldn't he think that golf is glorified *gulli danda* in slow motion?

All this speaks to the extraordinary assemblage of corporations that have made Gurgaon their base and have attracted more 'high net-worth' residents to the city than bees in a hive. Fortune (500) smiled upon the city: Microsoft, American Express, Indigo Airlines, Dell, Coca Cola, Genpact, Ericsson, Nokia, Samsung, Sony, Pepsi, Alcatel, Wipro, TCS, Flextronics, Hero Honda, IBM, LG, Maruti Suzuki, Nestle, Oriental Craft and several others. These are internationally recognized names of Fortune 500 companies sprinkled amid those of some very strong indigenous ones, but the list is far from complete. Suffice it to say that more than half (or 279 in 2013, to be precise) of the former have either their headquarters or branch offices in Gurgaon, creating over 400,000 white-collar jobs by the end of the first decade of the millennium. Gurgaon soon acquired the moniker of 'Millennium City', referring to the astonishing transformation with which it greeted the beginning of its next thousand years. A new, exciting and prosperous life was to be found in a city that offered plush residential buildings and indubitably the smartest office space in the country, with rents half of that of Delhi, all within a short distance of the new and expanded international airport.

However, my wont as a historian is not to overwhelm the reader with piled-on detail, like descriptions of all the scores of businesses that have opened branches in Gurgaon; it would be unbearably tedious. I have therefore selected mainly those companies, with few exceptions, that were incubated in this city and have become national and international players. The other famous corporations, banks, five-star hotel chains or the big names in the hospitality business are not discussed here even though they have had a very positive effect on Gurgaon's economy and have created hundreds of jobs and attract thousands of customers. Omitting them from this narrative is to be interpreted as a compliment to their already distinctive profile in the world and their role in enhancing the prestige and pelf in Gurgaon.

A businessman from Mumbai, who was enjoying his martini at the architecturally inventive Oberoi Trident Hotel on April 2014, where flames dramatically rise from a mirror-like water surface, summed it up rather aptly: 'Gurgaon is now the corporate headquarters of the country. We Mumbaiwallahs have to make frequent trips here now and this is the best place for locating a business today. Mumbai is old and overpriced.'

At dusk, when travellers arrive at Terminal 3 of the Indira Gandhi International Airport, the lights of Gurgaon make the south Delhi farmhouse belt look like a dark coverlet with a glinting brocade border. Driving south on NH-8, beyond the Delhi border into Gurgaon, they would pass Cyber City, a massive constellation of chrome-and-glass buildings. Even those of us who have lived here since the mid-1990s, when this was a sketchy two-lane road with the barren fields of Nathupur village on one side with an impressive big-horned Brahmini bull silhouetted against the horizon, are quite dazzled to behold the glittering vistas that have cropped up on the *gauchara*, or grazing lands.

While building Gurgaon, the major real estate corporations gravitated to a generic global urban appearance and style in their high-rise apartments and business towers and gated communities. The earlier colonial style adopted by DLF for its clubhouses in each of its residential colonies gave way to the unabashed embrace of stacking storey upon storey in columns that created Belvedere Towers, Regency, Windsor, Hamilton, and Hampton Court clusters. The architecture is impressive all right but it emulates that of older new cities like Dubai, which copied New York with its pioneering skyscrapers. A mimicked Western sensibility and design superficially inform many of the buildings of Gurgaon, but alas, not in its infrastructure or its governance. There are sections of the city, like Cyber City, that defy one to believe that this is good old Gurgaon or Gurugram, whatever its name, it never lets us forget that it was once a village. Developers have impetuously cobbled together residential neighbourhoods and business parks into the 'new Gurgaon' while others, like nearby

Faridabad, so staid and planned and controlled, slept uneasily under a blanket of regulations.

How on earth did all this happen in the once drowsy village of Gurgaon?

After the Japanese Suzuki Company jump-started the small car, it took the rest of the nation by storm. Honda and the other automobile and spare parts manufacturers flocked to Gurgaon, and its recent extension in Manesar, and they are now at the forefront of the automobile industry in India. After cars and motorcycles the next engine of change and prosperity came in the service industry sector that now brands Gurgaon. Voices from Gurgaon's call centres are heard around the world, patiently guiding anxious owners of malfunctioning computers or other electronic equipment back to normalcy. Gurgaon is also the site where the Business Process Outsourcing (BPO) industry was seeded in India.

Most recently the young airline, Indigo, conquered India's skies by determinedly soaring above its competition. The garment industry carved itself a large niche in a rapidly growing manufacturing landscape. Many other global companies found their way to Gurgaon, like the beverage and food giants Pepsi and Coca-Cola, but they were not the game changers, even though they came in the early 1990s and occupied offices in DLF Corporate Park's comparatively modest buildings, where several important business infants began their growth into giants in the corporate world.

But before we go any further, I have to confess my bewilderment when I first encountered the term BPO. In my interviews with those connected with BPOs, I did not interrupt their acronym-peppered answers, but consulted Wikipedia and found a lucid summary, studded with links to other sites, to comprehend this relatively new phenomenon in the global knowledge-based economy. Its creation was tantamount to striking oil or inventing the formula for Coca-Cola, the older resource-based economy. Wikipedia defines it rather lucidly:

Business Process Outsourcing (BPO) is a subset of outsourcing that involves the contracting of the operations and responsibilities of a specific business process to a third-party service provider. Originally, this was associated with manufacturing firms, such as Coca-Cola that outsourced large segments of its supply chain ... BPO is typically categorized into back-office outsourcing, which includes *internal business functions* such as human resources or finance and accounting, and front-office outsourcing, which includes *customer-related services* such as contact centre services ... BPO that is contracted outside a company's country is called offshore outsourcing. BPO that is contracted to a company's neighbouring (or nearby) country is called nearshore outsourcing ... Often, the business processes are information technology-based, and are referred to as ITES-BPO, where ITES stands for Information Technology Enabled Service. Knowledge process outsourcing (KPO) and legal process outsourcing (LPO) are some of the sub-segments of business process outsourcing industry.

It was not entrepreneurial smarts alone but a combination of several factors that enabled the second wave of business expansion in Gurgaon. Since the pre-Independence nationalist movement, India had been imbued with the Gandhian notion of swadeshi. This was followed by the even deeper Nehruvian 'import-substituting industrialization' policy that allowed few foreign companies to plant their stakes in India, and some years later, Prime Minister Indira Gandhi constricted foreign investments further. But it was the Janata Party government's emphatic small-scale 'self-sufficiency' plank and suspicion of the West that shut the gates of India to foreign companies after its landslide victory in 1977. The new government obliged the computer giant IBM and Coca-Cola to move on in 1978. The economy languished under this stern regime, and it was only as the result of a severe financial crunch in 1991, when the government was scratching the bottom of the barrel for foreign exchange for essential imports, that a powerful blast of reality blew away the cobwebs of insularity. It was do or die, and so it did under the unlikely steerage of Narasimha Rao: he took the daring step of loosening the stranglehold of the government on the economy.

American Express (Amex) was already a well-established international travel and credit card company in Delhi when it brought in the first BPO to India. As Sanjay Rishi, its very knowledgeable CEO, informed me in an interview on 6 June 2016, at their headquarters in Cyber City, the company transferred its Japan and Asia Pacific Corporation's (JAPAC) operations to Gurgaon. The choice of Gurgaon was pragmatic; it had an anglophone and talented workforce that cost far less than its American counterpart. Equally important was the seduction of newer, smarter and cheaper office space than in Delhi offered by DLF's KPS in his tireless quest for corporate tenants. Pepsi had moved its offices into the first of the many business parks to come—the DLF Corporate Park on M.G. Road in Phase III. With its bright, big and smart modern offices, this group of four boxy buildings with a mirrored facade a kilometre from the Delhi border and about 10 from the international airport became the first stop for corporations seeking desirable quarters.

American Express also rented space there for its BPO operations, renamed as the Financial Resource Centre-East or FRC-E, with the help of the extraordinarily gifted Raman Roy who went on to be called the father of the BPO industry in India. It thrived and this back-office work became something others would soon covet, imitate and expand. The brand-new genre of service industries—the BPO, Knowledge Process Outsourcing (KPO) and Information Technology (IT) corporations—injected iron into the anaemic blood of the economy and linked Gurgaon to the global heart of business in the US and Europe.

The arrival of the BPO industry in the early 1990s was an augury; it had sparked the next big trend that was to catapult Gurgaon to the status of India's third richest city in the space of the next fifteen years. Other players in this industry made tracks to the same destination. Gurgaon led the pack and soon Mumbai, Bengaluru, Hyderabad, Chennai and Pune were to join it; 70 per cent of the world's outsourcing business was snagged by India by 2007, Rishi confirmed. This was the peak. The IT and BPO industries are still robust a decade later but India is facing serious competition from Sri Lanka, Vietnam and other countries with even lower wages.

For some of the details of this transformation, we must weave together the accounts of the two major protagonists, Jack Welch and K.P. Singh (KPS) from their respective autobiographies.[2] KPS, as we have noted in the previous chapters, had revived the struggling DLF by building the first corporate parks in the country in three phases of Qutab Enclave in Gurgaon. General Electric was already a player in the BPO business and was looking to expand its global reach when its dynamic CEO, Jack Welch, made an exploratory trip to India. KPS, who had been asked by the Sheikh of Bahrain to facilitate this visit, had thousands of square feet of business spaces to rent, and he followed this scent of opportunity like a bloodhound. He orchestrated a tri-city welcome extravaganza for the Welches in Delhi, Jaipur and Agra that left his indifferent guests exhilarated. Welch recounts in his book that he was so impressed by the magic of the Taj Mahal and the exotic grandeur of the hospitality accorded to him and his wife, which included caparisoned elephants and fireworks at the maharaja's palace in Jaipur, that he flatly declared that he had 'fallen in love with the people of India'. This love affair paid rich dividends not only to DLF but also to Gurgaon. GE Capital moved its offices in 1997 from its stuffy office in Delhi into an expansive and elegant suite in the self-same Corporate Park. This spiked the trajectory of Gurgaon's growth and it is today the prime location for call centres of major global businesses.

Pramod Bhasin, who rose to head GE Capital International Services, was discerning enough to persuade Raman Roy to leave Amex and join GE Capital to found their offshore outsourcing division. Roy's coming with a prized team to GE Capital was transformative. The company grew from a nucleus of 300 workers to a muscular behemoth with 65,000 workers worldwide. 'I certainly did not suspect this unprecedented potential,' Bhasin said, 'but unforeseen business continued to grow exponentially over the years and it hasn't peaked yet.'[3]

Raman Roy ingeniously proceeded from strength to strength with his entrepreneurial wizardry. After pioneering offshore back-office capabilities for American Express and GE Capital (now Genpact) and Spectramind (now Wipro BPO), Raman established his fourth start-up, Quatrro Global Services Private Ltd, of which he is the CEO, and based in Udyog Vihar in Gurgaon. It was to fulfil 'underserviced and unaddressed needs of mid-market companies with its integrated platform based services' through a mix of incubation, acquisition strategies and leveraging 'cloud architecture'. It is estimated that he is responsible for creating 35,000 jobs thus far in his career in these four companies.[4]

Incredibly profitable, 'GE Capital sold 60 per cent of the firm to private equity investors in 2005,' Bhasin explained, 'after which it was renamed "Genpact", and is today among the leading outsourcing firms of its kind ... Its name is a contraction of the 'im*pact*' it *gen*erates for the businesses it draws into its systems of processing by cutting waste, increasing efficiency, and making organization more rational.' He was soon to become the president and chief executive officer of Genpact and is now retired, but he remains its non-executive vice chairman.[5] Well, Genpact quickly outgrew its crib in Corporate Park and moved to king-sized accommodations. Today it owns and occupies two colossal towers in prime locations in Gurgaon. It had captured the attention and business of many Fortune 500 companies and its turnover was now more than two billion US dollars. 'We could have bought eleven acres for twenty crores,' Bhasin recalled, 'but we passed up the opportunity. I wish I had had the sense to buy it for myself—I would have been a billionaire,' he said wistfully, gesturing to that parcel of land on which now stood the DLF towers visible from glass walls of his former corner office with its 'smoking' balcony. 'I used to stand there and smoke and see these towers rise.' Way down below from this dizzying height, he recalled, he looked out at a chaotic crossroad where, daily a herd of glossy 'black goats made their unhurried way across the intersection while the traffic honked madly; the shepherd was always in his red turban and kurta-dhoti, and somehow this daily occurrence epitomized India. The world is sending us its business to process and a herd of goats can bring everything to a standstill.' Beyond that he also overlooked, in a field behind a recently built wall, the pit where part of the city's sewage was emptied. This is where Gurgaon's affluent and effluent meet, I thought. Bhasin, a shrewd leader, has no illusions about Gurgaon: 'Gurgaon is a great place to be in, the best in India, but let me assure you that Genpact would move to the next new great place if the terms and conditions and labour costs were better than those offered here. If the water shortage persists and the sewage system is not built as promised, the company would have no qualms about moving out of Gurgaon and going elsewhere taking many of their workforce with them. That is how successful corporations operate; there is nothing in Gurgaon to be sentimental about.' I thought long and hard about the candour of his statement. Noida could be that next place if it got the international airport proposed in its neighbourhood, I thought; Gurgaon better pull up its designer socks and get its unfinished jobs done.

The present CEO and president of Genpact, N.V. Tyagarajan or 'Tiger', as he is known, was, in 2013, on a relentless prowl for even greater kills in the global jungle. Today, he has expanded Genpact to unforeseeable limits since he took over in 2011 and has made socially progressive decisions. Its latest venture as part of its corporate social responsibility shows a laudable sensitivity to gender biases in the country. On 23 March 2015, *The Economic Times* announced Genpact's partnership with Ashoka University in Sonepat 'to create and launch the Genpact Centre for Women's Leadership' (GCWL). Ashoka University is the remarkable fruit of private philanthropy and its spokesperson claimed 'this industry–academia partnership is an effort to drive gender-inclusive growth with a vision to create a balanced distribution of resources and decision-making powers across sectors'.

Tyagarajan said, 'Through the GCWL, we aim to create an ecosystem of knowledge, resources and advocacy that will help create the next generation of women in leadership roles.' These are the imponderables that make a place like Gurgaon's new and enlightened occupants the hope of India's dismal social record.

Genpact's unqualified success opened the floodgates for many other BPO companies to arrive in Gurgaon. Some of the other major players, among the fifty of such companies, are Convergys India Private Limited, with 70,000 workers and sixty-eight customer centres. Even the smaller companies have global reach: WNS Global, a British Airways spin-off, has offices in Gurgaon and other parts of India, China, the UK and the US and in many countries in eastern Europe.

On a Sunday in March 2015, I met with five young call-centre employees in a café—they all appeared to be in their twenties, smartly dressed and extremely forthcoming. The two men were Punjabis who had grown up in Chandigarh, and one woman was from Andhra Pradesh and one from West Bengal, a regional mix of people that would have been impossible to find in Gurgaon only a decade and a half ago. My questions were general—about job satisfaction, salary and benefits, and social life in Gurgaon. They seemed not to disagree with each other and preferred to remain anonymous—they all liked the working environment which was often 'fun and easy-going', they felt like they were 'with family' and they all felt, surprisingly, that they 'were not paid well enough given the hours of work we put in every day'. Making an average of Rs 55,000 a month, these BPO personnel were making four times as much as a schoolteacher with arguably far greater responsibilities and intellectual challenges. 'I resent those executives, who were unbelievably overpaid with awesome perks,' said one of the men who had been on the job for three years. 'What we do is very hard and stressful work, especially the night shifts when you are required to be very polite to rude and sometimes abusive customers,' said the bespectacled one who spoke up more than the other three. This brought on a flurry of complaints about the night shift, which they did not choose but to which they were assigned.

Their perquisites included medical insurance and contributions to a retirement plan that were pronounced to be niggardly. 'We have to pay for our own transport and we do not get paid holidays, like the bosses,' the Andhra woman elucidated. I asked about upward mobility in management levels and of this they seemed very dubious; stagnation at a bottom rung of the ladder was their greatest fear. 'There is one manager for about a hundred of us, so not many can hope to climb the corporate ladder.' The two men saw it as a starter job; the women thought they would stay longer, even after they got married, to have a better standard of living. The men commuted from Delhi by Metro and the Gurgaon Rapid Metro; the other three used autorickshaws to get to work on Golf Course Road from a three-bedroom apartment they shared in a gated community that was secure, comfortable, and enabled them to save some money on rent and electricity bills.

'We three also share a part-time maid: she cleans the apartment and makes basic vegetarian meals—dal, vegetables, chapatis or a pot of rice. We come home at different hours so we just warm our food in the microwave and eat whenever we are hungry. We live simply at home but we do spend money on going out,' they said. The best part of living in Gurgaon, they agreed, was that 'it is a sociable city for young people'—lots of pubs and restaurants, and plenty of malls to shop in and see a midday movie—'because we work in the evenings'. They had never noticed that Gurgaon had any power cuts or a water shortage—their office and apartment buildings had 'totally, one hundred per cent' water and power back-up. They had the air of standard global white-collar workers; computers and smartphone expert, used the gym in a nearby mall, had professional aspirations and hung out together. The men had joined them because they too felt their chances of meeting other women were better this way; no, they were not dating—they were just friends and had come in two cars. Yes, the women went to the beauty salon in one of the malls—spent roughly twelve hundred rupees a month on personal grooming, manicures and hair care. 'Yes, we need to look presentable at work; it is expected,' one of them said. One of them frankly admitted that she preferred this independent life to living with parents, who were far too conservative; in fact, she had a similar job back home in Hyderabad before she moved to Gurgaon. 'I would suffocate if I had to live with my parents like my brother and his family do.'

Financial independence had empowered these young men and women to think they had a right to shape their own lives. Only one of them got any help from home; her father had given her a small car to use which she did only on special occasions—finding a spot to park in Gurgaon was a major hassle and it was best to leave it in the garage in the basement of her condominium. One of the women sent money home regularly to her parents, because her mother was frequently unwell. Yes, marriage had crossed their minds, and the parents did nag them, but there was no time to look for the 'right person', one of the women said. 'I will definitely not have an arranged marriage; I am too independent-minded for that.'

Surprisingly it was the men who were more anxious to get married and would easily settle for matches arranged by their parents. This was a small sliver of life in high-income Gurgaon, a far cry from the life lived only a decade ago when employment opportunities were restricted and less well paid.[6]

These fiercely competitive BPO companies with their large applicant pools keep the pressure on employees to perform to the limits of their potential. There have been instances of more than 5,000 applicants for a single position in a BPO company. With an enormous workforce of some 300,000 young, educated women and men in Gurgaon alone, which was more than 15 per cent of its entire population in 2011, the Fortune 500 companies are their biggest clients and the battle for their customers is intense. They compete for contracts as they do for primacy in the fields they service. The latter can be diverse and includes banking, retail and wholesale consumer goods, entertainment, health care, finance, insurance, manufacturing, media, textiles, shipping, telecommunications, travel and utilities, and most have service centres scattered throughout the world. This BPO explosion, it is plausibly argued, could not have happened anywhere else in India at the time when it arrived. New-age apartments with all the amenities that bourgeois living demands abound in the residential colonies and high-rises, and they were prepared for the BPO invasion and so were good English-medium schools, shopping plazas and the establishment of private security guards in these complexes.

The BPO revolution may sound like something limited to the educated middle class, leaving the uneducated poor out in the cold to do ill-paid menial jobs. I believed this until I discovered that the BPO contagion is spreading to villages in and around Gurgaon, and bringing opportunities to the doors of literate villagers. Atul Sobti, the publisher and editor of the weekly tabloid, *Friday Gurgaon*, until it regrettably closed in 2015, alerted me to HarVa, a BPO that is setting up centres in rural areas, run and staffed entirely by village women. In Tikli Aklimpur, a small Brahmin village in Gurgaon district with fewer than 250 households, this project is now an established reality. A team of sixty women have been trained to hone their English, use computers, and deal with clients in other parts of the country and the world, reports journalist Shilpi Arora, who first broke this story.[7] 'It is creditable that, in a state known for its cultural rigidity and male-dominant social pattern,' she writes, 'HarVa has made it possible for women to move out of their houses [which they formerly could not], and be exposed to the latest technology and education.'

HarVa is not an NGO or a charitable organization. Ajay Chaturvedi, the founder of HarVa, took his engineering degree from Pilani and MBA from the famous Wharton School of Business at the University of Pennsylvania and is as aware 'of the rural labour cost arbitrage' as he is of the social issues of education and employment in villages. These women make 7,000 rupees a month on average (in 2014); he plans to expand paid work opportunities for women— these barely exist in villages and may help loosen the shackles of a misogynist society. If this initiative proliferates, as have its corporate counterparts, we can expect a real social revolution to be quietly under way. The women at HarVa insist that their daughters are educated and their extra income is making this possible. To see a woman make cow-dung cakes in the morning, milk a buffalo, and then sit and deal with clients over the computer in the afternoon, after her cooking and cleaning jobs are done, is like experiencing something remarkable. One can certainly hope that this is the beginning of a trend and literacy will give women more choices.

What makes Gurgaon proud is that it is not merely a recently fashioned hub for call centre services and back-office drudgery, but also the birthplace for some very successful IT corporations. In 1997, a small IT start-up, Nagarro Software, was literally cultured in a small apartment in Gurgaon that belonged to one of the two engineer co-founders. When I met with its co-founder and CEO, Manas Fuloria, in March 2014, it was a thriving and highly respected international player with 3,000 engineers employed worldwide. He chose to meet not in his corporate offices but in a delightful, organic outdoor café called Roots, set among spreading trees. He explained to me the risks his company had taken and the creativity it had shown on its rapid journey to the top ranks of such companies worldwide. In the last two decades, after a judicious merger (with a German company) and other acquisitions, Nagarro is now a booming global BPO and IT business.

'Nagarro stands for a new corporate type: a company with a global footprint, but agile and with highly independent local teams,' Fuloria explained as we snacked on the delicious organic vegetarian treats for which Roots is famous. He was more than happy to be based in Gurgaon, with links to Sweden, Silicon Valley in the US, Salzburg in Austria, Munich in Germany, Romania, and other countries where its engineers create customized software codes for businesses to solve problems and expand their impact. I lingered to talk to its employees, two of whom seated at a table nearby claimed that it is such an intense learning experience to work for Nagarro that they are among the best-trained software specialists anywhere and, by their own account, the company remunerates their expertise in a very fair manner.

More was going on in and around Roots than met the eye—they were growing organic vegetables and salads adjacent to the buildings and grounds of the large government enterprise, The Rajiv Gandhi

Renewable Energy Park, with the support of the Ministry of New and Renewable Energy (MNRE). To see a state-owned industry that was environmentally committed and growing in its influence came across as a pleasant surprise. The government proclaims that it is now trying to raise awareness of the acute energy problems and resultant pollution in Gurgaon and in NCR more widely.

Fortunately, public attitudes are changing but officialdom is still insufferably leaden-footed. My own experience in getting solar-powered hot water for our home in 1997 documents the change that has occurred in this field in twenty years. Our house in DLF Phase III was the first house in the area to have solar panels and tanks fitted on our roof. The obstacles we encountered were many and dismaying: on inquiring about who might provide such a thing, our architect's contractor (a wretch you will meet again in Chapter Seven) gave me a name and phone number. I called that number and a man showed up who postured as a manufacturer of solar hot water systems (but without a calling card or a brochure), who estimated Rs 96,000 which we accepted rather meekly. We had nothing to compare it with, so we accepted it. In our pioneering enthusiasm we ignored the warning signals that he was emitting at every stage. He demanded a cash advance of 50 per cent, but insisted on payment by cheque but to be made out as a 'self' cheque, as if I was taking the money instead of him so that he would remain untraceable. He promptly cashed it (our bank statement proved that) and absconded—which we suspected when he would not answer his phone nor appear with the promised goods. After much sleuthing (read: threatening our contractor with dire consequences) we found the swindler in a small shack in Shahdara on the outskirts of Delhi in his underwear and a week-old beard and bloodshot eyes. We retrieved a fraction of the payment in cash; he seemed to have invested the rest in alcohol, judging from the empty rum bottles littered on his 'company premises'.

Despite the loss we were still determined to live a green life. Our next move was to consult Rajan Gandhi, a very knowledgeable friend who had worked for Tata BP Solar and was up to date with the state of solar power generation in India. Their engineer arrived at the then isolated land of Gurgaon to assess our needs, gave us a proper invoice (for two-thirds the amount the swindler had estimated) and took a cheque; it was a professional response. However, it took three months of nagging phone calls (from our landline that was often out of service thanks to the erratically functioning Bharat Sanchar Nigam Ltd [BSNL]) to see any action because of the paperwork that the Haryana government expects you to complete to approve such a move. Finally, when the stipulated panels, insulated water tanks and pipes were installed on our roof, we discovered that while waiting for the official nod, squirrels (or are they chipmunks?) had laboriously chewed the synthetic insulation wrapped around the galvanized iron, hot water pipes, and appropriated the bits and pieces to construct their nests. (They did not wait to get HUDA's approval to build on our property, nor did they perish from chewing the plastic; they blithely continued their onslaught on our pomegranates and custard apples.) We made several trips to the Haryana government office to obtain the subsidy offered, and after a long silence of about a year a cheque for 14,000 rupees arrived, not an inconsiderable sum in 1997. Our Tata solar water system still works in 2018, with regular wiping of the solar panels on the roof and the annual replacement of the heating coil in the back-up tank that is needed when the annual inversion and 'fog' (read smog) smothers the northern plains in winter and the sun is obscured.

Exactly twenty years on, in June 2017, there was a happily startling change. While surfing the web we found ZunRoof, a young start-up company created by IIT Kanpur graduates, that installs the latest photovoltaic solar panels (made in Noida, I believe, with German collaboration) to generate the energy for household needs. The team arrived within an hour of my call, aided by the fact that they were in the adjacent block, only a few minutes away. After looking at a few past electricity bills—and June was a good month to do this since our consumption of electricity was at its peak—they suggested a 4 kW system that would suffice for our modest usage and promised to have the entire system ready and running in five weeks. This included getting approvals for the subsidy from the Haryana government and the two-way meters from Dakshin Haryana Bijli Vitran Nigam (DHBVN)—we would be spared the agony of having to deal with these two bureaucratic agencies. They would recover the subsidy from the government after the installation—we paid them only the balance. Even our total outlay of Rs 250,000 we expect to recoup in three years with reduced electricity bills, with our 4 kW of solar power returned to the DHBVN grid, and our outgoing supply and usage clocked on separate meters. The difference between the two readings would constitute our payable bill. Of course, the government would never pay us for any extra electricity we returned to the grid after deducting our usage, but they would charge *us* if our consumption exceeded the output. Be that as it may we are happy at the thought of living in a green house and would recommend it to all who own their own houses in Gurgaon and elsewhere. Wondrously, the ZunRoof team worked hard and efficiently and the system was up in less than a month.

But there is always some snag when a company is dealing with government agencies. In this case, the new meters were not installed for over four months because the two-step approval from DHBVN was inordinately delayed. My anxious phone inquiries every week from New York—my second home which I visited right after the solar panels were installed—elicited the same response from ZunRoof who tried their best to speed things up: the 'two-stage government approval is still pending'. They sure work slowly and in mid-November the approval came through but not the meters. 'Isn't the government asking us to install solar power in our homes? So why the delay in approving something they actually wish to encourage and for which the paperwork was done months ago?' I asked rather rhetorically, having dealt with the red-tape-strangled responses of DHBVN personnel over two decades. I could sense the frustrated shrugs of the ZunRoof engineer 10,000 miles away. He explained that the Haryana Renewable Energy Development Agency (HAREDA) approves the application first and then it proceeds to DHBVN, which examines the project and supplies the meters and ZunRoof installs them. So six weeks later, the time of heaviest usage of electricity, the august HAREDA and DHBVN were still ruminating over their approvals. There are now thirty-five homes in Gurgaon that have the installation but the approvals for many of their meters are pending. ZunRoof confessed that they too were baffled at the delay. 'In Delhi, the approval process is very quick and we have got the meters installed in our customers' systems within ten days,' they told me. What is wrong with Gurgaon—is it not supposed to be the speedy place?

That said, things are improving gradually, one home at a time over these two decades. In *The Times of India* of 20 June 2011, a rather exaggerated headline declared 'Gurgaon Switches to Green Energy'. How one wishes that was true. Bhawna Gandhil reported that Suranjana Rai Luthra, a resident of DLF Phase II, had installed a solar-powered inverter and water heater in her home and has been a conscientious green crusader requesting friends and neighbours to do likewise and appealing to RWAs to do the same in their buildings.

'This is a totally eco-friendly technology and helps significantly in saving electricity. The expenses of installation can be recovered within two years because the government is providing us with a lot of incentives and discounts ... All things considered, this is really the need of the hour in Gurgaon, and in all of India to start using solar energy and save electricity.' True, the desire to persuade others to do the right thing is laudable but residents need to be educated to think about clean energy that is within reach and that will save them plenty of money in the long run while contributing to cleaner air. The government agencies must start their own crusade for solar energy in a city as sunny and arid as Gurgaon, and cease to be the bottleneck for approving their own schemes; the delays only reinforce the prejudice about government intentions. 'Oh they are waiting to be bribed,' a neighbour who is also getting his installation done told me. We are hoping that Qutab Enclave Phase III, mercifully not zoned for high-rises, can become the green zone of Gurgaon instead, extending to the Aravalli Biodiversity Park contiguous to it. It certainly is an answer to the needs of the people who are living off the grid in the village centres, like Nathupur. Instead of isolated flickers we need a conflagration of solar power.

In spite of the power cuts and temperatures just shy of 50 degree Celsius in summer, the builders and architects of Gurgaon applied little mind to incorporating structural features that might conserve energy; instead the thin-walled, low-ceiling stacks of concrete of new apartments are more appropriate for baking than living. Buildings of steel and glass mandate air-conditioning, lifts, and high-wattage outdoor lighting that render energy conservation and climate change as quaint notions. The condominiums can run their generators 24/7, they brag about it to householders who have conscientiously not installed generators. Solar power is still a novelty introduced with discounts and subsidies to sceptical buyers. Meanwhile, it must be said that to encourage more and more people to switch to alternative sources, HAREDA needs to promote its solar appliances, such as solar cookers, street lights, torches and toys more enthusiastically. Wouldn't it be a marketing coup if the liquor vends that have been summarily vacated from within half a kilometre of a highway on 1 April 2017 (on which more later) could be converted to HAREDA outlets for these items? I remember bringing a rechargeable torch as a gift for a friend who lived in one of these high-rises. He admired the engineering of it but confessed that they didn't really need a torch in their apartment: 'We have twenty-four-hour back-up, you see, so there is never really the need for torchlight.'

I did give that torch to my maid who received it thankfully; she and her young family live in a jhuggi in Nathupur with a single light bulb that gives light for a few hours every day. And the toilet is off in the distance on a path difficult to negotiate in the dark. When she plugs in a table fan the connection often blows out. For her there is no *new* threat of climate change; the seasons are harsh enough and she has lived in light-deprived evenings and tossed and turned on steamy nights all her life. The jhuggis need solar panels more desperately than the houses of the rich, who have generators and inverters to tide over the erratic power supply. A ban on generators and a mandate to install solar panels in the villages of Gurgaon would be far more useful to this environment than the ban on cow slaughter. I strongly feel that the state should be installing these free of cost in all the fifty-two village *abadi*s where the poorest migrants dwell. I Am Gurgaon, the NGO that has done remarkable work on the environmental front, as we shall see in Chapter Seven, would, perhaps take this up as its new crusade.

What adds to the pollution is the inadequate arrangements for public transport, which constitutes the backbone of a successful city. Instead there is a heavy dependency on private cars, radio cabs, vans and autorickshaws that cause that other bane of life in Indian cities: traffic jams. This is no revelation but neither the government nor the construction companies planned to minimize vehicular traffic on city streets. Instead, private transport operators and their scores of wildly driven minivans took charge. With passengers stuffed to the gills of the vehicles, these deadline-bound, call-centre workers made the perilous commute for want of a safe and reliable bus service. Many would choose to shift to Gurgaon as high-rises with apartments began to crop up. By 2010, the much-awaited Metro arrived and its first station in Gurgaon, Guru Dronacharya, straddled the MG Road next to Corporate Park and the many tall office buildings of the Global Business Park opposite it. It has been an unqualified success. Droves of office workers used the purring escalators and lifts to board the gleaming coaches, now eight in number on some trains, and the frequency of trains in either direction has since increased to meet the ever-growing demand for safe, fast and air-conditioned transportation all the way to HUDA City Centre. It was as if a large piece of the city jigsaw puzzle had been finally put in place; the many other missing pieces will also be slowly fitted and the construction to expand the system to connect Gurgaon's spread are well under way in 2018.

A man who did more than merely lament the lack of any public transport in Gurgaon is Sanjiv Rai, then the CEO of the

Infrastructure Leasing & Financial Services (IL&FS) Company, whom I interviewed on 7 March 2014. The corporation has pioneered a totally privately funded light rail system that connects to the Delhi Metro's Yellow Line that exists between HUDA City Centre and Delhi, at the Sikandarpur Metro Station. Rai demystified the reason for a private company taking this bold and unprecedented initiative in India. He had spent thirty-five years first with the Asian Development Bank and then with Bombardier, the Canadian company, before he moved to India in 2008 to join IL&FS. His company evaluated the many infrastructural projects that they already had and the new projects they wished to create.

In Gurgaon, the Haryana state government had already tendered a project that would connect the Sikandarpur Metro Station to NH-8, with DLF winning the exclusive rights to do so. Rai spotted this as a promising area for his company to get involved. He negotiated with KPS's son, Rajiv Singh, the CEO of DLF, who agreed to sell IL&FS 26 per cent equity in the deal to build this link that the Delhi Metro had refused to do when it plotted its route in Gurgaon. It drew a straight line to HUDA City Centre—not allowing the small loop that now goes into Cyber City. With IL&FS Metro Rail firmly on its way, DLF, citing financial difficulties, wriggled out of the deal and sold its shares, permissions, and agreements with HUDA to IL&FS. The cost of the project was Rs 1,088 crore, with an additional agreement to pay HUDA—that had not invested a penny nor given a concessional rate for the twenty acres of village lands for the project—a sum of Rs 760 crore over thirty-five years as royalty for granting permission. In November 2013, six stations on a 5.1 kilometre-long track became operational, and in 2017 the second phase, going through Golf Course Road to Sector 56, was inaugurated, bringing the total to 11 kilometres with eleven stations—a journey accomplished in twenty minutes. Siemens got the contract for supplying the coaches and all the electrical switches, and if you've taken a ride on-board, you'll agree that a smarter or cooler ride is difficult to find anywhere else in the world.

The third phase of this pioneering transport system, now on the drawing board, will connect the new city to the neglected old one, coursing through Udyog Vihar and Sadar Bazar, terminating at Gurgaon Railway Station. The first phase employed a total of 250 workers, of which 140 are operational staff and the rest to keep the system safe and clean. It runs all the year round, without a break from 6 a.m. to 12.30 a.m., and is steadily improving its ridership. The people who have started to use this have the convenience of having a single card to transfer from the Metro to the Rapid Rail system.

I asked Rai if this was an act of pure altruism to put up the staggering amount of capital to construct this because metro systems have never made money anywhere in the world and are heavily subsidized by the governments of the countries where they operate. He explained that they are anticipating two revenue streams—85 per cent from the sale of tickets and the rest from advertising. The corporations could rent and get naming rights to stations; the individual cars would have wrap-around branding, including panels inside the cars.

This has proved to be such a lucrative strategy that the Delhi Metro followed suit and in 2016 it began to replicate it in their far larger and heavily used system. Enveloped in 'corporate graffiti' as I call it, the coaches move on elevated tracks, making for a very colourful display. The ticket sales haven't caught up to the expected levels, but the advertising revenues have far exceeded what was anticipated. While the construction was very disruptive to city traffic, Rai believes that the patience of the people will be rewarded when the entire system is complete. He hoped that Gurgaon, so callously dissected by NH-8, will be rejoined together by the overhead tracks of the Rapid Metro. None of this has happened too soon and there is scepticism and rumours that the third phase of the plans might peter out as the fiscal health of the company is under strain. The state government will probably have to step in and reduce their share of the payment to enable this rather vital plan for a public utility to be completed. The hope is that all of Gurgaon will, say five years on, be seamlessly connected with a modern metro system that very few cities in India have. And IL&FS has a very important repertoire of companies that look after waste management, water, roads, toll bridges, and everything else that Gurgaon is trying desperately to build. Perhaps HUDA needs to reorganize its own cluttered operations along these lines into departments that will function more efficiently.

⌒

While the streets of India crawled with Maruti Suzuki 800s, the air lanes in the sky began to thicken with the sleek grey-blue aircraft of Indigo Airlines. Apart from the automobile industry that gave middle-class Indians the power to own their own wheels and give Gurgaon its lift from obscurity, the biggest commercial airline in the country, Indigo, also claims Gurgaon as its birthplace. Very quickly after its birth in 2006, it bested the government-operated Indian Airlines and buckled up the largest number of passengers on domestic flights in India. It grew exponentially with its sale-and-lease-back model of financing, which works when a company buys the aircraft from the airline and leases them back to it. I am not sure how this financial wizardry is actually accomplished but it liberates the company's capital and allows it greater freedom to invest it in achieving overall excellence. Indigo had the vast majority of its aircraft on this plan. It attained the indubitable reputation for being not only India's largest, but its *finest*. More than two in five air travellers in India fly Indigo and its market share in May 2018 was already 41 per cent. As a frequent flier in India, I had occasion to ask fellow passengers what had made Indigo such a high flier. As an American colleague who insists on taking only Indigo flights as far as possible when in India put it this way: 'What's not to love about Indigo? They know the value of our time; they are never late, their pilots compare favourably with the best in the world, and their cabins do not smell of curry.' My thoughts exactly, I have to confess and it does sound like copy for an advertisement—except that it is sincere appreciation of a well-run airline. That last clause describes an ineffable asset.

While waiting to board a flight to Bengaluru in 2016, I decided to take a poll of fellow passengers on why they had chosen Indigo. They remarked in a similar vein: it has the best record for punctuality, with impeccably clean cabins and tastefully done interiors of its planes in smooth navy blue leather and white antimacassars, and, most important, it also offers the best prices. Some commonsensical ideas, like politely asking passengers to replace seatbelts in their original positions before leaving the aircraft and taking their garbage and newspapers with them saves valuable turnaround time. Its in-flight announcements, I noticed, are warmly inclusive—they always include 'boys and girls' along with the usual 'ladies and gentlemen' and its management has a sense of humour which no other airline had ever evinced, except perhaps Air India with its turbaned maharaja in his red achkan welcoming passengers like a valet, which appears unintentionally funny. Their cargo department in the Indigo headquarters opposite the Corporate Park, where I mistakenly first went to find my interviewee, was labelled boldly 'Get Packing' and it made me smile.

Since 2009, only three years after it began operations with a single aircraft, the airline has turned a steady and growing profit, even when the older Jet Airways and its competitor SpiceJet were losing money. Of this I had apprised myself before I interviewed Aditya Ghosh, its then 'President and Whole Time Director' on 25 August 2016. The airline is the offspring of Rahul Bhatia's Interglobe Aviation, the hospitality giant with a portfolio of some 8,000 rooms, which was ensconced in the aforementioned Corporate Park, where General Electric and Pepsi and other multinational corporations also lurked, and which it now partially owns. Indigo hatched in an office room as a fledgling start-up but it soon took over the office tower in the business park across the road. With a shrewdly frugal sensibility that goes with his entrepreneurial genius, Bhatia, who is today a billionaire and on the Forbes list of the richest men in the world, stands in stark contrast to the other airline magnates like Subrata Roy of Sahara or Vijay Mallya of Kingfisher, former high fliers who seem to have crash-landed.

The anteroom, where I waited briefly for Ghosh to arrive, had the air of a well-appointed drawing room with striking oil paintings that an aficionado of modern Indian art would look upon with pleasure. There were vitrines displaying twenty well-deserved trophies that had been bestowed upon Indigo for being outstanding in every imaginable category for which an airline can be judged. I walked around looking closely at the paintings sipping the coffee that had been promptly served after I was seated; it felt like business class. I was particularly intrigued by a large triptych of an arresting landscape in oils, which began with a green field with a building crane looming ominously over it and a car in the foreground; the next frame had a set of high rises and there were two cars in the foreground, suggesting creeping urbanization. But then, perhaps wishfully, the third frame had the crane and the empty green field again, and the incipient city had vanished.

Ghosh walked in dressed in jeans and a bush shirt, refreshingly young, affable and unassuming, and laughed and said he was embarrassed when I mentioned the *Business Standard*'s article of that morning that revealed his sky-scraping salary. He described his journey very sparingly—he was a lawyer working with the well-known law firm Jyoti Sagar Associates in Gurgaon, assigned to look after a prime client, Interglobe Aviation. Rahul Bhatia eventually offered him a position in the airline at a time when it was not off the ground yet, and which he accepted in 2005, as its president and director. Bhatia, who has retained 51 per cent of Indigo's shares, is happy to delegate responsibility to men who are brilliant and are passionate about their work. Ghosh is both, it became evident in a few minutes of conversation. He loves his office and home in Gurgaon that is barely twenty minutes away from the airport where the aeroplanes are, he declared with unabashed glee. He didn't overwhelm me with the numbers Indigo had ratcheted up. Instead he handed me a copy of their annual report for 2015-16, which was also a very restrained corporate brochure, mainly about its CSR operations all over the country.

Ghosh, without knowing that I was a feminist, revealed with considerable pride that 35 per cent of Indigo's employees were women and so were 25 per cent of the administrative and executive cadres, and believed that parity may one day be possible. But the better part of the hour was spent in describing the role that Indigo was playing in helping women and children, education and the environment with their CSR, not just in Gurgaon but nationwide.

'When our fleet acquired its hundredth aircraft we did not throw a party,' he recalled. 'Instead we chose 100 students, the very best ones from the poorest schools around Gurgaon, and got them admitted to Vidya School, a reputable English-medium school, and we will make sure they get the best education possible in the city.' This was a classic example of the prudent philosophy for which Rahul Bhatia is well known. From an article on Rahul Bhatia in *Forbes* in October 2014, I learnt that Indigo ordered a fleet of 180 aircraft, making it the largest order in the history of Airbus, for a staggering eighteen billion euros. Yet, I discovered, it continues to have modest vehicles, such as the Maruti Suzuki Wagon R, as the company cars, consistent with their policy of reducing waste and being thrifty. Instead of flashy SUVs or BMWs, they put their money elsewhere and believe deeply in philanthropy.

'We have adopted whole villages,' Ghosh informed me, 'like the two at the edge of Jim Corbett Park, and we take care of the entire population of those villages, up from street lighting and roads to schools and health clinics. Many people work as rangers in the park, so we provide them with their uniforms and equipment and take care of their families so that that they are not tempted by poachers to accept bribes. We are also building 400 small schools, with fifty to sixty students in the poorest villages in Bihar and Jharkhand, and we hope that all this will eventually show results.' The energy, sincerity, and the quiet pride Ghosh evinced in the good work Indigo was doing was heart-warming. 'And,' he added, 'in Gurgaon we have recently taken on the Pahari Road,' which is called Sunset Boulevard, 'and we will try to keep it clean and have new trees planted. That is a real challenge,' he added with a smile, which seemed to suggest that keeping roads clean in India was harder than managing a huge fleet of jet planes.

What Ghosh was most enthused about—not mentioned in the annual report—was the iFly Indigo Learning Centre, 'considered among the best in the world, where 800 employees are trained in all the services offered by the airline, such as security personnel, janitors, pilots and stewardesses'. He arranged for me to visit it the very next day and I must say that I never met a more energized set of students—and I have been a professor for over forty years. Summi Sharma, the manager of the centre, showed me around and any aspect of the training that I inquired about I was led to immediately. The entire building seemed to replicate various arts of an aircraft, and its connecting corridors were built like runways. I was shown two classrooms outfitted exactly like the interiors of the Airbus 320 planes where women were being trained as stewardesses to perform all the services that passengers require. Aradhana Hoon, an elegant young instructor, taught them poise, posture, body language and 'how to walk in high heels while carrying trays or pushing carts; her job was to transform these casual young women from varying backgrounds into well-groomed, efficient and good-natured stewardesses. In small cabin spaces with exact replicas of an airplane's kitchens, trainees stacked trays noiselessly, heated and served meals within a minute of the request, collected bills, made change. They got time out to have coffee breaks with colleagues, to meditate in a private room, sit on the terrace and take in the panorama of Gurgaon being built. In 120 days of such detailed and intensive training, the personnel are the most polished in the business, and it is this meticulous attention to detail that has made and sustained Indigo as the best airline in the country.

Just when the sky was the limit for Indigo, it met with some unexpected turbulence. In November 2017 a passenger was allegedly assaulted by a cabin crew member and a short video of the event went viral. This caused a major public relations mess and the airline met its greatest challenge with what some media reports called 'complacency' because the crew members responsible were not immediately fired. Every altercation has two sides, and unruly passengers are fairly common on all Indian domestic flights. This made headlines because it was India's most loved airline and I would vote for the management that hears out its own employees, which is what Indigo did, but in this age of instant responses Indigo saw its share price fall a bit.

Just as the brouhaha died down it met another air pocket. In March 2018 a Lucknow-bound A-320 aeroplane experienced mid-air engine failure but made a safe emergency landing in Ahmedabad. This raised the alarm and all thirty-two of the fleet's A-320 aeroplanes with Pratt and Whitney engines were inspected and half a dozen of them grounded when the technical complications were detected. Scores of flights were cancelled over three or four days until the problem was fixed. Fortunately, the company acted with alacrity and there was no mishap because of engine problems. However, delays and cancellations created a large number of irate customers who found themselves stranded. I was travelling with my in-laws from Varanasi to Delhi on 14 March 2018 when we were told that our flight would not leave until the next afternoon for which, they sweetly told us, we did not need to buy fresh tickets—this kindness was underwhelming. All six of us returned disappointed to our hotel and spent an extra night there, paying for our rooms and meals and forgoing the plans we had for Delhi the next day. Our US and Canadian relatives were very amazed that the airline offered no compensation for the expense and the inconvenience of cancelled plans. Indigo did offer an apology by SMS on my mobile phone. They got away lightly in financial terms but harm has been done to its image. Aditya Ghosh resigned in April 2018.

⁓

If an entire airline can incubate, hatch and take wing in Gurgaon, can an online airline-booking portal be far behind? In 2000, Makemytrip, also born in Gurgaon, appeared as a fledgling e-ticketing service for travel between the US and India, aimed chiefly at the travel needs of NRIs based in the US. It was created by a quartet of friends with Deep Kalra, another entrepreneurial dynamo I interviewed on 7

April 2014, as its chairman and group CEO since 2013. A graduate of Ahmedabad's Indian Institute of Management, India's premier institution for business management, he was inspired by the Indian Railways' online ticketing service: 'I worked with GE Capital and then another couple of companies but I always had the itch to start my own company.' Soon the four computer wizards put up Makemytrip's website. The idea was to empower the Indian traveller, but it went on to inspire the entire online travel industry in India. By 2005, it had acquired national heft by launching its India portal for Indian users to book domestic and international flights, and added travel packages and hotel rooms to their repertoire, in the manner of Expedia and Travelocity. It grew by leaps and bounds, and in 2011 gave itself a serious lift by creating mobile apps for Android and Apple phones making it easy for smartphone users to access its services.

'There are many online travel sites in India, several based in Gurgaon too, but we are the industry leader,' said Kalra, as I talked to him in his spacious office in Udyog Vihar in Gurgaon; he exuded confidence and good cheer and none of this was boastful; he was simply giving me facts and figures which I could easily verify. From 2011, it went on a shopping spree acquiring ten smaller travel companies to make itself the undisputed number one gateway to online travel arrangements in India and with enormous capabilities abroad. It was breaking national news in mid-October 2016 after its merger with the Ibibo group in a deal close to $2 billion, and bookings worth $3.5 billion were expected in the financial year 2016-17. Today, in 2018, it is the largest online travel service in Asia. Its meteoric rise paralleled Indigo's, a corporate sibling sharing a birthplace, and now Makemytrip makes thousands of bookings for Indigo daily. 'I am a great fan of Indigo myself. It has transformed the idea of what an economy airline should be. Its tickets cost less while its quality is unmatched,' said Kalra. I could hardly believe that both these companies, barely a decade old, were leaders in their class, and both were generated and based in Gurgaon.

There is an impressive cluster of MNC food and beverage companies that have also found Gurgaon an attractive operational base and brought thousands of jobs to the city. Pepsi, the soft drink and snacks giant, was one of the earliest tenants of Corporate Park, coming there in 1987. When it first arrived in Gurgaon it was unsure of its own product. It extracted the promise from its dealers and retailers that they would not stock any bottles of Coca-Cola. The battle of the colas was strongly waged but the 'real thing' was not thwarted for long and both were winners buying up their Indian imitators like Thums Up and Limca.

Nestle, the Swiss food giant, also moved its headquarters to Gurgaon, occupying an entire tower in another business park and its popular Maggi noodles and dairy products, despite the notoriety it gained with the adulteration found in the latter, can be bought in every grocery store.

Processed food, which had not been heard of in Gurgaon only twenty years before is now ubiquitous and an integral part of the middle-class diet. Looking from the outside, when I was building my own house on a plot behind Corporate Park in Phase III, I saw the parking lot of this business complex go from scantily populated to overflowing. Lunchtime customers at the Italiano, then the only restaurant with good pizzas south of the Delhi border, burgeoned. Its garlic bread and pasta sauces soon developed a faithful clientele and Pepsi served in wine glasses resembled dark Chianti to the wishful.

Older than these, and far larger in the numbers of jobs it created, was the trusted old garment industry. It found a hospitable nest in Gurgaon in the 1970s, a time when Gurgaon city barely existed. While the demand for Indian fabrics holds steady domestically, which absorbs 70 per cent of the production, Gurgaon has upwards of 300 garment manufacturing and export units, most of them clustered in Udyog Vihar and Old Railway Road near the old city. The depreciation of the rupee helped boost exports for a while but the industry is under siege thanks to competition from similar products from countries like Bangladesh, Sri Lanka, Pakistan and those in South-East Asia.

My early acquaintance with Gurgaon's burgeoning garment industry began in 2000, very close to my own home in DLF Phase III where some very successful buyers and exporters had also bought plots and built their homes. In this strictly residential area, a three-storey house was rented to a garment finishing and export office that was operational for a few years. Courier service vans and the cars of the white-collar employees continually blocked our lane and this caused me to demand to speak to the management. I went in chiefly to complain, but I found a congenial manager who explained to me that they would move once their factory in Manesar was built and the lane-blocking menace would be over. He surprised me with the figures of their annual turnover—it was well over $13 million for children's clothes alone. There were 'millions to be made', he said, because of the skilled and cheap labour available. I spoke to a young female employee of their carding and finishing department. She had attended school only till sixth grade, which she did not pass. Her skills, she said, were in her hands and she could finish 450 buttonholes a day; the very thought of it made my fingers cramp. I realized immediately that the firm was employing a class of people, uneducated or barely educated women, as its chief employees.

I had a chance to see this first-hand because Pramila, an immigrant from Bihar, whose husband was our caretaker, found a job in this 'factory' in 2000. They had been married when he was four, their parents were dirt poor, with a small farm in a flood-prone area. After her *gauna*, the post-puberty ceremony, she arrived as a shy teenaged bride, with her face totally hidden with the end of her sari, refusing to see or be seen by strangers or even speak a word in greeting, including to her husband, also a stranger. She was illiterate, spoke only Maithili, but was skilled at sewing. She began diffidently to help out in the kitchen where I demonstrated to her how to make tea and explained that it had to brew for four minutes in the pot. She looked totally bewildered. I thought it was the whistling kettle that baffled her, but it was the timer. Finally, she asked shyly, 'Minute *kya hota hai*?' She knew *chaar*, she said, holding up four fingers, but what on earth was a minute? The concept of measured time was totally alien to her, but not for long. Within a year she was conversing with Hindi speakers about as fluently as her husband did; he had been in Gurgaon for nine years, six of them with us. She had grasped many common English words too, and her confidence had grown to a level that she no longer hid her face and sported the wristwatch that I gave her. She bought clothes for her infant son at a sale of rejects from the factory next door. I gasped incredulously when she came back with a stack of export-worthy clothes and a job by talking to the manager and showing him her sewing skills. She also learnt how to read the time and the importance of punctuality and the rigours of a ten-hour shift, seven days a week, refinishing small, delicate, muslin blouses in a room swirling with lint. She earned Rs 4,000 a month, with a contribution to her provident fund and medical expenses for her family. This was life changing; I wondered where she and others like her would be had they been schooled and given vocational training. And where else would she have found the self-worth, the make-up she now wore, the handbag she now carried with a mobile phone in it with a deafening ring tone, never mind that she still could not read.

'I now sign my name when I get my salary—I no longer use the inking pad to make a thumb print,' she said with pride. But there was no real evidence to suggest that the garment factories were anything but sweatshops. They soon moved to the premises of their new factory in Manesar, where land and labour were cheaper.

I was disabused of this impression I had of the garment exporters when I interviewed Sudhir Dhingra on 24 May 2014 at one of his twenty-nine factories and saw it in operation. I heard his riveting tale of how he unwittingly got into the business and today sits atop the largest garment manufacturing and export empires in the country. Headquartered in Gurgaon, the flagship of his many companies is called Orient Craft. Coming from a family of progressive farmers and lawyers, Dhingra was expected to follow suit, but he hated the prospect. 'I hated law; I hated paper,' he declared vehemently, 'and the thought of reading files as a lawyer was intolerable.' In 1971, after finishing law school, he went on a trip to London where he stayed with an old college friend who was a garment 'day trader' selling shirts from India to vendors who flogged them from roadside vans. This friend requested Dhingra to buy a thousand cheesecloth shirts, popular among young hippies, and found easily on Janpath in Delhi, and ship them to him. Dhingra found a tailor who would make him the 1,000 shirts for Rs 15 a piece ('nine rupees for the two metres of cloth, four and a half rupees for the stitching, and one and a half rupees as his profit', but he needed the full payment in advance. Dhingra asked his father for Rs 15,000 to pay for the order. Although his father gave him the money, he disdainfully remarked that his son was going to give up being a lawyer to become a tailor.

Nevertheless, Dhingra paid the tailor and then waited patiently, making several trips to Delhi from Chandigarh, with friends who enjoyed dancing the night away, to urge the tailor to complete the order. This was decidedly a better career choice. He then had to find out how to ship these shirts. He was told that the BOAC office (now British Airways), opposite the tailor's shop was where he needed to go to despatch them. He naively went there only to learn that he would need an agent who could help him form a company and become licensed to export the garments. Fortunately, such an agent was lurking nearby and he helped Dhingra take these next tangled steps. This was hard work but Dhingra enjoyed it thoroughly and some months later he found a deposit of Rs 26,000 in his bank account. For all that trouble he'd been through and the additional expenses he'd incurred, he'd still made a neat profit of Rs 6,000. He wanted to return the profit to his friend in London, who refused to accept it because, in the meantime, he had tripled his investment. Dhingra liked the taste of this and now fielded requests for larger and larger dispatches. In one fell swoop he had become an accidental manufacturer and licensed exporter, and unwittingly laid the foundation of a sprawling future business empire. He made it sound facile but it took very hard work along with keen intelligence, a love for detail and a winning and egalitarian manner to achieve what he has built.

Finding the space in Delhi inadequate for his growing operations, Gurgaon was the obvious economical place to move to in 1977. At first, his workers didn't like the move from Delhi to Gurgaon—he had to hire a fleet of fourteen buses to shuttle them back and forth without charge.

'Now we have a total of twenty-four factories, and eighteen of those are in Gurgaon. With 30,000 employees at these factories, we're now the largest employer in Haryana; Maruti has only 11,000,' he informed me. Very few native Haryanvi men or women sought jobs in garment production and proportionately, they were the lowest in numbers. Most of the employees, however, are migrants from Uttar Pradesh and Bihar; others from Jharkhand, Odisha and Andhra Pradesh. Poverty had driven them from their homes to come to Gurgaon, where jobs were possible with fairer pay. He reckoned that each employee was supporting a household of five people at least; so about 150,000 people were sustained by this business. He remains personally accessible to his employees, and he claims they have his cellphone number and can call him directly with their comments and complaints.

I spoke to a clutch of women employees at one of the two major training centres; most of them were uneducated and unskilled from the poorest parts of Haryana, like Rewari, or Alwar in Rajasthan and Meerut in Uttar Pradesh, but after enrolling in their sixty-day intensive programme, they can join the workforce as regular employees. Surprisingly, only 20 per cent of the workers at the factories were women, and I also saw that there are crèches for children, canteens with subsidized meals, health insurance and dispensaries, and salaries well above Haryana's minimum wage. They said that for social occasions like weddings and funerals, workers are given special leave and they can also avail of interest-free loans.

Despite what sounded like contemporary policies and attitude towards the workers, there had been a great furore recently, and the newspapers had written of employee unrest. Dhingra explained that an employee had a stroke on the factory floor. A doctor was summoned immediately but the worker died, and it was certified as a death by stroke. This was picked up by the media and distorted into a story of managerial callousness with many more fatalities. This brought the factory to a standstill and Dhingra was still embroiled in the fallout from that event. But then the media has also been kind to him—I saw the album of press clippings that would have made any industrialist proud of their HR policies. While taking a guided tour of the factory floor with him, I noticed the informal ease and good-natured way in which Dhingra interacted with workers. There was no servile jumping up and wishing their master as he passed by; he appeared to know the names of the many he addressed and asked after their family members in a personal way. This lent enormous credence to all that he had said of his management style.

The biggest concentration of factories, including a very sophisticated design centre, is in Khandsa village in Gurgaon, off the highway. 'In the last twenty years—from 1992 to 2012, I can say we have grown twentyfold,' he said, calculating. 'I still hate paper and do not peruse accounts spreadsheets but the bottom line took care of itself.' He fills orders from well-known fashion houses in the UK and the US—he mentioned Abercrombie and Fitch and J. Crew, and when I toured the premises I found that there were many more famous clothiers who sourced their products from Orient Craft. These included popular brands such as Marks and Spencer, Gap, Banana Republic, Restoration Hardware, Tommy Hilfiger, Polo, Macy's, Armani and many others. It was an impressive operation.

'I am now on the board of a committee that wants to expand the garment manufacturing industry in Haryana,' Dhingra said as he ushered me through floor after floor, amid the clatter of sewing machines and the snip of giant clothes-cutting machinery where people worked at various stages of garment making. What also pleasantly surprised me was the level of cleanliness, the lack of lint in the air, the cool temperature in the workplace, and the separate toilet facilities for men and women on every floor; these are details hard to come by in general in India, particularly in the manufacturing sector.

The potential for job creation in the garment industry is incalculable in India because, as Dhingra had explained, the training was brief and the pay very good compared to other unskilled jobs. He also felt that the textile industry should be treated at par with IT and BPO businesses that are allowed 2.5 per cent FAR (floor area ratio) and garment factories were only allowed 1.5 per cent. If this sort of discrimination ends, the garment industry would grow exponentially, he felt. Dhingra's logic was mathematically simple: The garment industry is a $500 billion industry in the world and India's share, thus far, was only $17 billion, which is minuscule compared to its potential.

'For every billion dollars' worth of exports we create 2.2 million jobs. Here the government has passed the MGNREGA [Mahatma Gandhi National Rural Employment Guarantee Act, 2005] and they give away crores in paying for a hundred days of rural employment, which may or may not reach the intended population, because a lot is pilfered along the way,' he said with conviction. 'I had made an alternative proposal to the government. I said that workers could be employed all year in the garment factories that could be set up in the villages where the government would pay for a hundred days of work and the garment factory owner would pay for the rest of the year. This way we create permanent jobs with benefits such as EPF and medical insurance—not this useless dole for a hundred days that is riddled with corruption.'

Dhingra cited the example of India's chief competitor, China, where he said the government had been wise and had subsidized the wages of workers in labour-intensive industries—like garments and textiles—instead of putting its people on the dole. Indeed, China today has taken the lead in all kinds of export-based industries. I suppose our textile manufacturers need to be ready to build their factories in rural areas for such an idea to be effective. I cannot claim that I saw a flaw in his logic; in fact, knowing what I knew of the corruption in administering MGNREGA, I found this to be a brilliant way to create rural employment with far more sound and long-lasting results.

As businesses go, retail is a big one in Gurgaon and perhaps the commodity that ratchets up the highest numbers retailed here is alcohol. Gurgaon's relationship to alcohol has been as ancient as it is ambivalent. Today, what it lacks in infrastructure is compensated by an oversupply of places to buy imported spirits and wine, and imbibe Indian made foreign liquor (IMFL) and desi *daru*, the local brews. Gurgaon is not a major producer of either, but the lavish consumption of all varieties of alcohol, including imported wines and premium brands of spirits, generates an astonishing amount of revenue for the state government. The government, one might say, is addicted to this source of income and keeps raising the excise rates, so that more than a third of the value of a pint of liquor is excise duty. From 1 April 2017 an additional 20 per cent value-added tax has been introduced and this makes drinking in Haryana an expensive prospect. The total tax collected in the state this past fiscal year was Rs 4,071 crore that fell short of its target of Rs 4,900 crore; the target for next year is Rs 5,500 crore, but they are pricing a lot of people out of the pubs and drinking places. Much of this yield comes from the cities of Gurgaon, Faridabad and Chandigarh, but I could not find the disaggregated figure for Gurgaon. It might be sobering to get an accounting of how this revenue is spent. Liquor plays a very significant role in the economy of the city and its distribution and sale in hotels, restaurants, bars and pubs, and the recent introduction of government-approved drinking places (GADPs) attached to vends, employ almost as many people as the Suzuki factory.

This dependence of the state government on alcohol has echoes in the past, when colonial policies, seeking to extract ever higher revenues, virtually weaned natives of their country liquor and drove them to drink the distilled spirits manufactured by them—such as whisky, rum and gin—strictly on their licensed premises. Excise duty was the second largest revenue producer for the colonial government (the first being land revenue). It discouraged the manufacture and consumption of country liquor and brought it into the net of the excise department, depriving the villagers and the urban poor of their favourite pre-colonial libation that was cheap, far less intoxicating or addictive, and with nutritious properties as it was the fermented product of the fragrant flowers of the mahua (*Madhuca latifolia*) tree and the sap of the toddy palm (*Borassus flabellifer*). It had only 20–30 per cent alcohol content by volume, much lower than the levels in foreign liquor. Country liquor as it exists today is often adulterated with cheap ethanol, pesticides, lead from pipes, and other toxic substances. Not surprisingly, fatalities from consuming it make the news a few times a year. I cannot imagine the whisky, gin and beer-drinking consumers in the bars of Gurgaon asking for a pint of country liquor even if it was available; consumption of native drinks, which were once offered to the gods, now marks one as poor and lower-class.

The liquor industry in Haryana is enmeshed in state politics and the scourge of alcoholism among men recurs as a motif in reports of domestic violence. In the mid-1990s, women in Haryana, including those in Gurgaon, organized a Gandhian satyagraha against liquor retail. Haryani Bai, a prominent and vocal leader of the agitation, whose husband and son were both drunkards, pointed out that women had to travel about 5 kilometres to get water or fuel for their households but the men could buy their drink a few yards from their workplace. She also told of a rape next to a liquor shop in a deserted part of the old town in 1995. This enraged the women and they marched on the liquor shop and forced it to shut down.[8]

A rash of protests and sit-ins by women against liquor vends resulted in a campaign promise by Bansi Lal and other hopefuls of the Haryana Vikas Party (HVP) in the 1996 state election for total prohibition in the state. His motives were suspect because while he may have been moved by the plight of women and was strongly prejudiced against alcohol, he also saw it as an opportune moment to ruin the family business of his arch rival, Bhajan Lal. The latter's son-in-law, Anoop Bishnoi, owns Haryana's largest group of distilleries, and his father, Bheem Singh, is the distributor.

Bansi Lal made good on his promise almost immediately after he became chief minister but prohibition misfired in a major way. Had he done due diligence on the unintended consequences of prohibition in other places at other times he might have wisely demurred. Cross-border smugglers and brewers of illicit liquor had a field day, enforcers of the policies garnered bribes to wink at the goings-on, and the prices of what was available illegally more than doubled, making it an even greater hardship for the women, whose men were now spending twice the money than they did before. Violence against women did not subside either; in fact it increased, and there were a lot of adulterated illicit liquor tragedies too. Scores of deaths were reported in the period that prohibition lasted and many more were disabled or blinded. Clearly, prohibition proved to be a pitiless widow-maker.

In the meantime, Bansi Lal suffered enormous opposition to his rule for other ill-conceived policies as well, and the women themselves, who had clamoured to bring in prohibition, were now against it. In economic terms, it cost the state treasury Rs 1,200 crore in excise revenue in 1997 alone, and led to a loss of 20,000 jobs in brewing, distilling and retailing of alcoholic drinks. In addition, close to 40,000 truckers, farmers and bottle producers experienced a substantial decrease in their earnings. The state police filed 98,699 cases involving about 100,000 people caught intoxicated or in possession of liquor. Over 1.3 million bottles were seized and 7,000 vehicles were impounded. The state also saw an alarming increase in crime and violence against women. A bigger disaster could not have been created had the government tried to best this one. Khattar, the present chief minister, has expressed the wish to reintroduce prohibition into Haryana—he had better read some history, otherwise he is bound to repeat this grim tragedy.

To compensate for the fiscal deficit, the state inevitably had to resort to hiking taxes on necessities like electricity (10–15 per cent), bus fares (25 per cent), petrol sales tax (3 per cent) and additional cesses on businesses and self-employed people. Almost overnight, illicit brewing and liquor smuggling became one of the biggest industries in the state. Haryana's tourism industry suffered badly as tourists preferred to visit neighbouring states where there was no prohibition. Profits of most hotels and restaurants, including the state-owned Haryana Tourism Resorts, reached a nadir.[9] The HVP, which had allied with the BJP, was thrashed at the polls. Even Bansi Lal's son, Surender Singh, accosted his father in Chandigarh and blamed prohibition for a huge drop in real estate sales, HVP's electoral debacle, the departure of multinational corporations to neighbouring 'wet' states, and the emergence of a strong illicit liquor mafia. The death toll resulting from the consumption of spurious liquor by poor people continued to rise.[10]

Prohibition also left many middle-class homeowners like us reeling. I remember in May 1997, I arrived from New York to check on how the construction of our house in Phase III was progressing to find that one of the back rooms of the incomplete structure was being used as an illicit liquor vend and prostitution den. The architect had hired a contractor, a sly man named Mithu, a migrant from Bihar, to be the chief overseer of his building crew, who were also migrant workers from Bihar. Mithu, I discovered on a surprise visit, was also illegally selling liquor and disposing off some of the cement bags from our building site. He had an elaborately dressed and bedecked woman from Alwar, reputed to be his mistress, lodged in the room where this liquor vend had been established. The mason, who was not averse to the goods on sale, claimed that she was dispensing sexual favours and country liquor in small clear plastic packets to the workers and to people off the street. I found two men sprawled in an alcoholic stupor not far from where her infant was crawling. I ran and got the chowkidar, Bahadur, to deal with the men and destroy the contraband. Bahadur made short work of the hooch pouches by jabbing them with his khukri, although he was loath to explain why he had not taken action sooner or prevented this trade form being established there at all. The punishment for having liquor on the premises during those days of prohibition could lead to confiscation of the property and major legal difficulties; the newspapers were full of incidents of this sort. So I galvanized myself to act. We spent a few hours clearing up the traces of the liquor sale; the architect, when informed, claimed he had no idea that his trusted crew were a bunch of moonshine peddlers and rascals. The next day, Mithu's moll, who was aggrieved at the destruction of her moonshine stock, summoned the police (one of the policemen, it turned out, was her 'friend') and accused Mithu of not paying her for the construction work she had done for him (which may well have also been the case, Mithu being a total slimeball and liar, as I discovered). He was promptly handcuffed and thrashed by the police until the money he owed to her was recovered. I had barely calmed myself from that fearsome episode when, a few weeks later, my driver, Anand Kumar, died of poisoning after a binge on illicit liquor bought in Gurgaon from another building site. He left behind a young widow and three small children. I felt trapped in a nightmare. Clearly this signalled an end to my dealings with the architect. I owned an unfinished structure with a skewed courtyard, with funds close to rock bottom, and was thoroughly disheartened. Just when I thought I would have to abandon this project and return to New York, my very beloved friends with whom I was staying insisted I stick it out and they would help me. One of them was an architect who was writing what was to become a Booker Prize–winning novel, and the other was just beginning an inexplicable love affair with trees; and in their company it was hard not to feel exhilarated, no matter what the odds. There were the totally crucial interventions of a dear friend who was also an architect and artist, who took matters in hand. After six frenzied months, swirling with fresh ideas, designs and daily visits, we moved into our house and continued to work on floors and woodwork from within. When I think of those days, when living in Gurgaon was a foolhardy idea, I beam in gratitude at those three who made sure I would not give up.

Since the dark days of the 1990s, we now have a booming construction industry, better designed houses, executed with superior building materials and fittings, and architecture that has gained some applause on the national scene, giving Gurgaon an edge over Delhi in its housing stock. Yet, I hasten to add that building contractors, plumbers and electricians are still learners who give homeowners occasion for vociferous complaints. Formal vocational training is still a rarity; these men learn on the job and when proficient quickly turn into contractors themselves exploiting the unskilled migrants to do the jobs under their direction. Prohibition ended, not surprisingly, on 1 April 1998, when a thousand vends opened simultaneously in Haryana to shouts of joy and cheers. We named our house The Watering Hole where many pleasant evenings are spent with friends sipping gin and tonic on the back veranda.

And now Gurgaon must be the champion of all cities in India for the liquor vends here. On last count, done by the NGO I Am Gurgaon, on 10 September 2015, we get some very imposing figures: 210 bars, 172 IMFL and 147 country liquor vends had been licensed, and liquor is served in restaurants too, and these would be easily over 500 in 2018. To reduce the nuisance and threat from people drinking in open public spaces around these outlets, a new feature was added to the most frequented ones. For a period of time a private room was available, sometimes air-conditioned and furnished with tables and chairs, for clients to consume their liquor in privacy and present less of a hazard to the neighbourhood or to women who must travel in their vicinity. Customers could buy liquor from the outlet and consume it, along with any food on offer, inside these private rooms; now drinkers can be arrested for drinking in the open or in their cars, including passengers. This ease of drinking has been curtailed and bars and pubs are no longer open until 2 a.m. just like in Delhi where the last drink can be poured no later than midnight.

The contradictory signals on liquor regulations the Haryana government gives keeps the social drinkers baffled. It does not wish to jeopardize its handsome income from the liquor business or disrupt the other stakeholders, such as the distillers, wholesalers and retailers, and, of course, the drinking public at large and has decided that the liquor vends should be more hospitable to the drinking public. In fact, the plan is to construct the government's own very high-end liquor shops with private drinking parlours in fourteen locations where they expect to attract their richest customers. The government has set a target of Rs 5,500 crore in excise collections in the fiscal year 2018-19. In 2016, using electronic applications for the first time, they sold a total of 319 vends of which only 147 were for country-made liquor, raising a total of Rs 544.44 crore through e-tenders alone, surpassing the previous year's total by Rs 340 crore; the sale of liquor will be concomitantly greater. Since the beginning of April 2017, the excise duty in Haryana on each bottle of liquor is 38 per cent to meet fiscal targets and allegedly discourage drinking among the poor. *The Times of India* of 5 March 2018 reported from Chandigarh that 'since the beginning of the 2018-19 fiscal year the state government has made it mandatory to issue formal invoices for any sale of liquor that exceeds Rs 1,000. Haryana posted 13 per cent growth in excise and VAT revenue on liquor at Rs 5,682 crore over last fiscal's mobilisation despite the ban imposed by the Supreme Court on liquor vends within 500 meters of national and state highways, an official said.'

The state government's ambivalence about liquor is evident in its irrational pronouncements. In an interview published in *The Indian Express* on 17 March 2015, Aruna Singh, the deputy excise and taxation commissioner, Gurgaon, said: 'Drinking in the open is indeed illegal and the police should control it by all necessary means. But selling liquor is a legitimate business and [gets] revenue for the state and the contractors' vends [are] legally and transparently allotted, with sealed bids, and the contractor can establish his shop anywhere in the half kilometre radius that is given to him.' She also made it clear that all the areas are strictly monitored by excise inspectors, with the help of the police stations in the area. If someone were to buy a bottle and drink it in the open, they can only be apprehended by the police; it will not be the responsibility of the seller of the liquor. 'The police are the only competent authority to take action in this regard, and prevent all the crimes and incidents of hooliganism on the road,' added Singh.

So, on the one hand huge sums are collected from the sale of liquor and on the other there is the will to regulate, control and impose a moral code on the public. Reflecting this schizophrenia, on 1 April 2017 (April Fools' Day) the Supreme Court, seemingly having appropriated the right to legislate instead of limiting itself to settling points of law, pronounced a draconian judgement to be applied in the entire country. It summarily ordered that all places where liquor is sold or served, including clubs and five-star hotels, that are less than half a kilometre away (less than 500 metres) from a national highway, be shut down with immediate effect. Such serious overreach to legislate social control had a lot of people shaking their heads in disbelief. This instantly opened a box of loopholes to be exploited. Highways were summarily de-notified to become normal city streets; the entrances to restaurants were made more circuitous to beat the 500-metre limit; vends moved from where they were to a few metres beyond reproach. Other places found even more creative ways of dodging this rather ineffective and unnecessary measure. Surely someone who wishes to buy a bottle will travel beyond half a kilometre to do so, where the shop has relocated itself. What also emerged in the barrage of critiques on this judicial fiat was the fact that only 1.5 per cent of the fatalities on Indian roads are due to driving under the influence of liquor; the rest of the 98.5 per cent are deaths due to speeding, breaking traffic rules and sheer human ineptitude. However, the excise department takes no responsibility in this ruling. That is the job of the police, the deputy commissioner averred. The police, perhaps, haven't been informed of this duty or have simply been derelict, so the violations continue despite many complaints from the residents near these vends. And after all this drama, the government (again) did a sudden U-turn, rescinding the rule in Gurgaon for pubs and restaurants.

This huge stash of excise money, straight out of the consumers' pockets, is supposed to be deployed in the interests of the public in creating better civic and rural amenities, but the citizens find the government utterly phlegmatic, as I have noted earlier. In 2017, India adopted a goods and services tax (GST) where foreign liquor will be taxed at 20 per cent, so the government will be awash in funds. If the funds were effectively spent on civic improvements like dealing with the eyesores all over town—the heaps of garbage, the mounds of construction detritus and mountains of mud piled on the edges of roads, the chaotic traffic, the potholes and unfinished roads, the unsightly loops of electric wiring strung from pole to pole, the lack of foot paths or pedestrian crossings, or to tackle insanitary conditions where migrant families dwell in the heart of the urban villages, it would make drinking a civic duty of all good citizens and the tax on it an honest cess. Or if some of that money could be spent on education, like the profits from the state lotteries in the US, to improve the horrible condition of government schools and to create incentives to attract well-trained teachers, it would be a fair thing to do. I know this is not impossible in a city that aspires to be the equal of Singapore—it has the means, but it must acquire the will and competent personnel to execute it. It is well known that Singapore is immaculate, and even chewing gum is outlawed for fear that people might spit the gum on to the streets. Could one, for example, ban the spitting of pan juice on whitewashed walls in public buildings?

That is not going to happen, so let's not hold our collective breath. While we wait for the dust to settle on a hot evening, let's raise a chilled glass of some highly taxed liquid to our lips and quench our thirst safely outside the 500-metre limit. Cheers.

Six

Nathupur: The Village on Steroids

In August 1984, I was staying with my friends Anita and Arun Shourie in the latter's parents' home in Delhi. I had told them about my desire for having one foot in Delhi (the other is in New York) and H.D. Shourie, the force behind Common Cause, the NGO that fought for middle-class property owners' rights, suggested I look at Gurgaon, where the prices were reasonable and the Shouries had already bought two plots, one to build a house on and the other to sell to raise money for the building, in a DLF colony called Qutab Enclave. I was eager 'to look' and we proceeded to the DLF office. At the time, Phase III of Qutab Enclave was demarcated in Nathupur and its plots were sold from a modest tent, pegged just off Jantar Mantar in Delhi, the very spot where the grand DLF building now stands. The tent was furnished with folding metal chairs and a table at which K.P. Singh would sit and conduct business. A big blueprint of Qutab Enclave in its three phases hung behind his desk. KPS greeted us warmly and was memorably enthusiastic about the latest phase of Qutab Enclave; in fact, it was he who convinced me that it would be a wonderful place to live in. The first two 'phases' of Qutab Enclave had already been sold, he informed me, and the resale of those plots were touching three times the price that was paid for them a year ago. Phase III, which is closest to Delhi, was going to be the poshest colony in a dozen years, he told me. There would be a club, he said—better than the Delhi Gymkhana or Chelmsford (it's there now—though it doesn't surpass those Delhi clubs), there would be very fancy shops, and town houses and flats in a multi-storeyed building, all planned to come up in a few years (they all did). You cannot go wrong with this investment, he said, and he never spoke a truer word. There was talk, during that visit, of a light rail being constructed by the Japanese to connect Gurgaon to Delhi, make Phase III 'an extension of south Delhi', and that the Japanese were planning a 'Japan City as a retirement colony for their elderly citizens in the neighbourhood'. He was a persuasive salesman if ever there was one.

The idea that the Japanese, with their spare aesthetics, would have a hand in developing Gurgaon was very appealing to me. Most significant, however, was the fact that the money owed for my plot would be paid entirely by cheque in instalments; no cash payments would be involved (read black money, widely prevalent in real estate deals in India) and a formally registered freehold title in my name would be handed to me after the final tranche was paid. There was to be no disputable or complicated leasehold; a simple straightforward transaction in clean money in rupees or dollars with no middlemen involved.

The clean and transparent nature of the deal was so compelling that I wrote out a dollar cheque for 66 per cent of the cost of my chosen plot on the spot. Back then, Delhi simply had no such thing like a transparent real estate arrangement even if one had the money to pay for it. Foreign corporations, non-resident Indians and homeowners found this plain dealing in 'white money' extremely alluring—the real estate business in the rest of India was furtive with under-the-table scrambling. Land was rarely available on a freehold basis, and leasehold properties were mostly transferred by an informal 'power of attorney', a document that was not registered and could be challenged.

Advance paid by cheque, the next morning my husband and I repaired to the DLF office and boarded their minivan for a tour of Qutab Enclave. I encountered, for the first time, the vast emptiness of Nathupur. As we crossed the Delhi border into Gurgaon we saw clouds of dust rising from stone crushers on the edge of the quarry, grinding up huge rocks whittled from the picturesque Aravalli hills. My heart sank—not far from the quarry we now owned a nondescript 1,022 square yard plot, its corners marked by four bricks painted white in an expanse of plots on barren land. Suddenly it dawned on me that we had sealed a long-term relationship with this bleak mofussil outpost of Gurgaon, in a funny village called Nathupur, where our house was completed in 1997. In retrospect, I never dreamed that one day, the quarry would become the unique native forest in the Aravalli Biodiversity Park and the fields of Nathupur would blossom into a city that would compel me to write its story.

To build a city in the heart of a rural district, you need to absorb, willy-nilly, a village or two or maybe even a dozen; Gurgaon ate its way through more than fifty villages. All of them are in various stages of becoming Gurgaon, retaining perhaps only the indigestible gristle of their core. Scholar Ajay K. Mehra makes a useful distinction between 'urbanizing village' and 'urban village' in Delhi, and much of it is relevant to the villages that form the patchwork quilt of Gurgaon. The terms are often used interchangeably, but, he explains, that while the sociological processes of adopting and adapting that create an urban way of life are visible in both, the former 'reflects the natural process of transformation of a human settlement from one economic order to the other and one way of life to the other ... Thus, socio-economic and morphological changes taking place ... bring about attitudinal as well as socio-cultural changes gradually and naturally. An urban village, on the other hand, represents a process in which a rural settlement is caught in the process of rapid urbanization of a metropolis.'[1]

In Gurgaon we see this latter phenomenon more starkly than the former, of villages overtaken by the rapid changes around them while they fight the twin battles of preserving an old way of life and letting it go only to surrender and adopt the conveniences that material modernity brings. Gurgaon, with fifty-two revenue village settlements and the lands around them in various stages of absorption, is a work in progress—a pointillist canvas where new features are added when the need arises, and existing features are torn down because they are no longer appropriate.

While these villages of Gurgaon have followed trajectories that differ in detail, the common feature in all of them is the growth of bastis—large areas in the heart of the village settlement that have been developed into income-producing huts and tenements. They house the burgeoning numbers of migrant workers who stream into the city as construction workers, domestic servants, security guards, factory and shop assistants in the malls, whose services are utterly and totally vital to keep the city ticking. Even these urban villages have informal zones, for those who are natives and have houses and lands, for the menial classes that have also habitually lived in the village. And then there are zones for the better off, in pukka housing, and the poorer migrants live in jhuggi jhopris which they build and maintain themselves on minute plots. I discovered these on my several explorations through Sikandarpur, Chakkarpur and Nathupur, the three villages that constitute the first three phases of DLF's early development of Gurgaon.

To obviate the mind-blanking tedium of recounting (or researching or reading) how fifty different villages have adapted to the burgeoning of Gurgaon, I have chosen to tell the complicated tale through the vicissitudes of a single village—Nathupur. I found it both typical and unique to look at the patterns of change that have occurred in the three decades beginning in 1985, with the occasional comparative glance at neighbouring Chakkarpur and Sikandarpur. What is off-beat about its story is that it defies the conventional Bollywood storyline of a village invasion: rapacious city builders arrive

At DLF Qutab Enclave, what you cannot see is as important as what you can.

What you can see

1. 500 acres almost fully developed.
2. 10,000 metres of connecting roads.
3. Phase I development actualised.
   - superstructure of 1st 7-storey apartment block completed.
   - 400 independent houses under construction.
   - 200 have reached 1st floor level.
4. 10,000 trees and a nursery in full bloom.

Development doesn't all happen for the eyes. A lot of it goes underground for your convenience. When you visit the DLF Qutab Enclave, the results of only half our development actually show up.

Like you can see the first apartment block. Or the 400 houses in various stages of construction. But the sewerage systems, the pipelines and lots more is underground. And the planning for the facilities — the schools, club, shopping & commercial centres, hospitals & more — all this is behind the scenes.

All being planned at a feverish pace. Because DLF recognises that with the alarming population pressures on Delhi, the only solution lies in a rapid development of the regions within the DMA and NCR. Which is possible only if a full infrastructure of facilities is provided so that people can move both their homes and their workplaces to an open, cleaner environment.

DLF did it in the early '50s when there was a similar population explosion. By developing as many as 21 colonies. And DLF is committed to doing it again, today-at DLF Qutab Enclave. Total development. A complete infrastructure of facilities, including even security arrangements and subsidised transport. The way only DLF can.

What you cannot see

1. Zonal plans have been approved. Plot holders in Phase I can now submit building plans for approval.
2. 9146 metres of underground sewerage systems.
3. 3000 metres of stormwater drains.
4. 10,000 metres of underground pipes for tube wells & water connections.
5. Club plans have been finalised and tenders for construction are now being invited.

DLF UNIVERSAL LIMITED
R-22 Narindra Place, Parliament Street, New Delhi-110 001 Tel: 32285, 32562.

DLF Qutab Enclave
Plots, houses, apartments. **There's more than meets the eye**

maadhyam

A print advertisement made for DLF's then CEO K.P. Singh before even a single piece of land was sold.

SAUMYA KHANDELWAL

A family living in the
gaushala (cow shelter)
in old Gurgaon.

A street food vendor selling khasta
kachori, a popular snack on his
rigged bicycle-cum-food-kiosk
outside DLF Cyber City.

VAIBHAV BHARDWAJ

A cluster of high-rises reflected in a dying water body.

A collage of housing for labourers in the foreground seen in
contrast with the high-rises they built at a distance. A common
sight in Gurgaon in 2012, one could see this at more than a

The tony, upmarket condominiums on Golf Course Road. A sleek luxury bus carries passengers to their destinations late in the evening. Titled 'Vikaas ke aar mein', on the road to progress, by the photographer.

MANOJ BHARTI GUPTA

MONICA TIWARI

A couple seated next to a mound of garbage in Nathupur village. The immense circular towers of a business complex in Cyber City can be seen in the background.

MONICA TIWARI

DLF's Gateway Tower in Cyber City in Phase III that often serves as its icon. The first time I saw it, I thought it should be called the 'lipstick building'. It is seen here through the windshield of an auto-rickshaw decorated with stickers of gods and goddesses.

MONICA TIWARI

A cow stands still in the heart of Chakkarpur village abadi with tenement housing for migrants in the background. The vehicle from which this scene is viewed has a small dashboard shrine of Hindu holy pictures and paraphernalia arranged by the driver.

(top) A government school in Sector 46, Gurgaon, once abandoned; (above) The same school, now transformed into Vishvas Vidyalaya for mainstream students and for children with special needs.

ARVIND HOON

Here, at night, is seen the cavernous skeleton of the Sikandarpur Metro Station under construction. This is Gurgaon's link to the Delhi Metro and the Rapid Metro, the private light rail that runs intra-city in Gurgaon and is still expanding.

ARVIND HOON

गुड़गाँव 6

Old Gurgaon is 6 kilometres and a light year away from the new Gurgaon rising in bits and pieces as the rails of the Metro bind it together and connect it to Delhi and to other parts of the city. It has given Gurgaon the infrastructure that other cities crave. But the new Gurgaon could do with some bold new signage on its roads and neighbourhoods.

No stopping, no standing. A cow sees the forbidding sign on Mehrauli-Gurgaon road near the Metro construction, and it stops, stands, and ruminates about being as mindful of road rules as Gurgaon's thousands of drivers.

The twinkling, glittering glowing nightscape of MG Road with its bank of malls along both sides and a lowering sky above. The big new metropolis has arrived, the photo declares.

The common lane between tenements in a chawl at Chakkarpur village. The migrants who live here are chiefly artisans, plumbers, auto-rickshaw drivers, and other service personnel.

NATISHA MALLICK

Coping with water scarcity in the inner urban villages. This is a typical scene where a private water tanker fills a central tank, and residents, with no piped water facility at their tenements, arrive with buckets to fill and cart home.

NATISHA MALLICK

A young girl with her family in a chawl trying on the clothes she purchased in the market. Her dream of wearing fancy clothes is coming true.

Glimpses of the Aravalli Biodiversity Park, spread over approximately 350 acres, near Guru Dronacharya Metro Station.

in black SUVs in polyester safari suits, darken the doors of mud huts where poor and ignorant peasant landowners dwell. The evil ones twirl their moustaches, blow perfect smoke rings into the air and intimidate the innocent villagers into selling their land for a pittance. Their cowering wives are lasciviously treated while the sorry farmers lament their fate in the lyrics of Sahir Ludhianvi set to the catchy tunes of Shankar-Jaikishan. Those looking for a tale filled with cruelty, deceit and rapine or even melodrama will be sorely disappointed.

The story of Nathupur and scores of villages around it is in fact a rather unusual tale of peasants who believe that they were paid fairly, and a majority are more prosperous than they had ever dreamed they would be. The poor migrants who came in droves to live here as tenants and work in the many menial daily-wage and service jobs the city created is quite another story of a grimmer reality, but that too has its sunlit patches. Nathupur stands out as it has the best range of the city's modern development on its former 900-acre footprint and a dense and still self-conscious rustic interior. Its featureless expanse made many a builder's heart pound in anticipation and its impoverished landowners, who had for centuries eked out a bare living, found a way out of that timeless trap—they went on to become landlords collecting monthly rents instead of scraping their ox-drawn ploughs on their parched acres to garner a few sacks of millet.

Nathupur was soon carved up mostly between the big real estate companies—the Ansals, Unitech, and many others that followed DLF, with a sprinkling of small players (like those who built Garden Estate), including the leading village landowners. DLF, as we have seen, would soon become, under K.P. Singh's astute salesmanship, possibly among the largest real estate corporations on the planet; such was the prize of his gamble on Gurgaon. Snobbish Delhi-ites, unable to comprehend the upstart colony on the fringe, wrinkled their noses at the very thought of going where they believed India's rudest rustics dwell.

But the wind changed in 1980, when erstwhile Punjabi refugees and other astute Dilliwallahs (there is a subtle difference between

Dilliwallahs and Delhi-ites) cashed in their small dingy houses in the capital. Those homes had gained enormous value in the grossly overpriced colonies of south and east Delhi, and they could buy or build spacious, attractively designed houses and flats in Gurgaon for a fraction of that price. In addition, the same money bought them a car—instead of a two-wheeler—and left a sizeable bank balance that far exceeded their life's savings. All things considered, it was a very judicious move. Middle-class people were suddenly millionaires and could enjoy an upgraded style of living.

Sometime later, when Gurgaon no longer appeared as a distant blot on the horizon but an increasingly attractive place to live and work with civic amenities like restaurants and bars and the new temples of commerce, the modern shopping malls, people sold their older houses or apartments even in upmarket and prestigious colonies like Greater Kailash, Panchsheel Park and Nizamuddin to live in the opulence of newly built town houses and condominiums in Gurgaon.

DLF's parcel of Nathupur land was divided into some very impressive bits. Its largest area contained the residential colony of Phase III with blocks S, T, U and V, following the alphabetical sequence from the two earlier phases. Plots of varying sizes were delineated, interspersed with areas for schools, hospitals and pharmacies, businesses and a market with small shops and a bank, a fancy 'members-only' club and small, handkerchief-size 'parks' to resemble a well-planned suburban neighbourhood. Eponymous trees planted along the edges have created shady streets: Maulsari Avenue, Siris Road, Amaltas Marg and Jacaranda Marg, following the custom in suburbia in the West. However, unlike there, the same tidy lanes with footpaths, got chewed-up with homeowners extending their concrete or grassy sway over these strips, thus robbing the colonies of the space where pavements might have been laid on the borders of lanes. The houses are numbered in (vulgar) fractions where a house winds up with a romantic address like S 22/10, for instance, that is to be read as Block S, Lane 22 and House number 10, and this style of numbering is a part of India's colonial hangover. The addresses are unromantic but the individually owned homes show a verve of their own, with different levels of design and luxury created by different architects to match the owners' desires. Driving regularly through Qutab Enclave, one finds a laboratory of styles, materials used, and designs created. These range from charming to outlandish, from striking to ugly, with gardens to match. In 2018, the streets, though in need of repair, are leafy, and blazing with intense purple jacarandas, red gulmohars, and yellow laburnums in the summer heat; I have counted upwards of forty-eight kinds of flowering vines and trees. It would be a very great practical class for architects to study these homes carefully, see what works and what doesn't in the extreme temperatures and fragile ecology of Gurgaon, and create homes better suited to the environment.

The town houses with identical facades in all the three phases appeared like an attempt to replicate the row houses of South London. The houses proved to be very popular, and they sold like hot samosas long before they were built, and the money paid in advance helped finance the builder in constructing them. Mintu and Minty Pande, both highly respected professionals, now retired, were among the first to buy a DLF-constructed town house on a 275 square yard plot in 1983. They moved in after they parted with their Panchsheel Park apartment and have gradually transformed a cookie-cutter building into a stylishly appointed home, with beautifully tiled and renovated bathrooms and glazed verandas, and grown a spectacular magnolia tree in their front yard. They were quite tired of climbing three flights of stairs to their apartment and sharing the building with other inconsiderate owners who did not want to spend a penny on the common areas. Here they live graciously with a servant's suite upstairs inhabited by the cook and her family, with the best shopping nearby, and they have added a solar hot water system on the roof. Phase I showcases the best of these where the owners have proudly created handsome facades and gardens. The storm drains run beneath what would have been the pavements and debouch themselves into a pit or the bed of a canal or stream now dried up. HUDA and Town and

Country Planning Department had never made good on the pact they made with real estate developers at the outset, as we have seen, to connect their respective drain and waste pipes with the main sewerage system they would construct; this is not complete even in 2018. The residents' welfare associations (RWAs) do prod their developers and HUDA, but to little effect.

If one ventured on foot for about 200 metres out of Garden Estate, one would come to Nathupur's hidden resource: a vast traditional farmers' market that survived the rapid, modern build-up around it. It is an extremely large hive of uncounted stalls and compact shops along narrow lanes that sell arguably the freshest and tastiest vegetables in the world. There are also huge sacks of millets and chickpeas—what Gurgaon lived on and what nurtured its people's strength before the disastrous advent of colonial white bread (double roti) in the beginning of the nineteenth century. Women in colourful skirts and veils and heavy silver jewellery are quite numerous as shop owners here—they arrange their produce in glistening mounds, with scales made of two metal plates and attached with strings to a stick. I have made frequent trips to this market but dealing with open drains and clouds of flies does rob the experience of what it was when this was less hemmed in by the city. The fancy, sanitized shops in the malls that stock discounted groceries and a whole range of household goods have totally captivated the middle class. I find fresh okra, aubergines, bunches of fenugreek, spinach and herbs and turmeric and ginger root, the likes of which are not to be found in the other mainstream outlets—the government-sponsored Safal grocery stalls in major neighbourhoods where fruit, vegetables, refrigerated milk, wonderful ice cream and that Bengali delicacy called mishti doi (sweetened yoghurt) with palm sugar can be bought at fixed rates. The presence of thin plastic bags, however, quickly brings us back from this idyllic time to the present. The fruit and vegetable mandi of Nathupur should be preserved as a landmark and given the infrastructural help it needs to make the village core into a desirable and salubrious place where people can walk in and

share in its bounty. Instead it is hidden away like a shameful secret known only to the villagers.

The once thriving meat and fish market of Sikandarpur has barely managed to survive the building of the Metro station; it has squeezed itself onto a small rubble patch on one side of it, a sad sliver of its former self. In a truly world-class city with a creative vision, these old village markets would have become the fashionable draw for gourmets, cooks and health-conscious people—like they are in Europe, and now increasingly in the US—who are in the throes of regretting what they did to their farming communities in the intoxication to urbanize and embrace industrial and processed foods for their time-saving convenience. This market, once filled with the cries and jingles of hawkers and the bustle of customers, is still alive but it looks like it is breathing its last few desperate breaths. It will eventually fade away, stall by stall, as the crush of traffic drives away customers and forces the logic of paving it over and creating yet another parking lot for the SUVs that have proliferated like amoeba. There are thousands of poor migrant artisans who live in the village and cannot buy frozen fish in plastic packing sold in the grocery stalls of the supermarkets; and the large Bengali and Bihari population has raised the demand for fish. They like to see the fish still alive, swimming in shallow pans, scaled and dressed expertly into steaks or fillets. The dull glassy stare of dead fish piled in the air-conditioned counters of the giant grocery stores is less appetizing. And to actually talk to a fishmonger and discuss the virtues of his assorted products is to have the human interaction in a bargaining session that the anonymity of the big malls is quickly erasing. Do we have a glimmer of hope that the MCG will see the light and appreciate the charm of these old rustic shopping haunts and give them the necessary civic amenities, like good drainage and sanitation, to make them old-fashioned attractions in a city trying hard to expunge all traces of the past? A very interesting traditional market square can be created under the eaves of the Metro tracks to save the flavour and spirit of a living city. It is a pity that there is no voice or

NGO to take up the cause of the meat sellers and fishmongers and the MCG is not imaginative enough to help them survive as a part of the vibrant culture of the old way of life that is vanishing.

DLF capitalized on the remaining precious acreage in Nathupur, often in partnership with the owners who refused to sell, to create their biggest and boldest business park: Cyber City. In the mid-1990s, Nathupur, abutting the Delhi border, seemed to be the right spot for a business park, and DLF started the trend by building their Corporate Park in Phase III on the Mehrauli–Gurgaon road, which opened for business in 1997. It set a new standard of space and smart features for business headquarters and became the nucleus of the new city. While it signalled the migration of business houses from Delhi and Mumbai to its larger, modern spaces in Gurgaon, today it looks like a squat clutch of buildings compared to the elegant, pale, jade greens of Global Business Park across the road and is completely outclassed by DLF's own Cyber City a couple of kilometres away.

DLF's Cyber City is arguably the most impressive concentration of office space anywhere in India today and it does arrest one's attention even if one is driving past it on NH-8. It arose on 128 acres of Nathupur's south-west corner and its sophisticated presence has beckoned scores of Fortune 500 companies to locate themselves in Gurgaon. The panorama of the gleaming glass-and-steel buildings are, to use an overworked phrase, 'awesome' and architecturally it has style and spunk in each of its ten towers. The once stand-alone DLF tower, that was nicknamed 'the ship building' (or the 'lipstick building', as I call it) was visible for miles as the landmark to look out for. A photo of it was chosen as the back cover image of K.P. Singh's autobiography, *Whatever the Odds*, and is pictured on cover of this book. It now stands encircled and dwarfed by the dozen or more grandiose office towers that have neon-lit signs announcing some of the best-known names in the telecom, IT and banking business. At dusk, the panorama is bathed in hues of gold and platinum, evoking the buildings one has seen in downtown Houston. As the sky darkens, the lights come on and the towers glitter, while the curvature of the

Rapid City Metro tracks bearing its sleek coaches describe its path in streaks of quicksilver. We see hundreds of workers silhouetted in their glowing cubicles, animatedly helping customers on the other side of the planet, where it is now morning. If this sounds incredible, it is even harder to imagine that this was once Nathupur, which partially still exists, a village where men smoke hookahs and women cover their faces. In Gurgaon, the global and the local coexist, albeit uneasily, on the continuum of rural tradition and urban modernity.

The dream of the urban dweller to be able to walk to work and avoid the long commutes and traffic jams went on to be fulfilled here. The Belvedere Park and Towers, a phalanx of residential buildings on the two sides of Cyber City, are totally occupied by the white-collar gentry of Gurgaon—from young call-centre employees sharing apartments to CEOs of companies in capacious penthouses. A skywalk was completed in 2017 so that the main arteries that pass through Cyber City can be safely crossed above the tearing traffic. With the glamorous Cyber Hub, with its bars and restaurants a pebble's skip away (more on this in Chapter Eight), these towers, that might have been just another group of condominiums in Gurgaon, are now a highly prized neighbourhood of the business elite. In fact, there are no poor natives living in the Belvedere complex or the many others that sprang up in the fields of Sikandarpur, Chakkarpur and beyond in quick succession—the prices and rents of these apartments guarantee the exclusion of those without means or white-collar employment. Real estate offices mushroomed in small shops, in closets, in spare rooms. Their shrill sales pitches over the telephone gave way to their incessant text messages pinging on mobile phones, announcing one 'dream project' after another farther and farther away as Gurgaon sprawled, and found buyers who were willing to pay upfront and wait for their apartments to be ready in two to three years. Piles of building material on the edges of roads at construction sites were as ubiquitous as scaffolding, high cranes, cement mixers, and Bihari construction workers with head loads of bricks making their precarious way up a rickety ladder to the mason perched on the bamboo scaffolding. The old millennium and the new merge in that single camera frame on a smartphone.

The urban gale that blew into Nathupur (and also the scores of contiguous villages of the district that now are officially part of the new city) has changed much of it beyond recognition over the twenty-year period that I have walked in its alleys. A village with rutted dirt paths, shabby houses and many thatched huts that called itself a Gujar stronghold, with Yadavs numerically in second place, and a sprinkling of Meo, a few Sikh families, and Valmiki, Jatav, and other Dalit castes, and that added up to roughly 500 families in 1991, had swelled to 5,000 or more households. Manoj Kumar, a prominent Gujar landlord in the village, reckons that there were '50,000 people living in Nathupur'. He arrived at his calculation by counting the hundreds of informal homes, in February 2013, each one with an average of six people, and in his view most of them were from 'outside', implying that they were not Haryanvis.[2] I had several informal conversations with him over two decades, when he was forthcoming about how things were changing in the village. I first met him in 1997, as a man in his early thirties, married, with four daughters and two infant sons, who went from wearing a pyjama, with the typical male pot-belly overhang, and a checked bush shirt, and rubber chappals, often sitting on a string cot taking drags from a hookah and being very sceptical about the workings of DLF. But things changed and so did his views about real estate and even the 'meaning of life'. He had crudely scorned middle-class ways—they need a bathroom for each member of the family and the husband and wife sleep on the same bed in separate room—and now he was a vivid aspirant to that middle-class style of living. Since 2012, he looks a decade younger, is visibly confident, a trim-figured man in hiking pants, with sharply cut, dyed, and gelled hair, always sporting famous brands of tee shirts, anoraks and sneakers. He walks with a cousin (or henchman) in the Aravalli Biodiversity Park on the northern edge of Nathupur every morning, always greeting me with a large smile and a 'namaste behenji' whenever our paths cross. It would have been stunning to publish 'before and after' photographs which I had casually taken, but this he will not allow.

Manoj, now a village strongman commanding fear and deference, agreed rather reluctantly to be formally interviewed. He appeared, an hour and a half late for his interview, surprised to see that I had waited for him, offering the excuse that he was in his 'private gym, *jaha sab machiney laga rakhi hain*' for an hour's workout with a variety of exercise machines he has installed in it. 'Health is the most valuable thing in life,' he tells me, knowing that I would not disagree. I find his hookah retired from active duty and now displayed as a venerable antique in the completely rebuilt office, with a new sofa set, curtains and carpeting and an inner air-conditioned private room, where he sleeps in the afternoons, as he said.

Manoj had told me earlier that he and his three brothers had not sold all their land, even though there was gossip that the government would acquire it. He had told me about how backward and poor his people, the Gujars were, because the lands they owned were not cultivable; that they had little in their storerooms, their women had very little gold to wear. '*Vahi jameen ab sona ugalti hai*' (the same land now regurgitates gold). He looked thankfully at the sky where God lives. Manoj would not divulge the extent of his own sudden wealth or the current properties he owned (fearing, I suspect, that I might inform the income tax department). But with some wise investments in real estate in the village, his vast clan of over a hundred members, he claimed, now commands what is rumoured to be an astronomical monthly rental income. 'They earn in crores,' said Manav Kumar, a Bihari migrant who works with a security company and lives in the basti area of Nathupur and is a source of endless stories about the goings-on in the village. He estimated that Manoj's personal rental income is Rs 2 crore a month, and I have heard rumours of an even larger sum.

Manoj is the village's poster boy for the dramatic changes in the consumption patterns of villagers. In a rare moment of candour, he explained that he and his Gujar kinsmen—'*tau-chache*', paternal uncles, and their children and cousins, and grandchildren of his generation—'are what we are today because of Phase III colony of DLF. 'We made K.P. Singh into a billionaire and he made us *karorepati* (multimillionaires), no question that both have benefitted. Some of Cyber City is built on our lands leased to DLF,' he said. He stoutly refused to discuss the terms of the lease. Wealth had made him suspicious and discreet and he had lost the candour and bonhomie we had shared for years.

The village shops have over time undergone a discernible upgrade. It is another older cousin who, Manoj claims, owns the shops on Nathupur Road and the market square. That was surprising—in the past it was Manoj who would ask me for advice on how to renovate this area and even installed a fountain at my suggestion at a shopping plaza, even though the clumsy concrete structure that he had built was not what I had expected. It worked only briefly because of the plumbing problem and finally was demolished. The dirt path leading from Mehrauli–Gurgaon road to the village abadi was widened and tarred into the two-lane Nathupur road with street lights, which unfortunately are rarely switched on. The run-down village stalls that lined both sides of this street were tidily rebuilt with metal shutters, lighting, shelving and neat signage to announce their names. The obliging, credit-giving grocer, Ramesh, whose shop was open from 6 a.m. until 9 p.m., was the complete village *pansari*. He catered to both rustics and urbanites and the tightly packed shelves stocked daily groceries and even essentials like brooms, cobweb wipers, swabs, flyswatters and mousetraps, hard to find in fancier shops. One day, without a warning or a goodbye, he was gone without a trace, the shop empty and shuttered. A few days later, the two adjacent stores that repaired bicycles and mended pots and pans were also vacated and gutted in no time to make way for a swanky foreign wine and liquor vend. I was standing talking to those who knew Ramesh, the grocer, to find out where he went but nobody knew; it became clear that the indifference of the city of strangers had corroded the intimacy and concern the village once offered. I was looking wistfully at the shuttered doors when a large Land Rover came barrelling down the road and splashed me with the contents of a mud puddle.

'Our land is ancestral,' continued Manoj in Haryanvi during our interview, 'it is a gift from my late father who got it from my grandfather, who got it from his father. Now it belongs jointly to us four brothers. We have built some flats in the village, renovated our old haveli and added some new sections to it since our families have grown.' Again, he refused to divulge his income, or for how much his family land was sold, although he did concede that DLF gave them (Manoj and his brothers) Rs 48,000 per acre in the 1980s. Prices began to shoot up and then they decided to develop the remaining acres themselves. Manoj's two sons, who sat listening intently to their father being interviewed, now attend an English-medium boarding school at a hill station. They spoke to me in English when I asked them questions; that was quite startling, given that Manoj is not literate. The weddings of two of his daughters, who have been married off to politically well-connected families in Delhi, were celebrated with all the ostentation typical of a north Indian wedding: trees and buildings festooned with lights, gaudy brocade and tinsel finery, blaring Hindi film music loud enough to make glass windows in the neighbourhood vibrate, exploding firecrackers, a marching band that belted out colonial military tunes and a feast for over 400 guests.

These village weddings are perhaps the most conspicuous display of wealth that Manoj's clan ever manages. The morning after spoke of more pollution and garbage: there is the lingering pall of saltpetre smoke and used Styrofoam plates and cups, and empty bottles and scraps of buntings strewn everywhere. Stray dogs make a sumptuous breakfast of the spicy leftovers; I even heard a clutch of uniformed Bihari guards who patrol Phase III marvelling at the costly celebration for days afterwards—they were happy that they had been asked to partake of the feast after the guests had finished. In the morning haze, the five new cell towers that have materialized in the village look like slim minarets of the telecom companies responsible for the plague of cellphones owned by every adult in the city and village. Village landlords welcomed these installations—after all the rent for each of these mute, metallic tenants is Rs 50,000 per month. The Phase III residents objected to them being installed in their area because they are erroneously rumoured to be hazardous to health.

The makeover of the village continues; another saloon that grooms men has opened its doors where facial hair—and what remains on the heads—is massaged, shampooed, trimmed, styled, gelled, shaved or dyed (that single shade of boot polish black) and clients leave clean-shaven, with glistening pates and moustaches with a twist. But the large vegetable market, with scores of farmers still bringing in their produce daily from the hinterland, is very impressive and little changed. The fish hawker still brings in his catch in the evening in a large pail and perches himself on the side of the road with his sharp curved knife grasped between his toes, scraping and filleting fish amid a cloud of flies, to the precise requirements of his customers. The paan-bidri-cigarette shop has its gleaming holders of chopped areca nuts, catechu, lime, anise, a tin of perfumed chewing tobacco and other condiments, and the betel leaves kept moist in a damp cloth as he expertly composes a digestive *paan ki gilori* (triangular morsel) fastened with a clove. He has added jars of wrapped candy, and packets of chips and chewing gum to accommodate global tastes. Soon the old *atta chakki* (flour mill), the last vestige of the rural way of life, will vanish as will memories of poorer, simpler times and grandfathers with fuzzy facial hair and hands roughened with hard work.

A new market square came into being on Nathupur road just before it descended into the village. It had a modern grocery store, the first fancy one in Gurgaon with shopping carts and tidy aisles, and shelves stocked with everything from olive oil, Ovaltine, Horlicks, and Marmite to rolls of toilet paper and dog food, catering to the tastes and desires of the Westernized and non-resident Indians (NRIs) who were filling up the newly built residential areas. Then came the big blockbusters to the malls, like Big Bazaar, Spencer's and Reliance—while the pioneer struggles on.

Gradually some upmarket stores began to grace this square. The restaurant Italian-O moved in with its popular menu of lasagne, pastas, pizzas and garlic bread—it pulls in a large local clientele to this day. Opposite it is a small dhaba that makes tandoori rotis, dal, and meat curries (Hindu villagers seldom cook meat at home but will eat it if available outside). This area attracted a florist, a tailoring shop called 'A Stitch in Time', a pub, which opened above a dank and dismal dry-cleaner, and competed with the roadside fresh juice shop below. Wok-o-Mama, a classy Chinese restaurant, cheered up the market square no end; it serves authentic Chinese and Thai food instead of the Sino-Indian fusion cuisine more popular in NCR, can cater to large groups, and thrives in spite of the many oriental restaurants that have opened up in the neighbourhood's bubbling Cyber Hub (see Chapter Seven). A fashionable clothing store, with mannequins wearing brocaded finery adorning its windows, a chic beauty parlour with all the services you would expect to find in a five-star hotel, and a car repair workshop called Overdrive, sadly demolished and gone since 2014, elevated this square and the shops that line the road into a comprehensive local shopping centre that draws customers from the rest of Phase III, from its town houses and its private homes and the gated communities of Garden Estate and the Media Centre.

What was truly impressive was the arrival of Gita Singh, a well-known Delhi art dealer, who moved her elegant art gallery, Art Pilgrim, from Delhi's arty Hauz Khas village to Nathupur village. Its tasteful display of paintings, sculptures and artefacts was the first one to open in Gurgaon, pushing the young township up a few notches in its climb towards becoming a city. I asked her rather simply, 'Why Gurgaon?'—over mojitos in the DLF Golf and Country Club on a warm afternoon in April 2013. Singh, the canny curator, replied: 'Well, Gurgaon has developed a vigorous market for art. The young professionals, who have moved here to work in their lucrative jobs, live in the large fancy apartments or houses with tons of wall space. They come looking for something to dress up their living spaces. Someone walked in the other day and requested eight paintings—he wanted three in blue, two in yellow and three in neutral colours; he didn't specify abstracts or figures or landscapes. Of course, I found them for him and he was very pleased.' Art Pilgrim moved on to another Mecca in Sushant Lok, because, she said she was bothered by the flies that came in from the vegetable and fish stalls opposite the gallery doors in Nathupur, and business remains brisk because Gurgaon shows no signs of cooling down as a place to work and live. What dramatically underscores her point that Gurgaon has an appetite for art is that the Devi Art Centre—an architecturally spectacular art gallery—also made Gurgaon its home. Its special exhibitions attract visitors even from Delhi and get rave reviews in the national media. Undoubtedly, Gurgaon is increasing its gravitas as a place where art and artist find their niche.

The urban and urbanizing villages of Gurgaon or their way of life are not entirely obliterated although their most valuable asset, their surrounding fields, fallow, fertile or pasture, were mainly acquired and transformed by the state government and private builders. In fewer cases, the landowners themselves built residences and shops to rent or lease, and refashioned themselves from farmers into landlords and shop owners. They are both sheltered by and often in defiance of the *lal dora* regime. This regime, so named from the literal red line drawn on revenue maps outlining the area where buildings were allowed, was set up with the first settlement in 1813. It is still prevalent and a notional boundary, often a road, separates the new town from the abadi, the village settlement. The abadi is supposed to be strictly residential, permitting only small dry goods stores, a vegetable and fruit seller, and service providers, such as shoemakers, dhobis, locksmith, and traditional food processing such as milling wheat, pressing oil and other agricultural products. Some residents have retained their milch cows, buffaloes and goats, and allow pigs to feed themselves from the rubbish heaps, while a large number of stray dogs, fed on scraps, act as guards against strangers. Since the gauchara, the grazing lands, have been sold to DLF to create Phase III, these animals are left to browse where they can, in the colony's vacant lots, or the areas that have been marked off as parks and gardens, sauntering across heavily trafficked roads, crossing streets, sitting under the shade of the Metro tracks or in a cool puddle, as anyone who has driven through Gurgaon will attest. The villagers continue to keep dairy animals and poultry and grow vegetables on small beds near their houses. The Gujars, in particular, still have wrestling matches and pride themselves on their masculinity. '*Gujar ka londa,*' a new song that celebrates the machismo and fearlessness of these muscular young men with their guns and swords, has gone viral on YouTube and it booms out loudly from the fancy cars they have acquired and on the back window of which is often painted the word 'Gujjar' in English in fancy fonts.

What remains is the old core that the villagers hang on to for their own use and spend their new-found wealth from the sale of lands in a variety of ways. Some old havelis have been renovated, others have only the arched facades preserved, and a few have been torn down altogether to build modern houses. The poorer dwellings with thatched roofs and mud walls have been slowly morphed into brick-and-mortar houses, most with more than one storey, with direct-to-home dishes and antennae for television sprouted on their concrete slab roofs. The bonanza for those villagers of Nathupur and others in Gurgaon, who had even a few acres to lease or sell, was beyond their wildest fantasies. Many have leapt into middle-class status and several are millionaires. Their new or old houses now have stone, marble or paved floors with internal wiring and plumbing, with fancy gates to discreet compounds behind high boundary walls. These upgraded houses, at least the dozen or so that I have visited over time that had water stored in plastic buckets and clay pots, now have piped water from their own tube wells and storage tanks on the roofs of their homes. On my recent unannounced visits, I was offered cups of tea made proudly from tea bags, and packaged biscuits or salty snacks instead of home-made ladoos and halwa, and glasses of buffalo milk I was greeted with when I first visited Nathupur in 1986. I saw modern kitchens with gas stoves and washing machines, bathrooms with Western-style fittings, sitting rooms with sofa sets and refrigerators, and verandas with cane furniture. The crooked rutted lanes are paved over, bullock carts and bicycles, which were common even a decade ago, are mostly replaced with motor cars, the locally manufactured Maruti Alto 800s and Hero motorbikes, and some families who made it big by developing their land or leasing it to DLF, now have large SUVs and fancy sedans. Waste management, however, which lags woefully even in the urban parts, has not made an appearance in the village. Litter is noticeable everywhere, because the old organic garbage so easily consumed by the cattle is gone. Plastic wrappers and bags do not deteriorate; they clog drains and lie in unsightly heaps, while cows get poisoned as they feed on them. The unhygienic conditions *outside* the houses and in the common spaces are a symptom of an indifferent village sarpanch (the headman), a post now officially abolished and replaced by an elected MCG councillor (and non-existent municipal services).

While this is a fairy tale of sudden riches, it is difficult to ignore the dark, hairy underbelly when it comes to gender relations in Nathupur, especially among the Gujars and Yadavs. One day, I accosted Manoj, my Gujar informant, about the disrepute khap panchayats had brought to Haryana. Khap panchayats are traditional committees of caste elders to pronounce on social problems, like women's education, sex determination and female foeticide and infanticide, rape, inter-caste marriage, adultery, premarital love affairs, notorious in the rural areas of Haryana for their fierce punishments, including the occasional death sentence for transgressors. Mohan—and several others—vociferously confirmed that there has never been a khap panchayat in the Gujar community, and it was the Jats who've adopted the panchayat format, but thankfully, there are very few Jat families in Nathupur, they said. Be that as it may, patently the ingrained gender bias that prevails in the northern and western parts of India is found here. The Gujars clearly do not practise female infanticide—a brutal way of family planning—because the half-dozen families I met and visited several times have as many or more girls than boys, and all are now being educated. The Yadavs, who were content to talk to me in the street or in their 'offices' never invited me into their homes, and are a different story—their female sex ratio is abysmal. Haryanvi villages, especially those of the Yadavs, are facing a serious shortage of women—the young men cannot find brides among their own cohort or ethnic group. The coming of the migrants, particularly the Biharis and Bengalis, has eased the situation somewhat, but female foeticide remains a major problem where the police do not do enough to enforce the law.

The cramped living spaces of the new migrants have obliged them to give up on gender segregation, and women can be seen with uncovered faces by the strangest of men. There are no private toilets and the predawn visits to the fields are not possible here. When women are required to line up in the open, in front of a communal toilet, the delicate notions of purdah and privacy are severely compromised. Bengalis, Odiyas and people of the north-east did not share the purdah culture of the north, and 'are always with uncovered faces; they do not have shame', confided a local Yadav woman who still wrapped her sari end around her face, when I visited her quarters. I asked if she envied them. 'Our men are very different, we have to behave modestly—we are more custom-bound.' Her answer gestured at the rude patriarchal culture and ethos of Haryana, although the English-learning grandchildren of the old families, with their modern education, are having a hard time conforming to these notions of modesty that keep the women, quite literally, under wraps. One can still find the old hookah-smoking patriarchs, gathered under the big banyan tree in the village centre, or sitting on moulded plastic chairs on their verandas, their wives and daughters-in-law hidden in the kitchen or minding the children. Hookah smoking, which the women too enjoyed indoors, has declined as well, but cigarettes, chewing tobacco, and bidis have taken its place, and many young boys and girls are being discouraged from smoking as they attend schools and learn about lung and throat cancer.

On 23 March 2015 I visited the renovated home of a respected member of another prominent Gujar clan, sixty-year-old Chaudhry

Zail Singh. The Chaudhry is plain-spoken and still drives a delivery truck ferrying building materials from his store to building sites. His wife, Rashmi, was seated on the floor behind his chair, her face not visible, while I sat on another chair and sipped the tea she had prepared, while he answered my questions. I asked about this unequal seating arrangement. He said, in Hindi, that he treated his wife better than most, had put land in her name and now she gets a cheque every month from her tenants, but she sat modestly on the floor because the veranda faced a public thoroughfare. 'We have plots in S, T, U, and V blocks, in Cyber City, and some in Sectors 55 and 56 further away, so we have built flats in the village and get rent from about two hundred tenants. The cheques are deposited and she withdraws twenty thousand rupees a month to spend,' he said. She instantly retorted that the money was not for her to spend but for household expenses. 'I hardly have any reason to spend money on myself; I spend it on my family and my grandchildren, for the food and their needs. I don't ever eat out in a restaurant or go to the cinema, I do watch TV occasionally. I don't shop for clothes, I don't go to the beauty parlour, all that my daughters-in-law do.' She still tends to the buffalo and proudly serves the fourteen litres a day output to her grandchildren, churns the butter and *chhachh* (butter milk) and renders the ghee; her wealth had not spoiled her in anyway, except that she liked the indoor bathrooms and had a hot bucket bath in the winter.

Rashmi may have been seated on the floor, but she is no shrinking violet. From behind her *ghunghat* (head covering), speaking in a strong mixture of Haryanvi and Hindi, she interrupted her husband, even contradicted him and laughed delightedly when I possibly embarrassed him with my feminist inflected questions. I asked teasingly why she had married such an old-fashioned man and she shot back: 'I had no choice,' she said, 'my parents married me off when I was *naa-samajh* [ignorant]. We were from Kotla Mubarakpur in Delhi, far more advanced than this village.' The idea of companionate marriage to a spouse of one's choice was only a generation away. I pointed this out and he shrugged resignedly.

Zail Singh openly disapproved of the imminent end of the custom of purdah. 'My four daughters-in-law do not keep purdah inside the house, they openly laugh and joke with their husbands,' he said ruefully in Haryanvi. 'The idea of an old married couple sitting on chairs or on the floor together is still unimaginable; segregation and purdah are better, they lead to less complications'—but he was pleased that his daughters-in-law had passed high school, and one even had a bachelor's degree in arts. He and his wife were not schooled at all; in their time, they explained, it was not considered necessary to be educated because you learnt your skills observing your elders. Besides, she said jokingly, the schools don't teach you how to look after a buffalo—'that we Gujars know how to do instinctively'.

At some point during this conversation, their son arrived in a huge Toyota Fortuner and parked it next to their Honda Accord, removed his shades and reported the day's happenings to his father—of collecting and delivering orders of building materials. Many of his cousins are in the same business and he tries to stay ahead of the competition by working hard every day. He then went inside and I could hear the banter he engaged in with his wife and sisters-in-law.

We moved on to discussing living conditions in Nathupur. Zail Singh complained bitterly about the *nagar nigam* (MCG) and the councillor Pravin Kumar, who 'was totally useless', he said—he did nothing after he came to visit and saw the miserably filthy conditions, and how mosquitoes 'eat us up at night'. 'We used to have drains on either side of the lane and there was never any stagnant water, so there were very few mosquitoes. They are building a road in the village and have stupidly filled up the drains; the water now collects along the road, begins to stink and soon mosquitoes breed there. They cannot even install a pipe or make a channel. DLF does nothing for us either, although its coming to Nathupur did bring us prosperity. But they have made crores and crores by selling our village lands and not cared for the village that helped them.'

I followed Rashmi into the kitchen where laughter and camaraderie were in full swing; one of the sons was there and only two of the wives had their heads partially covered. The son proudly said he had married a 'BA pass lady', and all the children of the family were studying in English-medium schools. In the adjacent room, about seven boys and two girls were gathered around their 'master-ji' who came to tutor them in English. They were amid an English conversation lesson. We all switched to speaking in English and I was surprised at how the young boys made eager conversation and were very well informed of the family's financial situation. I complicated the English lesson by making them think up answers to questions I asked, rather than the questions in their textbook with answers they were learning by rote. It was a challenge that they seemed to enjoy very much. The older girls did very well at composing their replies and the younger ones piped up with jokes and giggled. The youngest boy seemed to be content with asking me every couple of minutes, 'What is the time?' and laughed every time I looked at my watch and gave him a precise answer. He then recited the two times table with a flourish, in English. One of the girls said that she had seen me in the Aravalli Biodiversity Park often, with a bearded sahib, as my spouse and I collected the rubbish discarded by others on our morning walks. They all enjoyed the park 'every single day'—even the ladies went out together for walks and private chats, they all thought they now had a place where they could be alone and enjoy themselves without the men looking over their shoulders and chores that nagged. I could sense that prosperity had initiated a sea change in this household and they were embracing it very happily, even though Chaudhry sahib wished it would all slow down. He was also distressed at the influx of migrants even though they were making him very rich. 'See what strange people, who don't know our ways, who don't speak our language have come to live in our village and now outnumber us; we keep them as our tenants. What will we do next?' He looked despairingly away from me and took another soothing drag from his hookah.

The interior of Nathupur has become the home of migrants from many parts of India, but mainly from Bengal, who are mostly domestic workers such as maids, cooks, drivers and security guards and found their new homes via kin who arrived earlier or through agents in the labour market. Only with the willing suspension of disbelief could one watch these recent peasants turn into construction workers, learning the skills on the job. Exploitation seemed to be the name of the game: after a couple of years of work as a plumber, an Odiya migrant would upgrade himself into a contractor and hire other Odiya migrants as his 'apprentices' that he would loosely supervise and thoroughly exploit, while he looked for fresh sites. Similar practices beset electricians from West Bengal and Uttar Pradesh and masons and carpenters from Bihar, or stone and tile layers from Rajasthan. Formal training in these essential professions is utterly lacking, and only those with innate skill and experience ever rise up from the casual day-labourer stage. The construction industry is a huge money-spinner, as we have seen, but there are very few large companies that train their personnel; private homeowners getting their houses built have to take their chances with whomever the architect or his allied contractor brings in his crew. Taking risks with machines and scaffolding seemed to be routine even for those who had never ventured from their villages before, and it was a miracle how quickly the city took shape and that we did not hear of more mishaps despite a remarkably untrained labour force and a lack of safety measures, like boots and hard hats.

Sikandarpur, on the other hand, has a central artery, which now has the Metro running through it overhead, dividing it into two narrow lanes, one in each direction, lined with shops that sell essentials for building: iron and brass hardware, cement, paints, sanitary fittings and plumbing, electrical goods, lumber and plywood, glass for doors and windows, and a huge market with wood and cane furniture for everyday use stacked in open air stalls. We made three to four trips a day to this market to get everything from brass tacks to inverters for our electric back-up and number plates for our car or a small electric motor for our fountain. The migrants that have settled here are chiefly construction workers and self-employed artisans, plumbers and autorickshaw drivers. Families of various ethnicities and religions seem to live together in very mixed conditions without serious tensions; in fact, they all speak to each other in a gender-free pidgin Hindi and seem to find a great deal to laugh about; yet the laughter dries up should sexual liaisons develop or when kitchen knives become instruments of murder.

I found groups of residents follow me around as I walked with my iPad, photographing and recording responses to my queries; they all seemed eager to be my informants. A mixed group of fourteen women spoke to me from the little kitchen areas in front of their individual huts on either side of a narrow lane, who seemed to be enjoying some time off from their arduous routines. They told me that they had found it easier to work for several families in shifts as short as two hours each, rather than all day in a single home. It gives them better pay and flexibility in dropping a job if the middle-class mistress 'speaks to them rudely or cuts their pay when they are sick or have to tend to sick children'. Shanta, a woman from Bihar, said she cooked in three homes now and made Rs 11,000 a month for three hour stints in three-households as opposed to the 4,000 she got for working for ten hours for a single family in Phase III. Part-time work is what they now seek, and have afternoons off and enough time to feed their infants and toddlers, and can even provide their children an education, which cost them Rs 500 a month per child in the poorly run government school nearby. They also shared baby-sitting duties and the neighbourhood was mostly safe and friendly. And, she added, her cooking is improved and enriched by serving families from Punjab, Uttar Pradesh and Andhra Pradesh. This was invaluable training and she will probably get even better wages as her range of dishes improves.

A knowledgeable elder, Rajendra Yadav, recounted a brief 'history' of Nathupur. It is a Gujar village, he said; the Yadavs are not as numerous as the Gujars, unlike Sikandarpur. I was told that the fortunes of the Gujars and some Yadavs changed in colonial times when they were recruited in large numbers for the British Indian Army. The rebellion of 1857 had come as a huge shock for the East India Company, which was dissolved a year later and the British

Crown took over via the military or 'fauji' route under the British, gaining land for loyal service. But the land did not reward their toil. It was not until their descendants leased their land or invested their capital with real estate companies that they began to get handsome returns. Many have bought cheaper land with the proceeds of the sale in villages farther away (as we saw in the case of DLF in Chapter Three), or invested their capital to earn a stable income. Some took the cue from the builders and constructed seven-storey tenements that serve as dormitories to rent to the inevitable flow of migrants who would arrive to take up jobs the city offers. They were not disappointed—they have come in throngs, and crowd the unofficial 'slums' or 'informal housing' (as sociologists euphemistically call them) in Gurgaon. To the horror of my Gujar friends, I always wound up in the jhuggi jhopri area, which is a world apart from theirs. The jhuggi dwellers do not pay rent to a landowner although they wind up paying about 500 rupees a month in cash to the self-appointed strongman in the area. The police make periodic visits to tear down the illegal shacks and the occupants live with this threat; very often they have a few hours' notice to remove their goods before the wrecking crew arrives.

In my several visits to Kohinoor's various jhuggis over fifteen years, I saw a steady 'improvement' in how she and her family lived. She is forty-three years old in 2018, a Bengali widow who lives with her only daughter, Regina (a name given to camouflage the fact that they are Muslims) and her two children, who have recognizably Muslim names, Israul (seventeen) and Amina (fifteen). 'There are more of us Muslims here now, and so they use our real names,' she explained. (I have used their real names at their request.) The family erected their own jhuggi on a 10x10 feet plot, with loose brick walls that have often been torn down by the authorities for being 'illegal', or collapsed when a dust storm or monsoon rains have lashed Gurgaon. They share the toilet, a communal enclosure, circled with bamboo chicks and old saris for women's privacy; bucket baths are taken outside their own shack. A small channel carries the solid waste into a pit not far from this basti area, a cesspool of stench and vermin, but they manage to ignore it. Their small space is crammed with goods because Kohinoor is someone who picks up all kinds of discarded goods from the homes she works in. She has a television set, three tin trunks and recently got herself a gas stove with two cylinders, and a small refrigerator. There is a small table and two plastic chairs for the children to sit and study under the glow of the electric bulb. In 2016, she earned Rs 12,000 per month cleaning two homes and her daughter made about the same money working as a nurse's aide in a hospital. They haven't moved to a 'pukka' tenement room because rents are in the Rs 2,000–3,000 range, she said, and therefore beyond their means.

Kohinoor speaks a Bengali-inflected, gender-free Hindi but Regina, who was a child of eight when she came to Nathupur, seems very well integrated into the north. She speaks fluent Hindi and a smattering of English, wears the Punjabi salwar-kameez, much like the other young women in this basti, and not the wonted saris that the older generation of Bengalis and Biharis wear. She married very young and her two surviving children attended school, unlike their Bengali neighbours; their father has been 'gone' for some time and not missed. Amina wore slacks and a T-shirt, like other teenagers in the basti, and the youngest ones were in frocks. Their latest worry is to buy a notebook computer for Israul—and even the cheapest one is prohibitively priced for their combined income, and the erratic electric supply makes the prospect even less attainable. Amina, bright and talkative, showed me her report card for sixth grade with an average of 90 per cent marks, but she lives in fear of her aspirations being cut short: 'My mother says I do badmashi [wicked things] so she will get me married off. I spoke to Regina, whom I have come to know well, and sternly told her about the law against child marriage. She informed me of a tragedy that had just taken place in their basti that the media had failed to report. It involved a young Bengali Muslim girl, one of four sisters of whom only the eldest was married. The other three were nubile and often got into the kind of scrapes that teenagers are wont to get into anywhere in the world. 'She was not of good character [*chaal chalan theek nahin tha*] and was always in trouble,' Kohinoor explained, in a lowered voice. 'One morning, her parents scolded her harshly before they left for work. When they returned, the fifteen-year-old had hanged herself with her dupatta from a tree not far from her hut. The girl was hastily cremated as there is no land for burials.' The police were not informed of her death. This sent shock waves in the community. Amina now fears that she is also perceived as wayward and will be hurriedly married off to prevent her from such a fate. In May 2018 her fears proved right. In a hastily arranged marriage with a young man who works as a mason, Amina was married off; the groom's father 'settled' the match by asking for three lakh rupees and an ounce of gold. I was angry but helpless and refused to attend the wedding, although I did give her a TV set that she longed for as a wedding present.

I asked Hiren, a resident of one of the pukka tenements nearby—he seemed to be educated and well informed about the politics that played out in this tiny alleyway—and he explained that these plots, where the poorest people, mainly Dalits and Muslims, live, are subdivided plots that were given to 'economically weaker sections' as part of a government scheme. The scheme, I discovered later, was the flagship initiative of the Ministry of Rural Development under Indira Gandhi, called the Indira Awaas Yojna in the 1970s, to provide adequate housing for those who were houseless and below the poverty line. In Nathupur, an acre of land was carved into sixteen plots of a hundred square yards each and given to the poorest members of the Valmiki (Harijan or Dalit) community. The men (naturally) received actual registered titles (pattas) with the strict proviso that the plot could not be sold, subdivided or rented. This area, which is now called the Indira Gandhi basti, has informally sprouted many illegal jhuggis 'rented' to poor Bengali and Bihari migrants. No one appeared to have a formal lease or title to his or her home. Their tenure is extremely precarious because the police come in every now and then to 'check', giving the residents a few hours' notice to pull out their TV sets and household goods, but often not, and sweep away the illegal constructions, smashing and kicking all household goods that remain.

The owner of the plot who is collecting rent illegally gets away without a penalty. Kohinoor's family picked up the pieces after such raids at least four times in the last five years alone, and live in fear of the next one. Although there seems to be no recourse against this periodic displacement, I have also witnessed how within twenty-four hours of the 'raid', the occupants rebuilt and rehabilitated themselves and helped their neighbours to do the same. We, the bourgeoisie, might shudder politely at the very thought of living in one of these, let alone rebuilding the hovels with alacrity, but these are their homes and their stepping stones to a better future.

This area, clearly the most squalid in the village, had a broken sewage pipe that emptied its contents into the unpaved and squelchy lane that passed between rows of huts. I turned to Hiren to explain why no one did anything about this execrable filth, where flies and mosquitoes swarmed as children played half-naked along it. 'DLF put in this sewer and the pipe carried the sewage straight to the pit next to Kohinoor's hut,' he explained. 'But after the 2014 election, a BJP MLA claimed this land and had the sewer line broken. Since then these hut dwellers live in great muck, while they spend their days cleaning fancy kothis in the DLF colony. We have no recourse against him [the MLA] since he belongs to the ruling party.' The MLA's action was indictment enough against the Swachch Bharat Mission of his own party,

In Nathupur, kin-related migration makes the Bengalis the largest group of Muslims and they often have multi-generational and extended families living in a single jhuggi. The few small mosques that exist are in the old city and cannot possibly accommodate the influx, so on Fridays, at the time of the evening namaz, one can see many selected spots on the roadsides carpeted with white sheets where hundreds of people collect faithfully, wearing their skull caps, to kneel in rows facing Mecca, to genuflect and pray. It is a visually striking manifestation of the orderly and peaceful piety of this community, a vivid contrast to the carnival like atmosphere of the temples where Hindus congregate and where women and children predominate. There appeared to be no tension between these two communities, except recently when some Hindu volunteers have been confrontational. As we have seen, in 2016, when a law banning beef, and another in 2017, forbidding the slaughter of all cattle, brought great hardship upon butchers, who are mainly Muslims. The next confrontation, mercifully verbal, was on the question of Muslims offering Friday prayers in open public places, lacking mosques where they could pray. The first such incident happened in the Wazirabad area of Gurgaon on 20 April 2018 (aside: 20 April is Adolf Hitler's birthday!) when a peaceful prayer session was disrupted by Hindu right-wing groups on the grounds that Muslims had not taken permission to use a public space for prayers. (We might make the same argument when Hindu religious processions or pilgrims move on public spaces—especially the Kanwariyas who disrupt traffic and make life inconvenient; and the many *jaagrans*, congregations to keep the gods awake by ringing bells and broadcasting bhajans at a eardrum-shattering volume, that robs the public of a night's sleep in many neighbourhoods—take place.) With shouts of 'Jai Sri Ram' and 'Radhe Radhe' and ethnic slurs, the namaz ended abruptly but there was no violence because of the presence of the police. The following Friday this activity escalated to other spots in Gurgaon, although security forces were on alert and violence did not occur. Chief Minister Manohar Lal Khattar, who did not order this harassment to cease, finally proclaimed that namaz should only be read in mosques and idgahs and not in public spaces for that was the law and he would uphold it, giving courage to the disrupters. He did not say what the 700,000 Muslims were to do because there was not enough space to accommodate them. A spate of several media reports and analyses on both sides of the divide filled the pages of newspapers and TV screens, making Gurgaon the focus of unsavoury happenings once again. The matter was still simmering at the time this book went to press, although ten public spaces had been specified for the purpose of reading namaz. Religious vigilantism has increased under the aegis of the BJP government and threatens a city and country whose conceit is that it is modern, secular, and a major business hub with foreign corporations that could pick up their bags and flee. Religious violence is abhorrent and has no place in a civilized city and this matter ought to be brought to an amicable end before Gurgaon's reputation for such events wrecks its economy that is greatly dependent on foreign companies.

Eid is celebrated with new clothes, a feast of goat meat curries, biryani and halwa. Kohinoor's granddaughter was outfitted in a tinsel-trimmed garara and choli and the grandson wore a very well-tailored achkan-pyjama and black leather shoes. Kohinoor beamed at them in her new sari and gold earrings. 'We could not celebrate like this in West Bengal,' Regina said, looking very glamorous in her dark green salwar-kameez embellished with a green-and-gold dupatta. 'We did not have any spare money and we were starving on most days.' I accepted a glass of bright pink soft drink and sat on a chair and began to comprehend their joy—they seemed to ignore the squalor and feel very positive about their move to Gurgaon. Their Hindu neighbours from Bihar and Rajasthan also accepted sweets and embraced them while wishing them 'Eid Mubarak'.

In June 2017, on another visit to their home, when Kohinoor was sick—a frequent occurrence, given the far from ideal conditions she lived in—she paid a 'Bangali dagdar' for dubious powders and injections, and I saw her huddled on the floor under a cotton blanket. She had an upset stomach. I visited again a few months later to see how things were; I had given her an infusion of extra cash and I found that she had a mason construct a neat brick and mortar dwelling with a strong tin roof. She had also grown purple bean vines on the poles of her shack, tiled the small plot to keep it clean and planted flowers on its edges. 'Ours is the best jhuggi in the area now,' she beamed, 'and the rainwater no longer seeps into our home. I also have a good electricity connection so that my grandson can use the computer you gave him.' Two of them now have bank accounts in the local State Bank of India branch nearby; they all have cellphones and Aadhaar cards, their ticket to becoming documented residents of Gurgaon and being able to refill their LPG cylinders for a subsidized rate every month. A small refrigerator was also recently added to the home. With a substantial contribution from her employer, she has bought land in West Bengal and will build her 'real home' there and dreams of running a little tea stall and grocery store—the income will help her once she retires from her two jobs in Gurgaon. She can only go back to her village as a person of means and the ownership of a pukka dwelling with land around it; she will not face the shame of confessing that she made her money cleaning other people's bathrooms.

On the periphery of Nathupur's abadi, landlords have constructed tenements, refurbished shops and jhuggi jhopri clusters, where 'outsiders', the migrant labour from other parts of India, 'informally' rent rooms or huts. 'Informal housing' or 'informal rentals' which seem to have replaced the disparaging word 'slum' are set at a discreet distance from the villagers' homes. This is *not* gentrification, which happens in derelict urban areas where the well-to-do buy properties and 'improve' them for their own use. This phenomenon, of building tenement housing, is widespread in Gurgaon's other villages, and represents the opportunity the village landowners availed of to build housing to meet the demand created by migrants. It has given them a source of income and provides accommodation for the desperate migrants in the unregulated *lala dora* areas.

In looking at a cluster of these buildings, I operated on the premise that if you have seen one you have seen them all. The building I found myself huffing and puffing to get to the top of was seven-storeyed, with small railway-compartment style rooms, about a dozen off a common corridor that had very basic bathrooms with sewage piped into the open pit below, tiny kitchens tucked under a stairway, and their waste simply spilled on the streets around. For a 10x10 feet room the rent can range from Rs 3,000–4,000 rupees, and Rs 6,000–8,000 for a small flat with a toilet and kitchen (compared to rents in the condominiums that begin at about Rs 30,000 for a one bedroom and about Rs 200,000 a month for the palatial ones). Running water and metered electricity is supplied to these tenement flats—for which extra money has to be paid—even though much of the electricity is possibly drawn illegally by the landlord. The tenants I spoke to had no formal leases, even though they had to rent their flats for a minimum of two years, and rents were paid chiefly in cash and, sometimes, several months in advance. I imagine that this 'informal' income is not reported—the landlord I spoke to said he received very little rent—'someone pays me a thousand, someone two thousand,' he said, and refused to allow me to take his picture or divulge his name. He also gestured to two Bihari tenants, who greeted me, to ignore my questions and move on. The *lal dora* areas are enclaves that operate below the radar of the law.

I caught up with one of those tenants later. Mahesh (name changed on request), a Bihari migrant who has been there for fifteen years, and has moved up to the position of a contractor, employs three masons and a handyman who can make electrical connections and fix bolts and hardware to the shacks. He became my self-appointed guide around the basti.

There is a pragmatic bond between peasant capitalists and the peasant proletariat inside an urban slum. It is true that in any other aspirational city, the slums of Nathupur would not be allowed to exist and an empowered civic government would unleash their bulldozers and obliterate them, as Delhi has frequently done. But no one in Gurgaon is ready or willing to take responsibility for building better homes for the economically weaker sections (EWS) of society outside the *lal dora* areas, as we have seen in Chapter Four. Builders falsely promised to build affordable housing in allotted areas but only to get concessions offered for building for the EWS of the population. And when they did build some quarters, these were promptly bought up by middle-class buyers either to allow their staff to live nearby for their own convenience or were upgraded for their own use as extra storage or office space. I visited the wood-panelled, air-conditioned offices of a chartered accountant amid bare and dark rooms where families of cooks and drivers dwell. The builders, who received tax discounts to build such housing, were later pardoned for not keeping their word; a real estate agent claimed that there were under-the-table handshakes for immunity granted. Few well-to-do apartment dwellers would have seen where their team of domestic workers who serve as their drivers, cooks, maids or guards who patrol the buildings, actually live—for their hovels in Nathupur and Chakkarpur are invisible from the flats and villas. The most high-end spaces in the Nathupur abadi area is a Western-style hostel, with 12x12 feet finished rooms, with an attached 6x4 feet kitchen, a small hot plate, a fridge and the same sized space for a bath with a geyser fitted in it that goes for Rs 12,000 per month. The landlord, Manoj Kumar, explains that the monthly rent includes house cleaning and electricity usage.[3] A group of Korean tenants showed up outside this 'hostel' as we were talking and I could confirm the rent they paid in 2014.

There were many small landowners in Nathupur who did not fare well. They sold their land and failed to reinvest their capital gainfully, and quickly ran through their stash by consuming conspicuously: buying cars and SUVs, drinking and spending huge sums of money to celebrate weddings and birthdays. It is no surprise that many of them were quickly reduced to penury. They mostly had to move out of Nathupur, where land prices had shot up, and left for the more remote parts of Haryana. Jat farmers, once Haryana's dominant landowning caste but educationally backward, and now stressed with their imprudent spending, were happy to join an agitation to get recognition as one of the Other Backward Classes (OBC). In 2014, the BJP came to power in Haryana and the Jats, who had been in power for most of the existence of the state, felt disenfranchised. The Gurgaon Jats stayed out of the fray but those in Rohtak, Sonepat and Jhajjar districts went on a rampage in March 2016 and staged violent protests demanding OBC status for their caste to get jobs in the government from a quota set aside for such classes. It is rare that a caste, in the traditional scheme of things, seeks to downgrade its status; the Jats, however, saw no other route out of their landlessness and their lack of education.

Astounding as it may sound and as deplorable as their living conditions are, rural migrants have raised their standard of living compared to the lives they left behind in their remote and impoverished villages of Bengal, Bihar and Odisha. My informants gave me pause when they categorically assured me that they would not think of returning to their villages, despite the appalling conditions in which they lived and worked in Gurgaon. They quickly disabused me of the idyllic life in India's villages. They had left their homes, stricken by drought or flood, with no available health care, no schools for their children, with no prospects for the future. Even though they found Gurgaon alien and inhospitable at times, they considered it the land of promise—there were everyday hardships and a lot of filth, yes, but nothing to compare with starvation and a variety of sicknesses back home. They came because 'one person in their village set off to change his luck and sent home news of a better life'. Soon the word spread and people who had ventured as far as the next village set off to buy rail tickets to travel a thousand miles towards Delhi and Gurgaon. Their hopes and acceptance of abysmal living conditions in no way justify what they endure or exonerate the government from their lack of concern for their lives, but the poor migrants' priorities are focused on working at jobs that will allow them to provide for a better future for their children and the hope that they will move to better living conditions.

'I packed a small bag and came to where my *chacha* [father's brother] was in Gurgaon, working as an overseer in a construction company because he had passed high school,' said Mustafa, who now worked as a welder in a factory that made wrought iron goods. There is always one courageous person who blazed the trail from the village to the city and the rest follow in groups. It is now well established that Gurgaon is a destination where one prospers quickly, even though there are hardships, and working hours are long. The kin networks in Haryana, western UP and Delhi I found among people I thought were strangers was startling. It was more like losing the curse of fate, explained Nuzrat Ali, an articulate Bengali who was no longer a victim. He and his family had changed their own destiny, as he pointed to the shiny new autorickshaw he had bought a month before. And he had dreams of owning a car and a flat not too many years from now and, of course, have children who would speak fluent English and have office jobs.

Construction workers, the actual builders of Gurgaon, are nomadic migrants who build and live in temporary shacks outside the construction site, cook on wood fires (adding a great deal of smoke to the morning air) and use empty lots as their toilets, although recently I have seen the use of portable sanitary closets. They live there until the job is done, and the contractor may choose to retain some of them for his next site, where this temporary camp will move. But none of this, however, is new or strange or invented in Gurgaon—it is an inevitable and pervasive element in the process of urbanization in the Third World and there are many scholarly studies to document it. Ruthless as this may sound, it represents an opportunity for those who have come to find a better life in these hovels. This is a step up from the desperate conditions they left behind, and they at least have a wage at the end of the day to feed their families, and even set aside a pittance for a rainy day, or send money home to the families they left behind. I know about fifty people of this underclass who remit money home to widowed mothers, for sisters' weddings, for medical expenses, or to buy land or build a house, and they are fairly typical. The city supports many in their villages in this rather invisible fashion and has a positive impact on the countryside.

The tenfold explosion in the population of Nathupur has made it a more prosperous place, even though the jhuggi jhopri section of it remains squalid. Now the migrants far outnumber the natives but remain powerless and unorganized because they have no formal standing in Gurgaon. They have no voting rights, since they have no permanent addresses here and their ration and Aadhaar cards (the official proofs of identity) are of their home addresses hundreds of miles away. Migration is tantamount to disenfranchisement because they are not able to afford the time or the money to travel to vote in elections at home. The plan for individual Aadhaar cards, the unique IDs that the United Progressive Alliance (UPA) government at the centre initiated and are being pursued with missionary zeal by the BJP, are as identity cards and these may give these migrants a right to vote in the next state and general elections in 2019. Although it is not entirely clear at this point as many migrants are forced to give their official address as their original village home rather than the address of the jhuggi they occupy in Nathupur.

But there was much rejoicing in the Bengali huts when Mamata Banerjee was re-elected as the chief minister in West Bengal: '*Woh hamra asli lee-dar hai,*' said a man with a salt-and-pepper beard and paan-stained teeth. '*Woh hamra dekh bhaal karta hai.*' They hailed her as their true leader and credited her with looking after them not long after confessing that whatever the conditions they endure, they are far better off here than they were at home—so the exodus of Mamata Banerjee's vote bank from Bengal has only increased over time. They know it will be different for the many children that have been born in these hovels in Nathupur. The consensus seems to be that with better education, the younger generation will aspire to lift themselves out of the insalubrious morass to more lucrative jobs as taxi drivers, plumbers or in fields that have something to do with computers, and find proper apartments to rent.

With so many migrants now living in such a close-knit community, Nathupur was no longer peaceful, Zail Singh's daughter-in-law, Komal (not her real name), had warned me. There were incidents of disorderly behaviour and drunken brawls, she said. Petty crime, especially thefts and robberies in the upmarket residential colonies, were on the rise, although murders because of land disputes and inter-caste love affairs were known to have happened in the village. As recently as 9 June 2016, thirty-three-year-old Sandeep from Jind district, who was employed as a driver by the Maruti Suzuki factory, was found stabbed to death in the basti area; it sent shock waves throughout the village. Manav, the Bihari security guard, who had been living in the Nathupur basti for over twenty years in one of the tenements, recounted the gory story. 'This happened ten feet away from my own door,' he said in Hindi, 'and I found the body with multiple stab wounds sprawled in the lane with pools of blood around him. They say that he was having illicit relations (*kuchh chakkar chala raha tha*) with the wife of his friend; the husband became suspicious and returned home during the day to find them behind a locked door, his child despatched on an errand. So he must have finished him off. But he did not kill his wife … so far,' Manav added ominously. The police from the DLF Phase II thana got there later and arrested the Bihari husband who committed the murder, and he is now in judicial custody. According to *The Times of India* of 10 June 2016, Mahi, a twenty-two-year-old woman who worked in a club was beaten to death and her two friends injured near Shankar Chowk by a gang of four, including a woman, who were unemployed residents of Nathupur. All four, who were known to the victims, are under arrest.

That said, even though Gurgaon has attracted a wide spectrum of migrants—from CEOs of MNCs to lowly domestic workers with their varied hopes and fears—it gives the village a motley effect, with the two extremes of riches and scarcity patched together. However, it didn't take much persuasion to get the soft drinks giant Coca-Cola out of its HQ in Mumbai and the cubbyhole in Nehru Place in 1992 to head for Gurgaon, and more specifically to the transformed part of Nathupur. The company relocated its corporate HQ, along with 650 of Coca-Cola's highest-paid jobs in India, to three plush buildings, including the executive offices, in Cyber City. Srinivas Kini, its CEO, walked me through what seemed like cool and quiet acres bounded with transparent walls through which vistas of other towers of Cyber City shimmered in the sunlight. 'Yes, KPS lured us here,' Kini averred, 'but will Gurgaon be able to keep us here, by fixing all that ails it, or will it lose us to the next aspiring city that might be better managed?' He had captured Gurgaon's pride and fears in a succinct statement.

What happened to Nathupur's barren fields is, in sum, the drama that is being staged not only in many locales all over Gurgaon district but all over India also where cities are expanding and swallowing many villages. It has many distinctive assets that make it stand apart even among the other villages that Gurgaon absorbed. It is the home of the first gated community, Garden Estate, as we have seen in Chapter Four, and of the most luxurious five-star hotel, The Leela, and the most coveted Sri Ram School on Maulsari Avenue, where many students travel from Delhi and beyond if they are lucky enough to get admission. It is also awash in hospitals and clinics that meet the highest standard of health care, and to top it all, a vigorous, highly energetic and engaged civil society that has taken it upon itself to make improvements in the quality of life that they yearn for and the city is slow to implement. And the capstone of all this is the stunning Aravalli Biodiversity Park, regenerated from the same ravaged quarry that greeted all comers first. Now after three decades of delicious and disorderly growth, Nathupur could not have had a happier fate. If all this could happen to the fields beyond the revenue village, surely the village core can be re-imagined fully and rebuilt to afford quality living to the thousands of migrants that have settled there. Nathupur is the microcosm of the city and a sample of the changes in the cores of the dozens of villages enveloped by the city. No one had planned or predicted how Nathupur would evolve but there is an opportunity here to make it blossom into a safe, sanitary and salubrious environment.

There is a strong common thread that emerges from the stories I heard from the many CEOs perched in the towers of Cyber City, the residents of fancy houses and apartments who moved here, the dhoti-kurta-clad villagers who had sold or leased the land beneath these towers, and the poor migrants who had come to look for a better life: they all smiled and they said, in different words, that Gurgaon was where they wanted to be.

Seven

Destination: Bourgeois Lifestyle

O nce upon a time, Gurgaon, with its earthy odour of a 'gaon' rather than a city, had modest aspirations on the pleasurable side of life, having been conceived as a bedroom suburb of Delhi. Liquor was cheaper than in Delhi, but there was certainly little else there to seek except a long day's rest at night. That was in the 1980s and '90s. Then came the new millennium and the city abruptly turned a new leaf to become an unlikely sin city: it began to sleep later and eat later as restaurants, nightclubs, pubs and clubhouses became abundant and attractive. Malls sprang up and their brightly lit facades cast a neon glow on formerly dark main streets. The traffic thickened; camel and bullock carts and bicycles began to disappear and lines of cars, minivans and flocks of motorbikes took their place. Often, these fast vehicles, driven impatiently and without regard to rules of the road, clogged the lanes with seven cars abreast when there was room for just four, so they barely moved to the discordant symphony of blaring horns.

Gurgaon's old somnolent reputation melted like an ice cube in a glass of hot buttered rum as it developed its own personality and panache. It is not the staid embodiment of a planner's blueprint, like Noida or Chandigarh—it is an exuberant, if erratic, doodling by several real estate players who conjured its fabric. Its stylish housing and immense office spaces, schools and shopping malls have made this metropolis a magnet. Crowds of NRIs live here and so do people from all over the world. They have sizeable disposable incomes to match the attractions that demand it. With comparatively better value for money in real estate and in domestic help for those who earn in dollars, Deutschmarks, or dinars, the NRIs can live the coveted bi-continental existence that keeps their roots nourished while their branches have global reach. Looking out at a parking lot one will find that the cars have as many number plates from Delhi, Chandigarh, Faridabad, Sonepat, and yes, even Noida and Ghaziabad, as there are from Gurgaon. And thousands of poor migrants from all over the country see it as a place of hope, of jobs and wages and sustenance, of a life better than what they left behind. It is contiguous to Delhi, yet it remains cheaper, bringing artists, writers, journalists, academics to live in Gurgaon, as it has done for doctors, lawyers and accountants, to match the growing demand for their services.

Gurgaon grew at an unbridled pace ignoring its own severe limitations. It acquired a sprawling body first, with a fair share of sclerotic arteries, and boils and blisters to go with it, and now it is surgically altering its birth defects and implanting tissues it was lacking, including … umm … a young and vibrant soul. Yes, a soul, because its creators didn't quite know how to infuse it at first, like the other things they omitted, because they were wedded to old-style residential colony building. It seems to be saying, with a boastful touch, 'Look at my astonishing brawn, look at the money bags I fill; I have more malls and offices and apartments with more space than anywhere in the country; the Metro and the Rapid Metro run on gleaming tracks overhead and the NH-8 connects me swiftly to Delhi and Jaipur, situating me in India's "golden triangle". I am a global city.' It contains a carnival as rich and varied as its array of global corporations that give it its lifeblood. I must confess, in writing this chapter I feel a lot like a carnival barker: 'Come one, come all to fun-filled Gurgaon!' The young and the widely travelled have brought a lively beat to the once gloomy nights of Gurgaon, where the natives went to bed, it was believed, as soon as their cows came home. They had had their simple repast of dal-roti and the last drags on their hookahs. Now it beckons like a siren, with its nightlife, in the bars and cafes in Cyber Hub and a rash of venues for grander evenings for the executive class in fancy five-star hotels, or viewing the phantasmagoria of Kingdom of Dreams in Leisure Valley. Eateries, with menus displaying Mediterranean sophistication, or the well-known American fast-food chains with their hearty platters, or robust Punjabi fare hot from a tandoor, seem to find their eager clientele among the hard-working crowds that swarm Cyber Hub in the evenings, thirsting for a chilled draught beer or a fancy cocktail. Dance floors with strobe lights get crowds of fashionable youngsters bouncing to the sounds of eardrum-splitting fusion music. The aching necks bent over computers, the glazed eyes that scanned for business dates, all are soothed here. The latest films from Bollywood and abroad are screened in the many cineplexes with adjoining food courts to satisfy a wide range of tastes. Gurgaon's entertainments are the lure. Half a dozen golf courses bring executives and professionals out of their sedentary jobs to stride on green links to tone the body and refresh the mind, while cutting even better business deals. And for those who just enjoy a walk without the implements to whack small balls into small holes, there is the scenic Aravalli Biodiversity Park.

'And, pray,' Gurgaon shouts back at the naysayers, 'what city in India is regenerating a forest in its very heart? We are repairing the environment that was ruined by bad colonial policies and the worst concrete onslaught of our present times. Come back in five years (2023) and we will have mended our shortcomings, and you will be astonished…and envious.' Crowds of NRIs have made this their base in their home country and so do people from all over the world and all have sizeable disposable incomes to match the attractions that demand it.

However, those of us who live here know that under its bespoke dinner jacket the city wears a hair shirt, and the continual irritation has created itchy patches in embarrassing places. The media spares no occasion to describe the rashes and eruptions, phrase by lurid phrase. But then, even Delhi has its own pustules to deal with. There was a justifiable hue and cry about the flooded streets in Gurgaon where life had come to a standstill after the expected heavy monsoon rain in August, but on those same days the photos and stories of Delhi sounded like Gurgaon writ even larger. I would go so far as to say that the urban panorama of our country would betray the same chaos, the same choked drains, the same floods, and the same stalled traffic after a torrential spell of rain, be it Delhi or Chennai, Mumbai or Kolkata. The embarrassment is that the HUDA and the PWD and other departments in charge of road building and drainage in a freshly constructed city like Gurgaon did not learn from the mistakes of its storied neighbour. It is because the builders of the post-1947 freehold colonies of south Delhi, especially DLF, are also the major builders of Gurgaon, and the civic authorities follow the same old rule book that applies to these other cities. Environmentally sensitive planning, innovative thinking and practical solutions are not their forte.

Since 2010 I have been scouring any writing on Gurgaon, whether in academic journals, the media, on the Internet, or in fiction or film where it is occasionally used as a backdrop for a a crime drama. The print media is the most prolific, and lilting, unflattering and alliterative epithets such as 'dysfunctional', 'dystopia', 'disaster', 'disorderly', 'drowning [in sewage]' are spewed into their stories like red spittle from the lips of a paan-chewing aesthete on to a whitewashed wall. Jim Yardley's 2013 piece on Gurgaon in *The New York Times* was forwarded to me many times. This negative verdict has been so infectious that it should be astounding to most that the city exists at all and has the highest growth figures of any in India; for migrants, NRIs and foreigners continue to gravitate to Gurgaon to establish their homes and businesses. So, Gurgaon must have something worth getting that eludes journalists. Then one day, as if penitent or forgetful,

The Times of India of 21 June 2016 sprang a wonderful surprise. The headline read: 'A Healthy Slice of Japan in Cosmopolitan Gurgaon'. Cosmopolitan? The adjective was used by a Japanese resident, as I read on. Of course, I thought, if the 8,000 Japanese who were registered as living in Gurgaon thought so, our media had better start changing their tune. Sakshi Dayal goes on to report that Tomonaga Tejima, a Yale University graduate from Japan, moved to Ahmedabad with his family to work in a pharmaceutical company. Ahmedabad, a city known for its heritage and liveability, did not meet his expectations in either food or education, so he transferred his family to Gurgaon and commuted to work in Ahmedabad. This proved inconvenient so he took the drastic step of resigning from his job but he didn't pack his bags and leave for Tokyo, he moved to Gurgaon permanently instead. He decided to be a self-employed purveyor and chef of Japanese cuisine in a takeaway restaurant called Sushi Junction, located in Udyog Vihar.

Why did Tejima do this? He said the atmosphere in Gurgaon was a lot more 'cosmopolitan' than other Indian cities, since so many foreigners resided here. He wanted good schools and hospitals for his family and Gurgaon ranks very high for those life's essentials and that's what sealed his decision. Needless to add, his family lives in a modern, spacious condominium in the safe and sanitary precincts of a gated community on Golf Course Road along with thousands of his compatriots. His patrons, nurtured on takeaway in Tokyo, need no instruction on how to pick up a tantalizing piece of raw salmon with a pair of chopsticks. The other residents of Gurgaon are eager for his offerings, some of which he has adapted to please the Indian palate, and the word has spread fast. Other shops and restaurants catering to their tastes have blossomed—miso, wasabi, sushi, sashimi, teriyaki, and more will soon be household words. With palates jaded on curry, people will chomp down grilled octopus and squid with relish, sipping cups of warm sake, the subtly delicious rice wine. If the Japanese can also bring in their spare aesthetics to the gaudy towers of Gurgaon, it will be the city's gain. The Koreans, in even larger numbers, have populated similar enclaves in Gurgaon with shops and eateries to match. Gurgaon is not Seoul, I know, but they will find that it is on its way to finding *its* own soul.

The Chinese have always had a niche in India since the nineteenth century, and 'Chinese food' in India is very popular and so inflected with Indian flavours that this fusion food is a much beloved separate regional cuisine now. Szechwan, Hunan and Canton have brought their strikingly different flavours to expand the meaning of the culinary riches of China and these can be found at the upmarket China Club or at many Asian restaurants that have sprung up all over Gurgaon. Also, if you are tired of the daily dal-chawal-sabzi-chapatti routine and crave something to satisfy the foodie in you, an authentic Gujarati thali, or a wonderful Punjabi treat from the tandoor, or a Kerala fish curry, or Parsi seafood and dhansak or a Kashmiri full-scale carnivorous waazwan, or a Lakhnavi biryani or galauti kebab wrapped in a rumali roti, you will not be disappointed in Gurgaon. Or simply head to the dozens of pizza and burger outlets and wash the food down with a chilled Coke.

One doesn't have to drive around on Gurgaon's still unmarked and unlit streets to find these delectable gems. On two polished granite-paved levels, in the cool breeze of fountains and waterfalls, Cyber Hub is an oasis, where upwards of thirty eateries offering a medley of international eats, including the inevitable greasy spoons and fast food joints, and there are bars with live music and dance floors and cafés serve coffee from freshly ground beans from the slopes of Costa Rica, Kenya or the Nilgiris, take your pick. For relaxation, the huge army of youthful white-collar workers (although that term is outmoded now because starched white shirts and ties are rare; informal or smart-casual dressing has taken their place) head to Cyber Hub. Having sat hunched over their computers all day, they unwind with their friends and families at this strobe-lit, throbbing heart of the new city where they congregate. It is a place to sip cool drinks from multicoloured glasses, from melon juice to tart margaritas and mojitos, or a shot of tequila or a smoky single-malt whisky, nibble on succulent bites of barbecued meats, and then go and find another spot to satiate the craving for a lavish cheeseburger or a Chinese chilli chicken, or a delicate prawn stew at SodaBottleOpenerWala, serving Parsi cuisine or, they might wend their way for a multi-course Bengali dinner to the naughtily named Oh! Calcutta What is sophisticated about this is that Chinese or Indian food is no longer a single generic offering— regional specialties are on offer in separate restaurants, so the chances of getting authentically flavoured dishes is almost certain.

If you happen to be someone who grew up in the 1950s and '60s and thought that cha-cha-cha or the twist was the height of hipness, you might groan at the eardrum-piercing music and the Bhangra-like stomping about that is now in vogue. Perhaps this is a little harsh—I have also seen some nimble dancers who glide and twirl, and sometimes the live band takes a break and a slow waltz or tango is played and the place briefly becomes charmingly romantic. It is a cheeky rejection of the homespun swadeshi era that was powerful in its time and steered us to self-respect. Today, in a more hypocritical era, mimicking the West and embracing its technology while reviling it is a popular stance. Gurgaon was a blank slate on which this chapter of India's new liberal economic policies is now hastily being scribbled, even as brash capitalism and corporate culture are altering society for better *and* for worse.

And for those who like the quiet colonial enclaves for their amusement after hours, or for day-long bridge sessions in the Gymkhana Club of Delhi, Gurgaon with its usual excess has more than a dozen private clubs, built and run by the builders themselves. The best ones, in an architectural style that can be described as modern colonial, appear to be in the five phases of DLF City, along with the DLF Golf and Country Club, of which much has been said before. Sushant Lok and other gated communities have their own clubs for residents, a feature introduced by the builders of Garden Estate and imitated widely. These are open to members and their guests, and the membership is limited to those who own or rent property in that neighbourhood, although they can visit the other clubs of the same builder. The membership fees are steep and enrolment has been low in several of these because the choices to eat and drink in Gurgaon are plentiful. The Phase III clubhouse makes its money, the manager says, by letting out its fifty-odd luxury rooms; with Cyber City next door, many businessmen on brief trips find it a very convenient and comfortable place to stay in. The dining rooms of these clubs and the bars, where I have sampled their fare, are of good quality, although there is nothing to set them apart from other eateries, except for the quiet atmosphere that is hard to come by these days. The City Club in Phase IV, the most popular one, it seems, has high-quality continental food and the barman served us a dry martini. On a trip to Club V on a very sultry afternoon in August 2016, I found its air-conditioned interior oddly deserted except for a round table of intent rummy players in the card room and a couple of women sipping tea in the lobby. The billiard table looked a bit forlorn, without players chalking their cue tips and the ivory balls clicking expertly. The suave manager, Dhruv Puri, showed me around the place. He was busy trying to deal with contractors and chefs and furniture people for preparations for a big event the next day, when he was expecting seven hundred guests with music, films, two famous film stars, and a twenty-dish buffet that would set the place hopping.

No matter how hard you try to cover the bases in Sin City, there are bound to be many things you missed. Aditya Arya, the photographer and archivist-collector, who will appear a few pages later in this chapter, informed me that there were some notable new players that had come to join the party in Gurgaon. In Metropolitan Mall, the very popular chain, Khaaja Chowk, by Vikram Nair, now a Gurgaon resident, has created a loud buzz. He told me that I was absolutely out of touch if I had not eaten there—'the best Punjabi food in town'—and not met the entrepreneurial Vicky Nair. In fact I should not then call myself a true lover of good food. I admitted that I hadn't done either, yet, but would hasten to make amends. But to not feel too gauche I informed him that I met Vicky when he was a little boy, and know his mother well, and I am on uproariously cordial terms with my friend Mira Nair, his illustrious film-maker sister, who is based in New York. I took Vicky's phone number and made a mental note to visit his place and reacquaint myself with him. An unrivalled pleasure among the sumptuous offerings of Punjabi food, in my view, is a hot, blistered tandoori roti with a piece torn off to scoop up some karahi gosht (curried mutton cooked in wok) at any time of the day or night—let us see what Khaaja Chowk has to delight my palate.

Although not part of Punjab, Gurgaon has adopted Punjabi food as its own. It has an embarrassment of riches when it comes to Punjabi places to eat. From the high-end places like Jiggs Kalra's Punjabi Grill at the Ambience Mall, where among a dozen fabulous dishes there's the little-known stuffed guchchis (morel mushrooms) that are your ticket to heaven, and the well-loved chain of Punjabi By Nature restaurants that give you your money's worth. The only place Gurgaon is lacking is a dhaba that showcases Haryana's rustic specialities.

As a Scotch whisky lover, I was upbraided by the same friend for not having gone to Whisky Samba—a bar on Golf Course Road that boasts the most extensive list of single malts in the NCR. How did I overlook this in all my diligent research on the liquor scene in Gurgaon? You will repair there at the next opportunity and hope many others will do the same. Another friend told me that I hadn't done any justice to the microbrewery because the music was too loud and I fled after sipping the head of amber coloured ale. So be it. I am sure there is enough I have said to make my point: this is a very hopping, exuberant place to wet your whistle. I would request the journalists who put out bad press to stop grumbling, let you be the hair around their balding pates and explore the fun one can have in this city. Women journalists are, of course, much too astute not to see the fun side of all things.

However, regrettably, the emphasis in all these places is strictly heterosexual and family oriented; a gay or lesbian bar is almost unthinkable thus far in Gurgaon, but I might be underestimating the progressive denizens of Gurgaon. On 25 June 2016, a fresh breeze wafted through Leisure Valley Park, a large space that has seen better days, where about two hundred young people gathered to hold the very first Lesbian, Gay, Bisexual and Transgender (LGBT) rally and parade. Puja Bajad (sic), who moved to Gurgaon from Delhi recently, found that its queer community had neither visibility nor space, nor any place to meet. A woman of enormous spunk and courage, she spent a great deal of energy and effort to get the permissions needed to have a parade of this nature in a HUDA park. I saw LGBT volunteers clearing the park of all the litter that collects there because HUDA maintenance is conspicuous by its absence. Soon, buntings and balloons were festooned and proclaimed the colours of the Rainbow Coalition, an international organization that spreads tolerance and peaceable coexistence with people of all creeds and sexual preferences. The march was a kilometre long, confined as it was within the park boundary. They protested Section 377 of the Indian Penal Code (IPC, 1860) that enforces the nineteenth-century colonial law that criminalized 'anal intercourse' alleged to be 'against the order of nature'. This section, written by colonial administrators in the heyday of Queen Victoria, reflecting antiquated sentiments, had been overturned in 2009 by a broad-minded and progressive bench of the Delhi High Court, but in December 2013 two judges of the Supreme Court, in their questionable wisdom, reinstated colonial bias of Section 377 without any reason to do so, except that, I was informed, one of them was retiring and wanted his fifteen minutes of fame. This infamous section is completely out of sync with millennial values and those of ancient India, and it also stands in inexcusable contravention of the Indian Constitution that guarantees equal rights to all Indian citizens; it will have to be wiped off the IPC and it will be citizen activists who will win the day for the country. What kind of invincible, self-aggrandising stupidity is this? Does he realize his deed is now infamous and will be overturned and historians will scoff at his desperation?

The Gay Pride march had catchy slogans like 'Ab Gurgaon Dur Nahi', Gurgaon is not so remote anymore, to signify that it is now modern and the time has come for its residents to show up in greater numbers and fight the good fight to oppose discrimination against people of all sexual orientations, castes and creeds. A few heterosexual families did show up but they busied themselves with plundering the colourful balloons for their children—showing their dedication to 'family values'. Such people at university in the US are called 'cookie monsters': those who come to seminars to devour the cookies and leave rather than stay and learn something. It is devoutly hoped that this 'balloon snatcher' attitude will change to match the conceit of the city as the city of the new millennium.

The cosmopolitanism of this city has come not just from foreigners but also largely from Indians settled abroad (NRIs) who have returned to retire or to enjoy their second seasonal homes. In fact, those who lived and worked abroad had previously made their presence felt only in the shape of remittances of foreign exchange for their families. In returning to the home country, they bring their eclectic tastes and a brassy sense of fun, even as they participate in religious rituals and gaudy weddings. In seeking a place where they experience the physical comforts they felt in the countries they lived in, and yet longed for the quintessential India while abroad, they find Gurgaon enables their two-tone lives. And the more these well-heeled NRIs and their families occupy the stacks of apartments, villas and professionally designed homes and gardens with twenty-four-hour back-up for water, electricity and security, the more they live in enclaves removed from the crowded old town, just as the colonials once did in their bungalows in the civil lines and cantonments. Lutyens' Delhi and Shahjahanabad are the starkest examples of this contrast. They are insulated from the reality that accosts the average citizens. Chauffeured around in their luxury sedans and SUVs, they find the malls a place for bargain hunting, and have domestic help that take care of home and garden—they feel they can ignore Gurgaon's fundamental flaws at least while they are enjoying themselves. 'Take a drive on MG Road past the malls at night and you will see how "happening" Gurgaon really is.

The pubs are crowded, young men are on the prowl, you can buy some bhang or stronger stuff, and you will see a few foreign blonde women who wait for clients right outside Sahara Mall,' I was dared by a young resident. (I checked. The scene was even more lubricious than I expected.)

The tawdriness of Sahara Mall is outdone by the striking elegance I met at the Urbanist. At the turn of the millennium, Puru Das and Brian de Muro met in New York. The former was in advertising and the latter was doing a corporate job, and both found their love for art, design and elegant living deep enough to leave the tedium of their jobs and move to Delhi. Puru, in a hastily arranged interview in the glamorous interiors of the showroom, told me that their shared passion led them to become co-visionaries and founders of the art, architecture, and interiors design company, Urbanist. Not long afterwards, attracted by the cheaper rents and spacious showrooms, they made the felicitous choice of moving Urbanist to Gurgaon and creating their tasteful design studio and showroom in Plaza Mall on MG Road. After a bit of probing, Puru confided that their 'clientele in Gurgaon was more sophisticated' even though Delhi was the bigger catchment area. Their 60,000-square foot factory is in Greater Noida where they manufacture furniture and the accoutrements they need to dress up the new and bare apartments in the high-end blocks, such as the Aralias and Magnolias on Golf Course Road. Theirs is an aesthetic that is as compelling as it is clean and cutting-edge too. Their own words describe what they do best and the Urbanist website is inspiring to explore:

Our showroom space [in the Plaza Mall on MG Road] in Gurgaon allows us to present not just our furniture, but also a fuller picture of our style. The aesthetic vision that we showcase is the same one we aim to translate into the distinct visual language of each client, maintaining our own voice while capturing the singular tone that makes a home special. This is where we work with clients to develop a palette of materials and to find the points of intersection between our aesthetics and theirs. A dynamic experiential space, the Urbanist showroom is the ideal place to see first-hand our integrative approach to design.

Their bold designs and art collection have been applauded internationally and their clients have wishlists and the wherewithal to fashion some extraordinary interiors. Artistes are often pioneers and Gurgaon has embraced them with outstretched arms.

Gurgaon continues to attract talent of high calibre and over the last decade and a half many more artists and their showrooms have founded handsome galleries and showcases. It indubitably offers a smorgasbord of attractions to the ambitious and upwardly mobile professionals and businesspeople just as it offers an incalculable upgrade to the poor rural migrants from other states of India. There has been a steady increase in the numbers of people with a higher range of incomes and desires who have come to live in Gurgaon in the past three decades. They find the city an ideal destination for their aspiration.

Retail Therapy for the Stressed and the Bored

Just as consumers in the West were happily overeating, the famished middle class of India welcomed a bigger share of the pie on their collective plate. The Soviet Union, a close Indian ally and model, had ignominiously collapsed and after 1991, American consumerism was sucked into the vacuum in India with a vengeance. The infusion of foreign goods and capital and the import of foreign retailing strategies embodied in American suburban-style malls soon proliferated like bacteria in a Petri dish. Even Delhiwallahs were drawn to Gurgaon because they did not have anything as thickly concentrated as the malls on MG Road, certainly not until almost a dozen years later. Clearly, these and its scores of bars and eateries that boosted its image as the Indian city where the prosperous regard extravagant fun as their birthright were not envisaged in the Master Plan of Gurgaon, 2011. They emerged as a potent response to the new affluence and the consumerism it both generates and sustains.

These glass-and-steel structures with their see-through effect at night when the lights come on made them a worthy novelty to gawk at. The brightly lit boutiques with their merchandise on display offer the kind of self-advertisement that conventional architecture and brick-and-mortar do not allow. And the effect is magnified as one sees this on floor after floor, reached by shiny aluminium escalators. In the same frame, I noticed that there is only one working pedestrian crossing light and it is the one on MG Road in 2017, which gave people a chance to cross that road from malls on one side of the road to malls on the other without risking life and limb but, alas, that too is gone.

The toniest of all the approximately two dozen (and counting) malls in Gurgaon is the Ambience Mall in the north-west corner of Nathupur, now DLF Phase III, lavishly built by its present CEO, Raj Singh Gehlot. It boasts 1.8 million square feet of retail space, and each floor, paved in polished stone, runs a full kilometre. And this gargantuan place is chilled to a Himalayan coolth even on a hot day in May. Attached to it is a residential complex, the plush Ambience Lagoon Apartments that overlook a golf course—a nine-hole, landscaped gem. That gives this exclusive enclave, with its luxurious five-star Leela Hotel, the aura of Dubai or Singapore. I entered the mall tentatively with a young companion from Beverly Park who knew it well, to walk from one end of it to the other—a kilometre-long aisle of mirror-polished granite. On both sides of this, spread across its floors, is a staggering collection of boutiques: 300 premium showrooms, ranging from Benetton to BMW, a 50,000-square feet food court with multiple choices from finger food, to a Mexican taco and burrito joint, to one that serves a biryani meal or a formal European repast. There are also half a dozen multiplex screens with the beckoning aroma of popcorn and hamburgers and the fizzing of chilled Cokes with the latest Hollywood and Bollywood films on view. There are playrooms with grandmotherly attendants and snacks for children that permit parents and teenagers to shop to their heart's content without having to deal with whining young children. The men gather around the digital games arcade or in the bowling alley, or gravitate to the pub where a cricket match is on the television screen and hot dogs and chilled beers keep them watching happily. And what really took me by surprise was a small group of youngsters clad in down coats and hats and gloves with thick boots descending on an escalator. I asked them what they might be doing, clad the way they were in the height of the summer. They said there was a full-fledged ice skating rink upstairs where they had just finished a session. We raced up to find that the session was indeed over and a few others were just removing their skates and their fur hats to brave the dust laden May winds outside this refrigerated enclosure. These are daring new ways of entertainment in India and they give Gurgaon a flamboyance that other cities probably crave. All this and more, all arranged accessibly under one roof in a climate-controlled environment, with underground parking to boot, perhaps passé in the West, is an irresistible idea that Delhi did not have until very recently. There is, of course, a hierarchy of malls in Gurgaon, as Sanjay Srivastava discusses, among many other things, in his marvellous exploration of *Entangled Urbanism*.[1] Much also depends on tastes and needs and budgets, so there is no single reliable arbiter of this in the clutter of retail possibilities in Gurgaon.

What is entirely missed or eschewed by the throngs of mall-goers is the old-world, colourful Sadar Bazaar of Gurgaon in its old cantonment area. It has that small-town feel, where wares of all sorts are not only found in the small shops but also on open carts along the main street, and specialized goods—like bangles on Churi Wali Gali—make the experience a different kind of indulgence. The colours, smells, sounds and the business of bargaining with a shopkeeper instead of being in a big store—where a sales person is hard to find and ignorant of where the item you are seeking might be—are completely bleached out in these temples of merchandise. One can touch the items, try them on informally on the roadside itself, and bargain for a better price, and feel that you still live in a world of real people who make a living off the goods on their carts, or make things with their own hands or repair shoes or machinery or a fountain pen as you watch them do it. One can even have a conversation with a real person—a woman on the pavement selling *parandhi*s or braids of tinsel and black thread to add to your hair, as she tells you the secret of long and lustrous hair like her own. 'I use boiled amla to wash my hair and that gives it the shine and silky feel and keeps hair black,' she said, looking at my short salt-and-pepper mop, which told her that I was not about to attach a *parandhi* to my couture. I moved on to a cart that was selling chaat, my favourite teatime snacks, and ordered a plate of gol gappas that I devoured in gulps of delight on the spot, where other customers were taking their turns at doing the same. Perhaps the unmuted spirit of Gurgaon is here, in these vibrant alleys, rather than in the hushed precincts of a mall where McDonald's or Subway or Domino's serve you everything embedded in bland white bread.

The cherries sprinkled on Gurgaon's cake are the many five-star hotels, each with its own daring architecture and claim to fame. The Park Hotel, for instance, boasts a 'kebab factory' that lures those addicted to these succulent and delicately spiced morsels with freshly baked naan that give hamburgers an inferiority complex. Le Meridien, a swanky hotel off the Mehrauli–Gurgaon road and the haunt of corporate clients, has a bakery that concocts mouth-watering confections and cakes and wholegrain breads. The two Oberoi-run hotels in Gurgaon are simply exquisite; they are destinations in themselves for there is nothing comparable in the huge assortment of modern five-star hotels in the NCR. This might sound implausible, given that the Oberoi Hotel in Delhi, built in the 1960s, has a facade about as fetching as a Holiday Inn. These hotels belong to a senior Punjab politician, Sukhbir Singh Badal, who was well connected enough to snag these two industrial plots in Udyog Vihar, get the usual 'change of land use' certificate, and employ the best talent to build two architecturally spectacular hotels, and the Oberoi—a highly venerated international brand with properties that inspire awe in Egypt and Bali or in Jaipur—to manage them. They are a high watermark in design, luxury, and style that even hotels in London or New York would envy. The contrast they present to their industrial setting is even more astonishing when you pass behind their high walls and enter a realm of gardens and waterways. What stirs the soul is Oberoi's Trident Hotel designed by two Thai women architects. At its interior entrance, there is a vast tranquil pool, mirror-like in its stillness, with water dribbling over the stone banks. As dusk falls, a live flame arises magically from the sheet of water that leaves one wide-eyed in wonder. Bedazzled, I chanced upon a wine tasting in the arched and high-ceilinged bar with Oberoi's head sommelier Rakesh Awaghade on a Friday evening; my brain switched modes from academic to lush as I swirled a goblet with a deep red Cabernet and inhaled deeply before taking a sip. It was agreeably dry with a tannic edge and I held out my glass for more. This might be a routine happening in Bordeaux France or Napa Valley in California but in Gurgaon, it was thrilling beyond words (and rapid weight loss for my wallet).

Even the Rapid Metro—a public transportation system superbly engineered, built and serviced entirely by a private company, in trying to catch the eye of those who are wedded to their cars, has become something more than its utilitarian purpose suggests. It launched the 'Joy Express' for children in December 2015, on weekends from noon to 4 p.m. It brings children and their adult chaperones to the Rapid Metro system. Not only does the train run its scenic loop, but it also has supervised games, art and craft workshops, puppet shows, magicians and quizzes which make the service popular and give children a new place to play, learn and socialize. The tickets, available at the Sikandarpur Metro station and online, cost Rs 250 rupees for a child for four hours, and Rs 100 for the accompanying adult, and for working-class children, it's free of cost. This is a bold social experiment to bring people of all ages and classes together, in a city, as elsewhere in India, where the fortunate do not mingle socially with their poorer cohort and it may attune kids to appreciate the Metro as a sensible means of transport, unlike their parents who are cooped up in their cars with varying degrees of road rage as they navigate their way through thick and unruly traffic.

In endeavouring to increase its ridership after a fare hike, Rajiv Banga, the young and enthusiastic successor of Sanjiv Rai as CEO of IL&FS in 2015, has introduced some very amusing and funky ideas that have brought a wider clientele to experience this new means of transport. He has had poets in the coaches, as an experiment to bring literary-minded people to listen and participate in poetry recitals—the cars are silent enough to make this a very interesting possibility for a mobile majlis even as the trains go around on its wonted route. For the sports-minded, Rapid Metro pioneered another first in India—or anywhere else in the world for that matter—called 'Lounge Cricket'. The concept of indoor cricket in a small indoor stadium sounds insane, but it seems to have caught the imagination of youngsters who don't have enough open spaces to play cricket. Such daring ideas would be unthinkable for a staid government-run transportation system, although one lucrative idea has been adopted with alacrity by the main Delhi Metro system. The Rapid Metro leased each of its stations and coaches to a single bidder, a corporation which redecorates and maintains the station as a corporate space with the company's wares vibrantly displayed. The coaches too are wrapped in advertisements in bold and colourful designs and it is the rent from these leases that keeps the company solvent. The second phase of this is nearing completion and soon we will have much of Phase IV and other parts of Gurgaon connected to Delhi via Rapid Metro. Neither the state government nor HUDA have contributed a paisa for this enormous addition to the city's infrastructure.

Other fragments of Gurgaon's incipient soul have come from some of its creative professionals, artists and their patrons. Take Aditya Arya, a renowned photographer, a man with a magnificent obsession who has created a glorious museum of vintage cameras amassed from all over the world in over four decades. Tucked away in the basement of his house in DLF Phase III, Museo Camera is a collection he started in 1970. I first met him in 2013 in Delhi at an exhibition of photographs of Gurgaon by eleven of its best young photographers. He had curated the photographs from the submissions for the Neel Dongre Awards for Excellence in Photography under the aegis of his India Photo Archive Foundation, established in 2008. But nothing in that meeting prepared me for the remarkable achievements of this man, the intensive preservation work of historic photographs done in his Foundation, the students he trains in archival preservation, the exhibitions he curates, and, of course, the astounding collection of photographic equipment. He is a storehouse of knowledge and generously spends time with visitors who come (by appointment) showing them some extraordinary objects that they never knew existed and enlightening them about their historical importance.

Aditya is a self-fashioned man who started from scratch with a keen eye, a small savings account, and a stroke of luck. Professionally, he is a successful commercial photographer in the advertising world, but that is not what defines or drives the man. His great-grand-uncles had a small photo studio in Lahore, Gopal Chitra Kutir, in the 1920s and '30s, where a young Kulwant Roy learnt his trade. He avidly recorded the rich historical period of India's freedom movement with his camera—from Gandhi's satyagrahas to the leaders of the Indian National Congress and the Muslim League, to the early decades of an independent India, with its huge projects including some rare photos of Nehru inspecting the construction of the Bhakra Nangal Dam. Aditya, whom he regarded as a son, was the sole legatee of his huge trove of photos and negatives. Aditya personally supervises the meticulous scanning, conserving and chronicling the context of each photograph. The tome, *History in the Making*, which he co-authored with the historian Indivar Kamtekar, has a fine selection of these.[2]

With the unerring instincts of a bloodhound, Aditya followed the scent of photographic equipment for nearly half a century in the warehouses of ragmen in Chor Bazaar, antique shops, in the reputable studios that thrived in colonial times and in private hands, in India and abroad. He scoured alleyways and attics in Mumbai,

Hyderabad, London, Paris, Hamburg and Washington. The shift to digital photography and computers to develop photos has made dark room equipment and film cameras worthy only as collector's items. And this painstakingly created personal collection is arguably the greatest one of its kind on the planet. I finally took up his invitation to view his museum on the rainiest day in ten years in Gurgaon: 29 July 2016. Driving though blinding rain, I arrived at his gates wading through ankle deep water that was lapping dangerously close to the basement steps that had been sandbagged. He accosted us graciously even though he looked nervously at the swirling waters inching up. We descended the stairs, past a huge camera the size of a commercial washing machine on a stout tripod, its polished wood and gleaming brass hardware announced that we were entering an enchanting world of analogue cameras—a world that enfolds you and gives new meaning to the phrase 'in camera'. This rich repository of possibly a thousand cameras and growing, that ranges from 1880 to 1990, (and 2018, if you count the latest smartphone which does take fairly decent pictures), from the earliest pinhole variety to the Kodak's Baby Brownie box camera that made photography possible for amateurs, to the large-format tripod-mounted Zeiss and the iconic Graflex camera with its flash bulb on an arm, to the miniature Minox spy cameras made by Minolta. There are many other examples of rare cameras, and it was enthralling to listen to him describe their features and how he came by them. He has made copious notes on each, and has carefully filed them in his office on the second floor, where the photographs are also archived. For instance, there were a dozen big, boxy cameras on the floor around a cabinet to which I pointed quizzically. 'These,' he exclaimed, 'are the very cameras that were mounted on the bellies of a fleet of aeroplanes that accompanied the aircraft that dropped the atom bomb on Hiroshima. Of this, 15,000 units were manufactured,' he said, 'and one of them shot the famous picture of the mushroom cloud seen the world over. A ragman in Delhi telephoned me and said that he had a very special K 29 camera. I didn't know what it was and told him that he was pedalling a piece of junk. Later I looked up the model number he had given me and discovered that this was the code of the cameras that were especially made for this historic combat mission. I acquired two of them,' he said, pointing to one. 'And, a few months ago he disclosed that he had a dozen more so I bargained with him and bought the lot.'

The commissioner of Gurgaon and members of the MCG visited Aditya's treasures in 2016 and after prolonged negotiations that were often contentious—I discerned this from Aditya's refusal to reveal any part of them—tentatively offered a vast 15,000 square feet of space to display them in a prime location in Phase IV. They deliberated quietly amongst themselves about the seven crore rupees needed to create and maintain this space as a state-of-the-art museum. The sum sounded paltry when I heard the depth of Aditya's plans. He wants to build not only a stunning display area for his cameras with his curatorial notes on the collection but also a learning centre with regular workshops in every aspect of photography, an archive of all the glass and albumin negatives, the stereo photographs that he has collected, and a dark-room for reproducing photographs from negatives. He is also in possession of the originals and negatives of the marvellous political portraits by the late Kulwant Roy, which would also be displayed. Aditya's vision and curatorship will create a national gem that Gurgaon would proudly house and become an internationally known venue for photography lovers everywhere. It would also become the repository for the relics of other studios that are being dismantled as digital photography erases the analogue age and makes film, on which images were captured, a thing of the past. In 2016 the matter was still tentative, the funding uncertain, the space there, but empty and in need to be furnished into a museum; Aditya waited patiently for the other shoe to drop. Finally, on 8 August 2017, I got a brief message in New York from Aditya: 'Pact inked today,' he exclaimed. The MCG and the Indian Photo Archive Foundation have entered into a pact to create this world-class museum in a very generous space. In mid-2018, Aditya still has to attend meetings and discussions with the MCG but the project is now under way although his hair is greyer. I hope the Gurgaon authorities in their wisdom realize what an enormous asset this will be in bringing tourists, specialists and international acclaim to a city that has found a place on the global map.

Another collector and antiquarian was Gurgaon's own, the late Vijay Kumar Jain, who created the legendary bookshop, Prabhu Book Service, in the Sadar Bazaar area of Old Gurgaon in 1962. My first visit to this veritable storehouse crammed with shelf upon shelf of antique and out-of-print books was in 1980, when two carloads of scholars from the US, including the late historian Ainslie T. Embree, took the bumpy ride to Gurgaon on the old Delhi–Gurgaon road, past the wheat and mustard fields into the alley where it is located. The Jains are an Old Gurgaon family, the patriarch being Vijay Kumar Jain's famous lawyer grandfather, after whom the book business was named. The antiquarian business was inadvertently started when the eldest grandson found his passion for collecting old books, and Vijay Kumar Jain turned his brother's duplicates into a retail business. A large quota of books in the shop were old colonial reports from various government departments—from census volumes to gazetteers, to revenue and settlement reports—a dog's breakfast of hard-to-find documents that could be affordably acquired by historians of that period. Vijay Kumar was proficient, and he soon catalogued this collection and shipped off printed catalogues to centres of Indian studies in Europe and America. He laboured to get an export licence, in the days of the Licence Raj, and once orders started coming in from places as far away as the Universities of Heidelberg in Germany, and Pennsylvania, Columbia, and Michigan in the US, he was constantly acquiring books to fill these large orders, making forays into distant parts of India to ferret them. Gurgaon was, surprisingly, a scholarly destination before it grew into the corporate hub it now is, and Vijay Kumar's son runs the business. Nothing like it exists in Delhi and amidst news of more and more independent bookshops downing their shutters for good, we can hope that his descendants can sustain this precious bookshop. Meanwhile his brother, Ramesh Jain of

Manohar Publishers and Booksellers, had plans to open a branch of his scholarly bookstore that has sustained us over half a century, at Gurgaon where he had moved with his family into a villa in Garden Estate. These were stymied when his land was grabbed by a Nathupur landowner who claimed it as his own. Years of litigation led nowhere and Ramesh still commutes to Daryaganj in Delhi where Manohar is in a large store off Ansari Road.

Another little-known retreat for scholars, particularly those interested in ethnomusicology, is a vast collection of recordings and texts on Indian music in the Archives and Research Centre of Ethnomusicology (ARCE) of the American Institute of Indian Studies (AIIS) in Sector 32 in Gurgaon. The collection has been meticulously documented, and it also has a fine library that includes books, journals and dissertations, chiefly in the field of Indian ethnomusicology. These items have come from the collections of some of the scholars of Indian music who have volunteered their recordings—some totally rare and singular—for the Institute to preserve. With state-of-the-art technical facilities and an archive maintained to international standards, ARCE serves as the model for comparable archives all over the world. There's been special focus on the repatriation of collections held in archives abroad for access to Indian scholars and institutions. It holds frequent seminars and workshops and has ongoing research projects in Rajasthan and Goa, funded by Ford Foundation.[3]

And that isn't the end of our list of passionate collectors and creators who share their treasures so large heartedly. Tarun Thakral is another notable *shaukeen*, who takes his love for old and beautiful things to a fitting climax in his privately created Heritage Museum of Transport. A collector of vintage cars, early aeroplanes and other means of transport, he has created a most singular and charming museum on Sohna Road. It attracts aficionados from all over the country and is also an increasingly popular stop on the tourist itinerary in the NCR. To chance upon a dazzling assortment of a hundred post-war American and European cars gorgeously displayed and annotated, in the pastoral fringe of the city, is to be startled and then overwhelmed with curiosity and joy. And that is not all. Here one also finds aesthetically striking arrays of wheels, of cars, scooters and motorcycles from their simple beginnings to the ornate chrome and steel beauties that speak power to truth. There is whimsy and wit here too—such as a matchless collection of matchbox covers that depict all forms of transportation over the ages. There are pedal cars for children and armoured cars for battle and there are convertibles redolent of cars that would be in period films with dandies in pale pink and cream suits, and Homburgs and white-gloved hands to take a scenic drive with a romantic partner. This is a stylish, Great Gatsby–like experience, which no one with wheels who lives in Gurgaon or comes this way should ignore. It cannot be found anywhere else in the country, not even in a maharaja's stable of old cars—this is one of a kind and leaves you wreathed in smiles and admiration for the fastidious and ambitious Tarun Thakral. The museum has an excellent website that gives a mouth-watering preview, and a route map, times when they are open, and more than a hundred and twenty verdicts of enthusiasts who have visited the museum and accorded it five stars and rave reviews.[4]

It is hard to discover all the people with exceptional gifts who have moved to Gurgaon for the same imperatives—space, security, gracious living—that brought the world of business and banking and trade to this rising city. There are many modern artists who have cut national figures for fame and fortune, whose names evoke admiration and whose exhibits bring, on the affluent art collectors for their exhibitions. Subodh Gupta, who needs no introduction as a celebrated sculptor and artist, his famous tree bearing his signature kitchen pots and pans adorns the garden of the Museum of Modern Art in Delhi. His vast and very riveting collection is on display in an entire building that serves as his studio in Udyog Vihar. On four resplendent floors, there are dramatic displays of his creations with everyday utensils and many sketches and living arrangements in various combinations and permutations, clearly making this place a Mecca for lovers of modern art. My visit there for a celebration in November 2016 with Gail Levin, the biographer of the American artist Edward Hopper, and a fellow Fulbright scholar, was to see a side of Gurgaon that even New York would crave. It appeared like the who's who of the art and fashion world—two hundred celebrities, artists, collectors and interior designers, with wine and spirits flowing and table creaking with a chef's array of delicacies. It beat any of the art openings and it seemed like Gurgaon's cultural life was the picture of good health.

And there are other people of repute—architects, academics, chefs, cartoonists, satirists and commentators with well-known bylines—who have found a comfortable niche in this city of many wonders. Aamir Raza Husain, the playwright, stage actor, director and producer, and his beautiful actress wife and co-producer, Virat Husain, have made their most interesting abode in Phase I of DLF city, which is richly decorated with props and paraphernalia from their theatrical productions and his background as a scion of a noble family of Awadh. Old family portraits, swords, shields and artefacts that could themselves be well worth a visit, and their old-world Lakhnavi hospitality—I was very fortunate to enjoy this when I went to interview them—affirm that high culture lurks in unexpected nooks in Gurgaon. Aamir acted in the film adaptation of Rudyard Kipling's *Kim* and has both historical and romantic roles in his repertoire. Stagedoor, the name of the theatre company Aamir founded in 1974, has ninety-one productions to its credit over time. Their daughter, Kaniz Sukaina, a law student at Jindal University, debuted in *Mehernama*, a play that Aamir wrote and in which he and Virat share the leading roles. He broke new ground and delighted audiences in Gurgaon with the English plays, *The Lion in Winter*, and his own play, *Mehernama*, at the Epicentre in Gurgaon. He was frank about the inadequacies of theatre productions at Epicentre and thought the venue needed a complete makeover by someone who was more involved in the production of plays. The building is a government construction and simply does not cut the mustard as a theatre. Aamir's critique proved prophetic—the place was struggling to survive and the rumour that it will close its doors came to pass in 2016. One suspects that it is too valuable an investment to let it moulder. A dynamic theatre person should be found to lead it, to breathe new life into it instead of the usual indifferent bureaucrats playing musical chairs in a job in which they have no expertise.

And, I was reliably informed by someone who is his neighbour that Gurgaon fans are on high alert for a sighting of the beloved captain and star of the Indian cricket team, Virat Kohli, who has bought a house in Phase I of DLF City. Cricket lovers, and I am no exception, hope that there will soon be a cricket stadium big enough to host Test matches, One-day Internationals (ODIs) and T20s watched by huge crowds cheering in lusty enjoyment. Gurgaon has the space, the youthful zeal and the capital, and if it is planned well, even traffic will not be a problem to accommodate 50,000 cars.

The Kingdom of (Gagan Sharma and His) Dreams

Nothing I have said so far about Gurgaon prepares one for the phantasmagorical complex for theatre, Hindi opera, and song and dance, and a food gallery that opened in January 2010 next to Leisure Valley Park in Sector 29. It is astounding and only after a visit to the place, appropriately called Kingdom of Dreams, can one begin to fathom the place in its architectural, theatrical and ornamental layers. Photographs capture its mystique inadequately—you must see it yourself. And see it I did, with none other than Gagan Sharma, the man who willed this into being, in an expansive and frank conversation on 7 August 2016. He is an entrepreneur and maverick who came to this after many successes in the worlds of commerce, art and hospitality, and the journey is as riveting as the destination. I walked through the ornate floors and up a white marble staircase and finally entered a starkly simple, unadorned buff-coloured office cabin of Gagan Sharma. He was in a plain, white shirt and trousers, his salt-and-pepper hair boyishly rumpled, sitting at a largely empty desk. The walls were bare too, except for a television monitor hanging on one side next to a small wooden shelf that held earthenware images of deities, Lakshmi and Ganesh. Using the land that their grandfather had wisely bought in the 1970s, and key political connections, he and his brother built the famous thirty-second milestone complex of shops and restaurants that was quite the destination in Gurgaon in its formative years. Gagan also built the five-star Galaxy Hotel, and the erstwhile Apra Motors, that was once the largest agency for selling and servicing Maruti Suzuki cars and made him a ton of money. There were other businesses too, like the first horticultural project in India, of exporting greenhouse-grown roses to Europe; the first microbrewery in Gurgaon, and other real estate ventures, including plans to build a casino. But some of these were less successful than others.

On one of his frequent trips to visit his daughter in London, he recalled, he saw the wildly popular theatrical performance of The Phantom of the Opera and was ablaze with the desire to create an opera house in Gurgaon. His Apra Group soon created a partnership with India's biggest event management company, Wizcraft International Entertainment Group, and The Great Indian Nautanki Company was born out of this union. After lavishing Rs 200 crore on the six-acre plot leased from the government for forty lakh rupees a month, an extravaganza the country had never seen before was planned and executed. It was sensational news and its arrival dazzled the entire entertainment industry, including Bollywood. Actor Shah Rukh Khan, one of Bollywood's reigning idols, was appointed as its brand ambassador. How would such enormous sums and running costs be recouped and earn a profit? Sadly, it hasn't.

I took a wide-eyed, open-mouthed tour. A psychedelic melange accosted me—a combination of an *Arabian Nights* scene, a dash of Disney Land, a technicoloured Bollywood set, with the ambience of a rainforest, sounds of the wild included. The flying trapezes and revolving, rotating and animated features of the stage of Nautanki Mahal left my eyes popping out, as I entered the cavernous auditorium with approximately 850 seats, where the picaresque romantic comedy *Zangoora: The Gypsy Prince* is staged live every night except on Mondays. It is a Bollywood opera by the famous Urdu playwright and poet, Javed Akhtar, and it attracted a full house after it opened to the public in September 2010, but by 2013 the novelty had worn off. Showshaa, the second stage of the Kingdom of Dreams, has many theatrical events based on Indian mythology and where the immortal and beloved actor and singer Kishore Kumar's musical legacy is also regularly enacted. To add to this totally incredible viewing experience is the International Indian Film Academy (IIFA) Buzz Lounge, a very attractive bar adorned with film posters, memorabilia and portraits of stars that lit up Bollywood. From here one can segue into Culture Gully that offers the fine regional cuisines of India in restaurants decorated to evoke their provenance. Lucknow, for instance, has a looming cut-out of its famous Rumi Darwaza and a room with white and blue sapphire motifs to conjure a nawabi interior, and the aroma of its famous yakhni pulao and kebabs makes the mouth water. Assam is represented by its elaborate bamboo craft and serves delicately flavoured fish curries. And it all costs a fair chunk of money to view the show and have a meal, not to mention a cocktail, so that a family of four would spend more than ten thousand rupees for an evening's entertainment. Not many, without a company expense account, would be lured to repeat a visit to see the same show (*Zangoora* has been running since the inception of Kingdom of Dreams). The day I walked into *Zangoora*'s theatre I cast a calculating eye on the rows of empty seats and thought that there were no more than a hundred and fifty people in there on a weekday afternoon.

Gagan had a fatalistic air about him. The government is after him for their monthly payments, he has incurred other losses—Apra Motors, the famous cash cow, was sold to the competition, and even his personal stable of cars, that once boasted a Jaguar and a Rolls Royce, met the same fate. 'I now use a Maruti Suzuki,' he said with a melancholic smile, 'but I have not stopped my charity work. Have you seen my *gaushala* [cow shelter]?' he asked. Yes, indeed I had, and had a long conversation with Dr Lokesh Abrol, who brought with him the first team of doctors to Gurgaon in 1991 and started the first multi-speciality hospital and now, willy-nilly, spends his spare time looking after the affairs of the gaushala. Gagan pre-empted my next question: 'No, no,' he said, 'I had never seen a cow at close quarters and was not a religious person. Rajesh Khullar, who was then the commissioner of Gurgaon when the Commonwealth Games were imminent, came riding on his peon's bike to ask Lokesh for a desperate favour. The cows had to be removed from the roads in Delhi and there was nowhere to take them—so would Dr Abrol take charge of a place where these cows would be placed? The government would allocate the land and do the construction of the cowsheds, provide the fodder, but they had no money to pay for the expenses of running the gaushala. If such a location could be found, a beautiful retirement home could be created for these animals that sit about on the roads. Abrol was taken aback, Gagan told me, when on the very next day when he was flying to Bengaluru, he happened to sit next to him and said wistfully that he had made a lot of money but he had not yet fulfilled his father's dying wish to create a gaushala, and asked if Abrol would help him get that done—he would fund the entire project. Their conversation, in 2009, quickly turned seriously productive: Khullar's official predicament with the unwanted cows, Gagan's obligation to uphold his father's wish to build a gaushala, and Abrol's fateful connection with the two men, resulted in the truly remarkable gaushala I had beheld on 16 May 2013. People may be obsessed with cows and banning the sale of beef in Haryana but no one would take care of them.

Khullar made available a field, where the garbage mafia was illegally charging two lakh rupees a month for the dump, as the site for the gaushala. Abrol was horrified at the smells and the heaps of rubbish, but Khullar despatched a squad of MCG cleaners to the spot and in three days the place was clean and promising. The sheds were constructed with unaccustomed rapidity, and in the hurry to get things rolling some extra rows were also built—which would have to be demolished. Abrol stepped in and said that the extra sheds could be used as a schoolhouse and the MCG gave in. The school quickly came into existence and is itself a marvel, I thought, as I leafed through its curriculum and looked at the drawings of the young children who attended the place.

I was exceedingly impressed with the imaginative and nature-loving programme that Abrol had put in place. In the other sheds, 300 cows were heard mooing contentedly, healthy and happy to be off the macadam, chewing their cud of fresh grass and many of them yielding milk for the schoolchildren. Not long afterwards, a shelter for bulls that rambled aimlessly on city streets was built nearby, and the bovines of both sexes seem to have found each other in joyous union. Stressed for funds, the MCG stopped paying for the petrol for the vans that brought cows to the shelter. Ever since that subsidy ended, Abrol said, there are no more cows than are brought here. Gagan Sharma exasperatedly told me that when he visited the two shelters not long ago, he discovered that more that 250 of the cows were now giving milk, and there was so much milk that Colonel Chauhan, the administrator of the shelter, was selling the milk to the public. This upset him—he ordered the milch cows to be sold, keeping only enough animals to provide milk for the students who attend the school. There has seldom been a happier ending to a Gurgaon saga, but this does not mean that there are no more cattle on the city's streets. The *gau rakshak*s, cow vigilantes, that have appeared since the ban on beef might wish to use some of their resources of time and money to build more cow shelters instead of being a menace to Gurgaon's meat-eating citizens.

The incubus of debt and taxes transmogrified Gagan's Kingdom of Dreams into a nightmare. Gagan is almost philosophical in adversity, hoping that the financial troubles will get sorted out, as they have in the past. Director-actor Aamir Raza Khan had warned his friend that Wizcraft was leading him down the road to ruin: 'Gagan is an absolutely wonderful person, but the deal was not viable,' he averred. 'But we hope that something will work out and the government might bail out this fantastic project. It cannot be let to die.'

The Kingdom of Dreams is indubitably a remarkable creation and the government should consider lowering its ridiculously steep rent and save a cultural asset for the people of Gurgaon. It could become a public theatre and opera house with a variety of high-quality productions in a city that has barely any institutions that have live cultural offerings.

However, my hopes are not high. The Epicentre, now defunct, but a building crying out to be refurbished, is architecturally modern in its simplicity and rather unimaginative in its overall personality in comparison but was frugally administered by the government. It began with the promise of bringing theatre to Gurgaon, and it did so sporadically and unevenly for many years. Being an official endeavour, it is insufficiently imagined as a theatre. Two actors whom I met after a show said that their experiences on the ill-equipped stage had been 'simply awful'. One of them went on to say that an architect who had probably never seen a play or even read a book probably built it. In spite of the events it hosted, the Epicentre remained a dreary venue, but it has the potential of a lively venue for concerts and talks and book launches in addition to plays, on the lines of the India International Centre, and someone with imagination fix it. In its existence of a dozen or so years, it remained one of those well-intentioned wannabes. It did spottily sponsor play readings, lectures and performances of Hindi and English plays, but they lacked the zest and vigour that draws people to spend money and see a show. I attended a lecture there on the general ecology of Gurgaon, which explained its rather unfortunate treatment of waterbodies that have either vanished or become cesspools with stagnant water and serve as sewers, and the general paucity of trees. There had been no publicity of the event and I went because the speaker is a friend of mine, but when I looked around the hall and counted, I found barely a dozen others in the audience and none from the management that remained resolutely distant from their own enterprise.

Be that as it may, the unusual medley of cultural, culinary and carnivalesque assets make for a city that is far from the humdrum satellite towns mushrooming around India's metropolises. It has the space, the appetite and resources for a great deal more and I am sure that patrons will emerge from its well-endowed bank of corporate executives who will support a superb cultural centre for the arts, perhaps even a world-class university (Haryana chief minister Manohar Lal Khattar is talking about such a project but I have not read or heard any details). Gurgaon desperately needs to cultivate its cultural and intellectual profile—research and think tanks that draw from the international pool of talented scholars, a hyper-local website that collects news, events and commentaries about the city, a readable newspaper with political sophistication and balance—especially since *Friday Gurgaon* sadly folded—that adds to the academic and artistic depth that a city needs to feel it has arrived, to feel it has outgrown its village mentality. It needs to convert its rich citizens into patrons—much like in the cities it aspires to become.

Eight

Gurgaon's Increasingly Civil Society

It is time to think of Gurgaon, as it approaches the end of the second decade of the millennium, as a growing and hormone-driven teenager with a blend of the brawny scent of a corporate body, the slightly musty odour of governmental apathy, and suffused with whiffs of the fresh and vital aromas of its young and energetic civil society. It is a unique intermingling of the three and one that could be branded and marketed as the 'Gurgaon Model' to many towns and cities that will be built or expanded in the coming decades.

The last ingredient, its civil society, has emerged as a vigorous part of Gurgaon's everyday life, with educated and responsible citizens who do not accept the inadequate infrastructure, public spaces and civic amenities and do not take 'no' for an answer. It is as dedicated to bringing art and culture to a city as it is in raising awareness and action to make a city that is green, clean and has an environment that is physically and socially healthy and harmonious. The citizens, who are coalescing to create a strong and enlightened civil society, will resist any calls to the contrary.

The many voluntary organizations that occupy the space between the public and the private constitute civil society, imbued with the belief that things can get better with better knowledge, planning, and management, which will result in a liveable, even a model city of the future. It prods the government to prevent public matters from stagnating and urges it to entrust to better hands what it has patently failed to achieve, while it seeks financial and operational support for ideas that will make Gurgaon and the scores of towns with similar problems better places to live.

While this is not the place to parse the vast theoretical literature on the definition, meanings and scope of 'civil society', what is germane to our narrative of Gurgaon is to understand how civil society has emerged in this city, how it has influenced its politics, and what its principal expressions have been and will be in the future. In brief and in layman terms, civil society, in this context, is the layer of independent organizations that are the creations of a concerned citizenry and not part of the governmental or corporate machinery— although it often works in alliance with its officials, institutions and corporations. Since economic liberalization began in 1991, the relationship of the state with its citizens has changed dramatically. An independent-minded 'consumer citizen', as John Harris calls them (in Chapter Four), who is more often a woman than not, has emerged as the principal actor on the stage where the new politics of action and activism are at play in Gurgaon and in cities across India. This kind of politics finds its inspiration in international social movements, like the women's movement, the peace movement, and the environmental movement, and deploys the same non-confrontational and non-violent tactics and zeal. They are concerned with civic issues, like children's education, public spaces like parks, pavements, or security, and infrastructural deficiencies. In Gurgaon, they have undertaken a huge range of projects—from the development of the Aravalli Biodiversity Park to the release of public funds for civic improvement, like pavements that do not exist along major roads, to the disposal of garbage and the elimination of plastic bags. Civil society is what makes a city less uncivil; it is its social and practical glue that holds its fragments together.

The commonly used rubric of 'non-governmental organization' or NGO is not quite appropriate to describe these new community volunteer groups. I find the label a trifle condescending since it defines their effort in negative terms—'*non*-governmental'—almost anything that sparkles in Gurgaon could be put in that category rather than under governmental organizations. Also, NGOs mostly have a cadre of paid employees and have the structure of a hierarchical workplace, even though they tend to be far more democratic than officialdom. These volunteer activist groups are formed within communities and neighbourhoods rather than in the workplace and attract educated middle-class volunteers, ranging from intellectuals of all persuasions, to professionals, corporate employees, and retirees among their members. Both, however, increasingly use cyberspace and social media than formal brick-and-mortar offices. So, we have to think about these new-age organizations as a public resource, created by the will and vision of private individuals with the cooperation of both private and public sectors. It is a kind of middle ground that uses voluntary personnel and raises funds to improve the quality of life in the city and within its many beleaguered villages. They are goal oriented, and take up tasks on which they unleash their professional and organizational skills and privately raised funds. They deserve a category of their own, so I call them urban angels (UAs).

UAs, fortunately, have been growing in number in Gurgaon with an agenda that promises a new dawn for the city. They demand transparency, accountability and efficiency in governance, try to hold private builders to their promises, network with the MCG, and with Resident Welfare Associations (RWAs) that are concerned with the practical aspects of maintaining their residential buildings and colonies, creating an intermediate layer of authority that is purely by the people and for the people. They generate projects for the public good that they oversee and underwrite, such as clinics for mental health, schools for children (including those with special needs), library resources for poor children, public parks, gardens, and usable public spaces. Funds were scarce initially, but since the law ordaining Corporate Social Responsibility (CSR) to the tune of 2 per cent of their profits, this has changed; the corporations got the nudge they needed to be philanthropic and also participate in the life of a city in which they had established their businesses. But we still need watchdogs to make sure that the money it generates is indeed deployed in the most effective manner for public and social uses. Efforts at adult literacy, vocational training, and helping poor migrants find their feet in the big and complicated city are some of the initiatives that are currently under way.

This style of politics is about having a voice that is heard (and listened to) in the corridors of power and about empowering the middle-class citizen consumer. Historically, the US Constitution and the Bill of Rights (1787) directly influenced the Rights of Man of the French Revolution (1789). This was a watershed moment in global history, and signalled 'bourgeois empowerment' that gave us the template of civil liberties which all liberal democracies cherish as their constitutional foundation today. So, activism by the well-to-do residents concerned—scornfully referred to as 'bourgeois activism' by their Leftist critics who neglect to acknowledge that they are undeniably bourgeois themselves—is part of the solution in a city where civic institutions are rudimentary or weak, and need the guidance and practical help that these groups can provide. This is not to be confused with other forms of political activism—like that practised by trade and labour unions, who are usually affiliated to a major political party, are confined to the conditions of work and remuneration in the workplace, and are active in the automobile and other large manufacturing industries. Violent confrontations between factory managers and disgruntled workers seeking more pay, as seen in the case at the Honda Motorcycle Factory in Manesar in August 2012 and the workers' strike at the Maruti Suzuki plant in Gurgaon, resulted in harsh reprisals by the management that won the battle in court.

Most of these new organizations, like I Am Gurgaon and SURGE, have developed websites and blogs, use social media as their chief means of communication with growing numbers of members, and are committed to strictly non-violent and legal means to achieve their goals. Whether it be in their protests, demonstrations, or calls to social action like the well-publicized Raahgiri initiative—modelled after the Cyclovia initiative in Bogota, Colombia—held every Sunday morning. It kicked off in Gurgaon on 17 November 2013, an effort to take back the streets briefly from vehicular traffic by blocking a section of the streets with the help of the MCG and the police, and using the space for cycling, plays, games, walks, sing-alongs, and other social activities on a Sunday morning. As the planning and participation in these activities grew, a Raahgiri Foundation came into being and raised consciousness amongst citizens about other civic problems; whole neighbourhoods have been ignited to action to raise money from private individuals and corporate sources that underwrite the cost of the activities and the street food sold. The movement has since spread to sixty other cities in India. The image of insular privilege, lurking in the sullen concrete towers and gated communities of DLF Phases IV and V, seems to lighten as hundreds of people of all ages and means converge on to the cordoned-off streets to march, sing, dance to the sounds of live bands and crooners, or to simply amble on traffic-free streets. True, the assemblage is mainly of car-owning families, which is only 10 per cent of Gurgaon's citizens, but Raahgiri is also a vivid protest against the lack of pavements or crossings for pedestrians and cyclists on major roads, making travel for anyone outside a speeding car extremely dangerous. When the MCG gets some funds, it may well undertake to make the roads less wide and give the city usable and uncluttered pavements, shady trees and less concrete to battle. The *Hindustan Times* on 24 October 2017 reported that the gathering held in mid-October would be the last as funds had dried up even though residents had urged the Foundation to continue this green effort, by then successfully emulated in so many cities. In February 2018, the state government came to the rescue and revived this organization with a one-year stipend. I am sure the Rahgiri Foundation will find a permanent way out of its financial problems because its management has been extremely frugal and transparent and a wide range of residents now take part in it.

Urban angels have gained hard-won credibility and are known for their professionalism and a laudable *disinterest* (not to be mistaken for a lack of interest) in the projects that are planned and executed by these groups. And as far as I was able to glean, the well-to-do officers of these organizations volunteer their time, raise money, and often contribute for the projects to pay the personnel hired to execute the project. The MCG fully understands this and has shown great enthusiasm for many initiatives but its own lack of funds hampers it from offering anything more than moral support. Perhaps HUDA will come to recognize that these citizen groups are professionally and altruistically motivated, rather than eye them with suspicion and see them as rivals or antagonists. Some collaborations have produced celebrated results, and we shall look at the best of these endeavours.

One of the earliest of such groups, provoked by the lack of a municipal body that cared about the young and fast-growing city, was the Society for the Regeneration of Gurgaon and Environs (SURGE) in 2001. It brought together a very impressive list of leaders of industry, CEOs, government servants such as two former air vice-marshals, a director general of police, a chairman of the Railway Board, and notable educators to pay attention to what can be described as the congenital defects of Gurgaon. As of 2015, Subodh Bhargava, once CEO of Tata Communications and CEO emeritus of Eicher, who had also served as the president of the storied Confederation of Indian Industry (CII), is its chairman; and Jyoti Sagar, eminent advocate and tireless litigator against the shortfalls of HUDA and the Town and Country Planning Department, is its vice chairman and clearly the legal mind and ebullient energy behind the organization. This body has done a great deal to bring the fiduciary failure of HUDA and the Town and Country Planning Department to account in a public interest litigation (PIL) that forced them to be audited for the first time. I interviewed him on 8 April 2014, in the office building of Jyoti Sagar Associates, and after an intense hour of listening to him, looking at documents and catching some of his contagious rage against the state of affairs, I emerged enlightened on all that ails Gurgaon. When he filed the PIL in 2010, HUDA had already been sitting on an immense pile of accumulated External Development Charges (EDC). The sum, he recalled, was approximately Rs 40,000 crore, not counting the interest owed on this money held by HUDA. Even in Gurgaon—the allegedly privately run city—civil litigation limps along at the speed of an engine run out of fuel, and the functioning of the courts is almost as bogged down as it is in Uttar Pradesh, which is strangled with red tape.

In February 2007, in utter disregard of all the detailed critiques offered for a draft of a master plan by SURGE, NGOs and RWAs, the Town and Country Planning Department published the Final Development Plan of Gurgaon and Manesar, 2021. This Plan, Jyoti Sagar said, was a typically cliché-ridden document rife with errors, lacunae, impracticalities and budgetary gimmickry. It also did not account for something as basic as population growth when assessing its future needs, as per the summary of their questions of the plan posted on the website of SURGE. The TCP Department, Jyoti Sagar said, was stuck on an imaginary 4 per cent growth, when the realistic needs of Gurgaon were growing at the rate of 40 per cent. He laughed and added, 'They told me that planning was done after a place was populated, not before. So they couldn't anticipate or estimate how much population there would be in Gurgaon in 2021 in their plan. How can this be called a "plan" at all when it is based on gross fiction?'

I nodded in agreement throughout his cogently stated objections; it was a revelation to hear him put forth so lucidly all the things that were on every concerned resident's wishlist. The inventory of inadequate infrastructure, so often recounted, such as inadequate water, electricity, sewage disposal, and rubbish collection, lack of storm-water drainage and discharge, and local public transport were on SURGE's to-do list. The plan is to spur HUDA and the Town and Country Planning Department to deploy serious resources to get the essentials done. 'In 2001, Gurgaon had little or no increased provision for public security, firefighting, parking, schools and hospitals, cultural activities, sports complexes, recreational areas, public parks and walking trails and so on that every city should have,' Jyoti Sagar reeled off the list without a pause, 'but here there was nothing.'

In exasperation at this, he had filed another PIL. This is also making its way through the cluttered judicial system in 2016. The defendants have answered the strong and clearly articulated questions in his complaint only vaguely. Jyoti Sagar's frustration reflects the anger that most residents feel about official apathy for not providing basic conveniences in a city they would like to be compared to Dubai or Singapore.

The Aravalli Biodiversity Park

If there is an archangel among the urban angels that hover over Gurgaon, it is inarguably I Am Gurgaon and its fervent founders. Gurgaon is fortunately endowed with a spur of the timeworn Aravalli range that runs south-westward from Delhi. At its northern boundary, on the Mehrauli–Gurgaon road, is a pair of ridges with a valley sprawled on some 350 acres of scrubland with immense crags, boulders and rocks. Decades ago, this rocky ridge attracted the attention of stone merchants and builders who treated this as an immense quarry to mine. As south Delhi was being built by DLF and others into its various colonies, this area was rapidly gouged. The tracks of trucks, bulldozers and tractors scarred the undulated landscape and an army of men with pickaxes hacked away at the great formations of orange and blue stones. These huge rocks were dressed into small chunks for foundation fill and boundary walls, but mainly crushed for gravel and carted off to the many building sites that south Delhi had spawned. A fine smoke-like dust rose from the stone crushers and it seemed that the planet's most ancient fold mountains, eroded over time into low mounds, would be pulverized into gravel for the thousands of houses. By 1980, the urban onslaught was upon Gurgaon, as hundreds of middle-class families began to make Gurgaon their new home, as we have already seen; the demand for gravel and sand kept the pickaxes flying. In this migration to Gurgaon lay the hope of this quarry to be saved from further degradation.

As fresh professional émigrés from Delhi in late 1990s, the late Atal Kapur and Swanzal Kak Kapur, both gifted and ecologically sensitive architects, and Latika Thukral, a banker who had given up her job to spend time with her family, wound up as neighbours and friends in DLF Phase III. A chance meeting with Ambika Agarwal at a rally—against the illegal dumping of garbage and carcasses off the scenic road that skirts Phase I—organized by her husband, the urban angel Prabhat Agarwal of Aravalli Scholars, led to a decisive conversation. Weary of the complaints that Gurgaon provoked, they agreed to become actively involved in tackling the problems and these three women—Ambika, Latika and Swanzal—founded what is today the most dynamic and active citizen group in the city: I Am Gurgaon (IAG).[1]

Swanzal told me the name came to them as they tried to build an agenda that they would execute responsibly and identify with the new city they had now called home for a decade. The functioning core of IAG quickly expanded to eight people, with a revolving door, as scores of interested residents joined the group. In 2008, in order to raise funds it was obligatory to register themselves as an NGO. 'This way, we began to grow and share our ideas of what to do. Our first project was very modest,' explained Latika, 'we wanted to beautify the roundabouts and triangles on the roads and we got permission to do this because we did not ask for funds but wrote personal cheques to get the work done.' (HUDA and PWD obliterated these in the widening of roads that Gurgaon was soon to experience, and they appear to be oblivious of the meaning of pavements and have been removing traffic lights and substituting U-turn loops in the misguided hope that these will keep the traffic moving.)

'We had other ideas about reducing garbage by distributing cloth and straw bags to discourage the use of plastic bags that were littered everywhere,' Latika continued. They also had bumper stickers printed to curb the danger on Gurgaon's roads and to instruct motorists to brake for pedestrians and other vulnerable creatures on the roads. Latika is I Am Gurgaon's unflagging spirit, be it a time of scorching heat or cold grey smog, knocking on the doors of government offices for permissions, renewals, negotiations, and of business corporations for their CSR funds to keep alive these new and astonishing initiatives IAG has undertaken to make Gurgaon a better place. She and Swanzal also manage the employees of the projects and keep track of the progress of those underway. There are at least eight to ten core members at any given time and they share projects, responsibilities and initiatives to make IAG a forceful engine for change.

On 14 April 2014, I formally interviewed Atal and Swanzal, partners in life and in SAKA, their architectural firm, along with Latika, in the Kapurs' vast and tastefully appointed apartment with views of Gurgaon stretching 360 degrees to the horizon—agricultural lands spiked with high-rises, cranes, earthmovers and skeletal structures that lent a surreal aspect to the landscape. Here was the man of rare talent who envisioned the Aravalli Biodiversity Park (ABP) along with two principal actors who had willed it into existence in the form it was to take. 'The really major thing that happened was the fact that right in our own neighbourhood in Phase III was the abandoned quarry on the Aravalli ridge and it had the distinct potential of becoming a beautiful park,' said Atal. His design for the ravaged landscape was instantly persuasive, to make the park he so wanted, when he set the ball rolling with Commissioner Rajiv Khullar, also the head of the MCG in 2008. He offered his pro bono services to the MCG to execute his design and be the consultant and supervisor for this massive transformational project. Khullar studied the proposition carefully and was finally convinced that IAG and its members were not conspiring to appropriate the land for their own use and gave it his green signal, and the greening could begin. A tenuous partnership between the MCG and I Am Gurgaon was born and the Aravalli Biodiversity Park opened in 2010. It was to be reimagined as a native forest of nearly 350 acres and by 2012 this miracle was in the works.

It began with Atal's initiative to restore this region as a public park that could be used by the residents—a facility that Gurgaon conspicuously lacked.[2] Atal played a crucial role as a consultant to the MCG for this project and reshaped this gutted quarry into an aesthetically remarkable park. To be fair, the MCG and IAG speak in two very different registers and it took a while to become mutually intelligible. Atal envisioned a place totally accessible to walkers, runners and cyclists, so the natural dirt paths were made wide and solid enough to not turn to mud in the next rainy season; the MCG dreamed of income-generating uses, such as an amusement park on the lines of Disneyland and had other even less amusing ideas. Fortuitously and serially, two enlightened and helpful commissioners, Rajiv Khullar and Sudhir Rajpal, took charge and played a very positive role in enabling this park and were receptive to ideas from Atal and the consultants he brought into the picture. An aesthetically pleasing wall, with motifs from nature, was built along the edge parallel to MG Road, and more utilitarian fencing and razor wire secured the other parameters of the park to prevent the intrusion of browsing cattle. A large gravel parking lot (not a poured concrete one), and a landscaped strip between it and the MG Road, with huge boulders sculpturally placed, has given this formerly dusty landscape a visibly artistic tone. Atal also selected and shaped a very dramatic rock face to create one of the handsomest amphitheatres that exists anywhere in the NCR or beyond. This is Atal Kapur's imperishable design gift to the people of Gurgaon, literally cut in stone and likely to survive the next several millennia. It has been a 'standing room only' venue for very successful concerts, play readings, and the hugely popular annual Gurgaon Utsav and many other cultural events. In November 2015, the opening night of the Utsav was dedicated to celebrating the memory of Atal Kapur, who had tragically succumbed to cancer earlier that year. The three consecutive nights of music, recitation of a stirring narrative by the historian William Dalrymple and novelist Githa Hariharan, poetry and play readings with hundreds of residents clapping and cheering from the seating built into the opposite hill, spectators perched on walls and standing between aisles and in the swath of grass before the stage was an incredible sight of the festivities. The star of the show was the dramatic rock-face backdrop of the stage of the amphitheatre itself, strobe-lit as the deeply robust voice of Shubha Mudgal coaxed the crescent moon to rise.

But all this doesn't betray that the punishing struggle behind the scenes to rebuild this degraded environment into a truly sustainable forest has been mostly the work of IAG. Atal wanted native species to repopulate the quarry, a huge departure from the practice of planting exotic ornamentals, like bottlebrush trees from Australia and the ubiquitous frangipani or champa tree from Central America, but in so radical a project he needed help. He summoned Pradip Krishen, a self-described 'ecological gardener' and the author of the outstanding field guide to *The Trees of Delhi*, who had just undertaken a major assignment to restore and create the Rao Jodha Park around the Mehrangarh Fort in Jodhpur on similar lines. Pradip endorsed the idea of native trees in conceptualizing the refurbishing of the entire Aravalli ridge, including the northern spurs of the similarly depleted Delhi ridge, but he did not have the time to get personally involved in the Gurgaon project. But on 1 July 2012, he wrote a letter to the MCG, in which he pointed to the wonders and hazards of the native species project, which is excerpted below:

I have no doubt at all that you will come across citizens who scoff at your efforts and your aim. Why grow a dry-looking thorny jungle, they might say. Why not plant quick-growing, flowering trees instead? You need to *convince* these naysayers, not brush them aside. Since it will take many years for your plants to begin to show their magic, you will need to find ways of convincing these people *now*. They need to be told that their negative attitude is based on ignorance—it is because they do not know how beautiful a truly naturalized wilderness can be. Show them some of the remaining 'jewels' – like Mangar Bani – that are among the last natural landscapes to endure in your part of the world. I am sure that once they see a natural wilderness responding to the changing seasons, they will change their minds and become your allies.

[Fellow citizens] will become your greatest allies if you are able to 'carry them' with you. Tell them what the Park is about, what you aim to do and why … Invite them to give their ideas and suggestions. There is no substitute for the participation of the citizens of Gurgaon in your efforts.

Pradip also suggested that Atal get in touch with the well-known naturalist and environmentalist Vijay Dhasmana, who promptly came to examine the area and grasped the project with alacrity.

Other auspicious factors converged: Sudhir Rajpal, IAS, once the city's deputy commissioner, returned to Gurgaon as its commissioner in 2011. He was eager, willing and enlightened, and clearly saw the environmental and social value of a revamped quarry. Vijay took him to Mangar Bani, a small section of primal forest that is still standing in the vicinity, to show him how he thought the park would look in a few years, and Rajpal played an important role in saving this precious section of the Aravallis. The MCG was created in 2010, but it had not been able to hold elections until 2013, so Rajpal took the reins in his hands and signalled I Am Gurgaon to go full steam ahead. A Memorandum of Understanding (MoU) gave it permission to plant native trees and in general do whatever was needed to raise funds to sustain the park. Latika, Atal, Swanzal, Vijay and others of the IAG team were greatly relieved. For denizens of Gurgaon this was an unmatched coup.

Latika declared, 'We would have no Biodiversity Park had it not been for Rajpal's cooperation and help.' Vijay had already rolled up his sleeves, apprised the group of what the real native species of trees suited for arid conditions were and began assiduously to acquire them;

he also created the nursery of these saplings. By 2016, it was thriving with 300 native species, including roughly 135 that were nearly extinct in the Aravallis. Vijay collected these rare native specimens and seeds from his travels in Rajasthan, Gujarat and Madhya Pradesh, to multiply and regrow the forest, and he is on the lookout for more. The ABD is a national resource because I Am Gurgaon is happy to share the expertise and native saplings with other gardeners and parks. Coca-Cola has become the patron of this amazing nursery and IAG is on a constant quest to get more corporations to donate funds to continue their many other projects in the Park.

With a solid team of workers toiling, it was important to keep this effort going, and a commitment (but not yet a done deed) from the MCG to dedicate the land as a people's park, soliciting funds from a larger number of corporations, was the next step. With all the publicity the park generated, and supported by the other initiative to Plant a Million Trees in the city, in addition to a healthy public–private partnership, I Am Gurgaon began wooing many corporate donors. Latika's conversion to the idea of the native forest impelled her to raise funds, and spurred forty-nine of them (thus far) to make major commitments, as part of their CSR plans, and that has become the lifeline of the park.

KPMG was the first donor and the planting began; even today they continue to give generously. Genpact came next with a substantial tranche of money to expand the greening operations. Coca-Cola continues to underwrite the nursery expenses. DLF contributed tankers of treated sewage water to irrigate the young saplings but it is still holding on to a large patch of contiguous land it owns within the park. The project is so compelling that in the subsequent months; scores of corporate donors came on board with annual pledges, with the largest sums coming from Sentiss Pharma and HDFC Life. Many more, it is predicted, will come forward in the coming years as the park turns into a gorgeous forest in what is now the heart of a concrete jungle. But this relentless grind of raising funds will wear out even the most ardent. What is imperative is to create a permanently registered, legally documented park and an endowment large enough to run all its operations with the income derived from it to sustain this in perpetuity.

A small stream of private funds assured that the quarry could get its makeover. Before planting could begin in earnest, it was imperative to eradicate *Prosopis juliflora* or the commonly called Vilayti kikar that has aggressively colonized the Aravallis, wiping out many native species, Pradip informed me on one of our nature walks, in September 2012. This pernicious tree was imported from South America and planted by the British in 1915. It now is the dominant tree on the ridge that spreads via its root system, cloning itself as it covers whole hillsides while secreting a poison that kills off undergrowth and neighbouring plants. Its leaves are not palatable for browsing and birds will not nest in it. Horrible as this sounds, no one at first believed that this tree had to go, and donors were not willing to give money to uproot trees. So Latika devised ingenious ways of finding or saving money to deploy a small gang of sturdy fellows, equipped with spades, to do the job. What is striking is the visible difference when compared to the contiguous Delhi ridge: the Gurgaon side of the Aravallis are now verdant with native species, but the contiguous Delhi side, which was walled off by its myopic authorities, is an unbroken canopy of Vilayati kikar with hardly a native tree in sight and where no birds sing. Wildlife is making a comeback, with rabbits, civet cats, snakes, moles, foxes, porcupines, monitor lizards, squirrels, and others on the prowl, many of which I have spotted myself. Young saplings are protected with metal cages from voracious browsers, the nilgai or the blue-hued antelopes that call the Aravallis their own stamping grounds. A walk in the park in the monsoon, four years since these endeavours have been under way, is to behold a palette of every shade of green with the young trees now attaining maturity. Perhaps the sight will move the authorities of the far larger confines of the Delhi ridge to follow suit, and perhaps even tear down that wall.

The Aravalli Biodiversity Park has a website that has made citizens of Gurgaon aware of this, and small individual donors added to the park's income stream (Rs 500, recently raised to Rs 650, to plant a tree and maintain it for three years). I would strongly urge my fellow residents to forgo a cup of latte and a pastry in Barista or Starbucks and plant a tree instead.

Other improvements followed. A drip irrigation system now covers more than half the park, its perforated black pipes snake up to large 10,000 litre water storage tanks placed at the high points of the Park to make more efficient use of precious water and save the back-breaking toil of watering plants manually. There are intelligently designed litter bins and comfortable, stylish park benches installed to make the place more hospitable to visitors. A tractor pulls huge piles of dirt up- and downhill, and the fencing posts were installed and painted an unobtrusive green. A few gardeners have now been employed, whom Vijay patiently trains and educates, while a team of labourers dig up unwanted invasive plants and remove the concrete and rubble that was dumped there for years. The MCG supplies the security, paying for only three watchmen for the 350-acre expanse and this, as we shall see, is inadequate. It had better brace itself to take its share of the responsibility in preserving this park and to treat the adjoining acreage, ravaged and overrun with vilayti kikar, with similar respect.

The whole process of developing this land was an uphill struggle and even today, pitfalls remain. Big and small private developers and HUDA were all individually eyeing this land to convert into a concrete and glass plantation of business and residential towers, in disregard of the fact that the ridge needed to be preserved and the forest was slowly growing back. Khullar understood that they had to be kept out of this space but was transferred before he could register this as a permanently protected area. The quarrying was stopped by a Supreme Court order in 1992, more because of the unsafe and unhealthy conditions the miners faced rather than a concern for the environment or the Aravalli's fragile ecology. Enforcement was lax and the illegal removal of stone continued until 1999 when trucks, under cover of darkness, snorted and grunted their way uphill with axle-breaking loads within sight of our house.

DLF still owns roughly 15 acres that remain a large arid patch in the refurbished park. The threat that those acres, and perhaps even the rest of what is now the meticulously replanted Aravalli Biodiversity Park, may be bulldozed to accommodate another batch of the ubiquitous high-rises, or be ripped apart by a sixteen-lane highway, although patently immoral and insane, still looms. It is the bounden duty of the state of Haryana and the MCG to unequivocally declare the region to be inviolable and protected as the country's natural heritage of the Aravalli range and a sacred trust. These dangers have been bravely battled, but given Gurgaon's history of arm-twisting land-use laws, the possibility remains that some future corrupt or ecologically insensitive commissioner may, with a stroke of his pen, erase the years of the reforestation project forever. This must never be allowed to happen.

The Aravalli Biodiversity Park is now part of Gurgaon's scarce natural assets as the green lungs of a city where macadam and concrete are lying thickly over its fields. It has become the space where scores of residents—on average 500 a day—come to breathe, to walk, to improve their health, or to idle the hours away in privacy under the shade of a spreading native tree. Apart from their morning constitutionals they do group yoga, walk their dogs, jog, cycle, or amble, and still others can be found gazing at the stunning landscape with smiles on their faces. As a Rajasthani woman, who carried headloads on building sites, said to me on my morning walk, her silver jewellery glinting in the sun: *'Yahan aake dil khus ho jata hai.'* And it's true—the park infuses a sense of happiness and well-being. I saw a man take a selfie in a clump of tall flowering grasses, smiling so widely that his face was totally creased; others try to capture blooms or birds with their phones, and there are lovers too, who find the vegetation both romantic and a suitable cover. I have overheard conversations in Haryanvi, Hindi, Punjabi, Marathi, Bengali, Tamil, Telugu, Odiya and English in all these accents spoken as we do our daily rounds of this idyllic place. Children race around in this huge natural playground, scrambling up rocks, or playing tag, or flying kites. Far from excluding villagers, like those gated communities, the park is egalitarian. The villagers, who were at first wary of these developments and thought the land might become an exclusive enclosure for their middle-class neighbours, now realize that the place is truly their own, and far more hospitable than they'd ever hoped; no more thorny kikar to contend with. The park has quickly become a vital part of their outer space where they can do things that are difficult to do at home. They come with friends, with lovers, with their children, in colourful jogging suits and running shoes, and many in their saris and pyjama-kurtas; they hold their meetings, share picnics, or just have the pleasure and privacy of the great outdoors to socialize. It is a special haven for women, I learnt on my regular walks, who come in groups from villages as far as Aya Nagar and Ghitorni in Delhi to share moments of privacy with their friends and breathe something purer than the grey, greasy air of Delhi. Some women I met one day wished that Aya Nagar, where a very large piece of land along the Mehrauli–Gurgaon road has turned into a dumping ground for rubbish and carcasses of dead animals, could, with luck and perseverance, meet the same fate as Gurgaon's quarry. 'Nothing like this exists where we live,' one of them said. 'We come here walking from Aya Nagar to get away from our families and to enjoy the air and the birds and trees because our open land smells of rotting dead animals and is strewn with garbage—here it is beautiful and pleasant. This [kind of park] should exist in every city. Delhi does not have the same dedicated people to do this for us; they have parks only for the rich.' Shy at first, many villagers from Nathupur, Sikandarpur and Chakkarpur also come here and even join the formal nature walks led by birders and naturalists, Vijay chief among them. Schools have large contingents of children who come to learn about native plants and observe many of the 150-odd species of birds that now nest here. And if we are lucky enough to have Swanzal Kak Kapoor, the ecological architect, on our nature walk, we are sure to get a sumptuous breakfast and steaming hot tea at the end of the trail. This urban angel has a very large heart and the exuberance of Kashmiri hospitality.

Despite this verdant outcome, there are some who grouse their disapproval because for them this park is a waste of valuable real estate. (Think of how much more value is 'wasted' in the 800 acres of the glorious Central Park in the heart of Manhattan in New York—an area that is totally inviolable. Not even Donald Trump, the rapacious builder and now the US president can obtain himself a few hundred square yards of that to stick up another of his gilded towers.) Here danger lurks with political connections. Some planners along with builders want to lacerate the ABP with a twelve-lane highway to ease the traffic on existing roads, an idea that is totally ridiculous and counterproductive, as we already saw in Chapter Four; others, more fanciful and a little dismayed at the idea of planting only trees and shrubs, have proposed to build an amusement park on the lines of Disneyland in this park; there are others who think that it will be greatly enhanced by instituting night safaris like in the jungles of Kenya, and some who want a café to let visitors indulge themselves and strew more non-biodegradable rubbish of disposable plastic plates and bottles. The mind boggles at the reluctance to accept nature on its own terms.

Unbelievably, those afraid of acquiescing in this superb natural restoration have dismissed it as 'bourgeois environmentalism', as if creating a natural habitat for native trees and wildlife is, somehow, a sham activity the middle-class indulges in for its own selfish purposes and to assuage its guilt. Perhaps they are sociologists barking up the wrong (non-native) tree. I am sure that their (mistaken) conviction will melt away if they spent some time in this park rather than pontificate on it from their ivory towers. Still, others remain distrustful or envious of the way private initiative and the funds from the private sector have created this oasis in the middle of the city. Regrettably, they aim, on one feeble pretext or another, to get I Am Gurgaon to leave, and the struggle for control continues in 2018. This would be unconscionable and counterproductive, and the brilliant work of restoring the Aravallis that has been done so sincerely and intelligently for almost a decade would be undone. It is devoutly hoped that the

MCG, which *owns the land*, will not allow any of those destructive and nefarious schemes to come to pass.

There are some villagers too, based in Delhi, who resent the fencing of the park where they would let their cattle graze. The goats and cattle had so denuded this area that there was absolutely no way to regrow the natural vegetation on the ridge except by prohibiting this practice. A few now have taken to hostile acts to express their displeasure at the cordoning off. Several rubbish bins and benches were once damaged and some villagers litter the place with garbage. In the dry months, the grass burns easily and in 2016, six separate fires were set, it is believed, either by mischief mongers or by careless smokers.

The MCG's security arrangements are pitifully scant with only three night watchmen to patrol this large area and there are no policemen around to arrest those who wilfully destroy things. Vandalism is a worldwide phenomenon and the only way to battle it, as I have seen in the parks of New York, is close the parks after dark, have good security arrangements, and repair the damage immediately and unremittingly until it becomes clear to the vandals their mischief will not defeat the larger purpose of the park. Here in Gurgaon the denizens have passionately embraced the park, now it is hoped that officialdom will also accept it as an inviolate feature of their daily lives, and receive pleasure rather than resentment from its presence. As a regular visitor to the park, I can assert without a trace of hyperbole that to see how it has developed over the past decade is to watch a miracle in slow motion.

'There are very few examples anywhere in the world where a city and its municipal authorities have had the foresight and wisdom to create a natural wilderness park within its bounds. I want you to know that should you succeed in your efforts, Gurgaon will have created something of amazing significance, and it will make all of us proud.' This is what Pradip Krishen wrote in that same letter to the MCG commissioner in 2012. I went for a walk with him in February 2017 and he stroked his beard like a happy man as he surveyed the young trees and began to spout their names in Latin. 'These are native trees,' I said teasingly, 'they would like to be addressed by their native names, please.'

So much more reclamation and replanting is needed to restore the entire Aravalli range to its former beauty that every corporation in Gurgaon should consider giving part of its CSR to this worthy project and the Haryana government should consider making the entire ridge in Haryana as a reserved forest belt—this is a sacred imperative. Aditya Arya, with his Aravalli photo project that was exhibited in Delhi in November 2017, is sending a strong signal to government and business houses alike that it is still possible to undo the harm development has wrought on the Aravalli ridge in the last 200 years with an intelligent and concerted effort. I would vote unequivocally for the I Am Gurgaon team, that helped sponsor the show, to be in charge of this critical and urgent project in Gurgaon.

Restoring the Chakkarpur Bund

One would think that the I Am Gurgaon team would need a sabbatical after the enormous achievement of securing and replenishing the Aravalli Biodiversity Park, and seeing dense vegetation smother the bald and desiccated landscape, but this was not so. But sabbaticals are for academics, not activists, I suppose. They soldier on determinedly— and yet another challenge is being tamed by creating a wonderful new public–private partnership of I Am Gurgaon, The Haryana Forest Department and American Express to rebuild the old colonial Chakkarpur bund or check dam. It is 5.2 km long and runs from the village of Chakkarpur to Sector 56 in Gurgaon. The restoration project was inaugurated in January 2016 by Rao Narbir Singh, the Haryana minister for forests, PWD and wildlife, a curious trinity; perhaps he will carry the message back to Chandigarh to engage in a statewide activity to bring back the aquifers of Haryana. The indefatigable Latika Thukral of IAG, who has undertaken to oversee this project despite her other commitments, took me there in July 2016 and a beautiful first 1.5 km of the dam had been reconstructed in the most wonderful manner. This is one of thirty dams that existed in Gurgaon around the time of Independence but since then, have been either paved over for construction purposes or neglected and allowed to deteriorate beyond usefulness. The object of building check dams is to conserve rainwater, recharge the aquifers, and prevent flash flooding when there is heavy rain; they are internationally recognized as a panacea for arid areas. Now, some seventy-five years after the last one was ever functional, with the proven diligence of I Am Gurgaon, the MCG's cooperation and with the largesse of American Express, a bund will become functional again, with only twenty-nine left to go. This is clearly a way to fight the aridity of Gurgaon while adding some much-needed pulchritude to its visage, and a clear signal to other corporations to point some of their philanthropy to the other bunds that lie neglected.

Special Schools

Gurgaon's civil society grows in diverse ways as more and more urban angels spread their wings. The Indian dream, of free and compulsory high-school education for all children between the ages of six and fourteen, incorporated into the Constitution as part of Amendment 21A (2002) and embodied as Law in the Right to Education Act (RTE, 2009) has, therefore, remained a dream in Gurgaon (and probably in the country as a whole), or should one call a spade a spade and say that the dream is a national nightmare? Government schools are customarily notorious for absentee teachers, rote learning, rusty curricula that do not meet the needs of the times, ill-equipped classrooms and for being without libraries, computers, even chairs or desks. Yet, the poor have nowhere else to go but into these overcrowded classrooms where teachers are as rare as the Great Indian Bustard and the dropout rate is horrifying. Private schools are supposed to reserve 25 per cent of their seats for the children of the poor and the government is to compensate them. The idea was grand but its enforcement, like in all such instances, is less than rigorous.

It's time to think of Gurgaon in broader terms than just a corporate haven with little else going for it. When Japanese residents, who live here now, are asked why they live in Gurgaon, they mention, among other things, its schools, and medical facilities and its superb housing. These exist from the very best to those that have room for improvement—but some of the best private educational franchises have their branches here, like the Sri Ram Schools and Delhi Public School, Goenka's schools, Shiv Nadar School, and other English-medium institutions that are greatly sought after. It is quite astonishing to see how many schools, colleges, academies and vocational training centres have come to enhance the opportunities for the younger generation. These franchises are recognized from their Delhi counterparts and need no explication here. I have talked to the parents of children who are attending these schools and they reiterate what one of the Japanese nationals in Gurgaon said—they decided to move to Gurgaon because there were excellent schools for their children to attend, without the nerve-wracking challenge of getting admission into overcrowded classrooms in Delhi. Needless to say, these are private schools and while they are excellent, they are expensive and have few scholarships, so the expats and wealthy Indians can have assured futures for their children. Poor immigrants are not entirely unhappy since many of the cheaper government schools and private schools are a step up from what was available to them in their villages.

The Government of Haryana (education is a state subject—subject also to its whims and official apathy) has pleaded that it has no funds to execute such a grandiose plan as the Right to Education Act has spelt out. In fact, what resources the governments do have are inadequately deployed and indifferently administered. Given this dismal state of affairs, the government showed remarkable wisdom in 2008 by permitting the enlargement of an excellent school called Vishwas, an inclusive private institution lodged in cramped quarters, to move into the expansive premises of a derelict and abandoned government school. It is an inspiring story. The focused vision and zeal of Neelam Jolly to establish such a facility in Gurgaon, where nothing at all existed for children with disabilities, came to fruition in 2007 in a small one-storey building in Sushant Lok. Her experience as a teacher and therapist at the pioneering Spastic Society of India in Hauz Khas, New Delhi, where children with cerebral palsy were taught and treated, prepared her for implementing the plan of combining health care with education. The demand soon outgrew the space; the number of children with special needs was so great and so urgent that Neelam began to look for a larger place. While scouring the neighbourhood, she found a government school in Sector 46 on a four-acre plot. The building was derelict with broken windows, the floor brittle with shards of concrete lying about. Bats flew in and out of the crumbling structure, its grounds a tangle of weeds and brambles where monkeys and wild dogs had made their home. Neelam was overjoyed—surely the government would not deny her the opportunity to rehabilitate this forsaken school into a much needed place where students with different abilities could study together. The days of educational ghettoes for the disabled were over.

I accompanied Neelam in 2008 to see what she had found to move her tidy little school; I could hardly believe that the ruin would serve at all. She prevailed on the government to trust her project and allow her to use the building and grounds for which she would raise the funds to restore; she triumphed against the usual sceptics. With grit, imagination, hard work, judicious use of meagre funding and unrelenting supervision, she managed the transformation of the place into an outstanding schoolhouse with a garden, trees and a playground in a very short time. The bureaucrats shook their heads in disbelief, I imagine. The attention to detail was laudable, down to the toilets that had to accommodate wheelchairs, and the entire building made user-friendly for children with physical disabilities. Ramps replaced steps and special furniture was designed and built in situ. As a good Haryanvi, Neelam said that she realized a long-standing dream to help the children of this city. I wondered at the possibility of what would happen to Gurgaon schools if they were freed from the clutches of an insouciant bureaucracy and if more such underserved institutions were made over to dedicated educators. The mind boggles at the possibilities.

In building Vishwas—the name, which means 'trust', 'belief'—old shibboleths had to be knocked down. The age-old idea of lumping all 'handicapped' children in a 'special' school is now passé and as per government rules, regular schools are supposed to include students with special needs, but most schools do not adhere to this rule. Vishwas has a mixed population of children from the mainstream and those with special needs, who are taught, at each level, in the same classrooms with a common curriculum. About 90 per cent of the children pay only a token fee of Rs 25 a month as tuition (yes, I blinked at the figure in disbelief) and even receive free uniforms and books if the parents are truly poor and needy. The mix has marked benefits for both groups; the goal is to integrate the two differently abled populations in a classroom, and children who do not have disabilities are exposed to the less fortunate and will, Neelam says, become sensitive to their needs and perhaps to all human beings. However, Neelam added, that the integrated model works best at the primary level but as kids grow older their needs diverge. The school has 280 students and goes up to Class VIII. It is a fully recognized inclusive middle school and has a satisfactory student-teacher ratio of 30:1 with one helper in each class. This last factor alone makes Vishwas stand out as a school where every child, however abled, gets personal attention.

I visited yet again, in 2010 and 2014, to see the place run and was stupefied at how many hats Neelam Jolly was wearing; she was the chairman and the principal, the accountant, the headhunter, the gardener, the fund-raiser, the interviewee (to extraneous people like me), the person who addressed many children by name and had personal conversations with them on her way to the staff room to talk to the teachers. (Luckily, the success of the place and the largesse of corporations have enabled her to hire the personnel needed for administering the institution.) I visited the staff in their cheerful lounge and attended a class with the mixed population and was very impressed. This is what our government should be investing in, I remarked. 'Oh,' said one of the teachers, who wished not to be named, 'the DC [district commissioner] and others inspected the school and promised to give a sum of rupees ten lakh only if we did something innovative!' Another teacher who also spoke anonymously, said, 'They did not think that this school was innovative enough. The DC did not give any ideas of what we should do to be regarded as "innovative". It was a ploy to dodge giving us even what they had said they would give. I am from Gurgaon and I know how little the government cares for education, and they really have no understanding or sympathy for why we even bother with the children with special needs.' I nodded, sipped my tea and thought: 'That may be true, but we have private citizens like Neelam and her well-chosen staff who will do what they can and more to change this ignorant stance.'

Vishwas, with its range of extra-curricular activities, such as special art workshops, special sports, yoga and theatre, and its many annual events, and its three school buses, two of them with hydraulic lifts for wheelchair users, is a complex and expensive affair to sustain. They also have a programme to train teachers for students with special needs and have workshops for parents where they can learn the skills they need to deal with such children in the most beneficial manner possible. Their operating cost in 2016 was Rs 700,000 a month, which included salaries for teaching and maintenance staff and the upkeep of special equipment in each classroom.

The government does not contribute any funds to run the school; fund-raising, from corporations and private sources, is done every term and adds greatly to the exhaustion and tensions of those in charge. Neelam is trying to eliminate this major anxiety by building a corpus of money that would serve as a permanent endowment for the school so that they could exist on the interest (it is a tax-free institution) and make their budgets based on the assured resources. The drive is on, but the amount collected so far is a paltry one, and efforts to raise funds will be redoubled in the coming school year. Any corporate manager can calculate what the endowment should be to yield this monthly income; I hope they will step up their donations to build up that corpus. The greatest gift an institution can be granted is an inflation-proofed, anxiety-free running budget and autonomy to shape its own aims, goals and curriculum, and in recruitment of teachers. Alongside, it can be open to periodic (three to five years) check-ups from a body of professional educators constituted for this purpose.

Equally inspiring is the story of Happy School—which needs to be told because it is a testament to the generosity and dedication of one Kamal Capoor, an urban angel par excellence, and a compelling tribute to the wonderfully civic-minded people who have come to live in Gurgaon and have laid the foundations of its civil society. I visited the Capoors in their home in Phase I to find out how this transpired. Her husband, Harish Capoor, is involved in the ennobling task to train and organize employees to clean streets and collect garbage in DLF's colonies. In 1998 they moved to Gurgaon, which made it inconvenient to commute to Delhi for her job. 'So,' she said, with disarming modesty, 'I sat at home.' She continued:

At home, I noticed that on the Silver Oaks apartment construction site in our neighbourhood, the children of the construction workers were playing in the dirt among the piles of building materials. I brought four of them home, cleaned them up, and fed them, and after a few days of doing this I started teaching them. And this was happening outside, so passers-by would ask me what I was doing and I told them that I was teaching these children. They immediately offered to help and soon there were others also teaching and some brought in books, food and clothes and before I knew it, there were fifty children coming in regularly to learn. So we moved operations from my lawn to the wide part at the top of Silver Oaks Road. It was right on the road under the trees, and meanwhile more and more volunteers showed up and now we had a hundred children. Even a beauty parlour sent in their hairdressers to give the children haircuts. Doctors came and checked the children right on the road. Some donated furniture and someone gave us an almirah to keep our books—right there on the road. At this point DLF asked us to move to their green belt, under the trees in the open air, and this was glorious. Our student numbers grew to 250 and the volunteers also grew. Not a single one asked for payment, and they were of all ages, mostly retired teachers from very good schools—DPS, Goenka, Heritage—all working hard and using donations and the kindness of strangers to manage this school. We have an amazing group of teachers—they were willing to knit scarves and woollen sweaters for the kids: some stitched clothes and even made costumes for their plays and outfits for the sports, and donations poured in—shoes, socks, woollens—for these children. We have picnics and collective birthday parties for all of them, which they never had before, and the corporates started giving help to organize events and transport children for picnics—especially the Indian branch of Corporate Executive Board (CEB, now Gartner) that started to donate milk to these children and does so even today. They also claim that ever since the company got involved in this charitable act their shares have gone up in value.

But just then, with 250 children attending the school in the green belt, HUDA's officials came and objected to their 'encroachment' on the green belt and wanted them to 'clear off immediately'. The project stalled, Kamal Capoor went with an influential person to Chandigarh to stop the eviction. She relates the story further:

There a very kindly officer of HUDA promptly rang his counterpart in Gurgaon and said that these 250 children and their teachers had to be given a schoolhouse. There was an abandoned school building on an acre of land upon which I had my eye, so I asked for that, even though my friends considered this very foolhardy. Out of the blue, my request was granted and we immediately set about rehabilitating the building, planting a thousand trees on the grounds, making playgrounds for games, getting the furniture for the classrooms—we had twenty-five classrooms on the ground floor of the primary school.

In 2012, a very nice commissioner of the municipal corporation, Mr Khullar, IAS, came to see the school and went to every classroom to see the children and the staff and declared it a very wonderful learning environment. He tested the children of class five—asked if they could recite the 17 and 19 times tables, and to his utter surprise two girls did so flawlessly. He was so thrilled, he rewarded the girls with a hundred-rupee note each and planted a kiss on the forehead of each. They were thrilled beyond measure; the others were also very encouraged by his kind gesture. Then he asked if he could help in anyway and I immediately said that we needed more space since we had over 400 children on the premises. After some discussion, Khullar agreed to build us another floor of classrooms even though this hadn't been done before in a government building, because they are all single-storeyed. He then said that this second floor would be his gift to the school. This way, the playgrounds for various sports—cricket, football, tennis, table tennis, and badminton—would not be reduced in size, nor any trees cut. He was as good as his word and the second floor came up within a year. Now they said they must call it School No. 46, since Happy School was not a name the government would accept for a government-recognized school. I have never had to raise funds or ask for money—it all just keeps coming and more and more children seek admission here.

The amazing thing is that there are three other government schools in the neighbourhood of Happy School, but they have barely any students or staff, and are far from happy places. They all need a serious upgrade.

In visiting other government schools in 2009-10, where no new ideas or energy had penetrated the thicket of indifference, I was not ready for the dismay I experienced as an educator. I walked around in unkempt premises, with dusty classrooms, the durries on the floors on which the students sat were stiff with dirt; the stench of the bathrooms pervaded the premises, the equipment was either broken or non-existent, there was no chalk to write on the boards, and no chairs for the students to sit on. Most troubling was the discovery that some teachers were absent from the classrooms without notice. One of those who was present, spoke to me in strict confidence—in fact she was nervous to reveal her name, so I called her 'behenji' or sister—and she said in Hindi that teachers were not recruited on merit, but for the money given to the chief minister to buy a position, and this sometimes amounted to several lakh rupees. It is seen as an investment for getting a regular salary, perks and a pension upon retirement and free medical services. I mistakenly thought she was exaggerating. After a bit of research, reading old newspapers and talking to those in the field of education, I discovered that corruption was endemic and began, unsurprisingly, at the top.

The Chautala JBT Recruitment Scam, as it is called, on the recruitment of 'junior basic teachers' is truly shocking in its venality.[3] In summary, Om Prakash Chautala, who had three stints as Haryana's eighth, eleventh and thirteenth chief minister during the years 1998-2005, was personally embroiled in a fraudulent and lucrative scheme in selecting teachers. When uncovered, it was found to be the reason for teacher absenteeism in schools across Haryana. More than 3,000 unqualified persons were appointed as primary school teachers on payment of the sum demanded of them to buy the position. Several lakh rupees per slot were received in return for the permanent government job—no qualifications necessary. A majority of the appointees were hopelessly inadequate for the job, some even illiterate. A CBI investigation was ordered by the Supreme Court during the term of the NDA government and the swindle was finally exposed in June 2008 with Chautala and fifty-three others charged in connection with the appointment of 3,216 junior basic teachers in the state of Haryana during 1999-2000. In January 2013, a New Delhi court sentenced Chautala and his son Ajay Singh Chautala to ten years' imprisonment each under various provisions of the Indian Penal Code and the Prevention of Corruption Act. No fines seem to have been levied for stealing state funds, and no restitution demanded, nor does Chautala appear to be disqualified from standing for public office again. Nothing was said or done about those thousands of teachers who populate these schools and don't show up for work—the government school system is horribly broken and it will be difficult to find enough good Samaritans to mend it, one school at a time. This scam explains why government schools are so neglected, the students barely getting an education and even the poorest migrants seek to send their children to private schools enduring great financial hardship. The urban angels are far outnumbered by what must be called 'urban demons', and Chautala and his co-conspirators are a fine example of that ilk.

Again, in stark contrast to government-administered education, another exceptional private individual, Prabhat Agarwal, has created a little oasis for young students called Aravalli Scholars in 2008. His wife, Ambika, is a founding member of I Am Gurgaon, as discussed earlier, and they make a remarkable couple with their rare spirit of public service. Prabhat gave up a successful career in the corporate world to dedicate himself to giving the underprivileged a better chance at learning. He has established a small library and reading room in a rented house in an alley in Sikandarpur abadi. The objective was to give promising students a place to study, with computers and Internet, books, and a lot of mentoring. It also has the value of a common room where young people can meet and talk since their homes do not have fans or adequate lighting, and certainly no space to invite anyone in; and Prabhat's generous supply of snacks—all organic, delicious health foods—and a drink that I relished, sattoo, made from roasted gram flour and drinking water. The books are well thumbed and can be borrowed and taken home or read at the large table in the well-lit reading room. Prabhat provides lunch and snacks because, as he says, many of the teenagers who come there are growing children and need better nutrients to stay alert and be strong. The students who come to Aravalli Scholars are children of migrants, who have 'less interface with the original inhabitants of Gurgaon than with people from Odisha, Bengal, Uttar Pradesh and even Bangladesh'. These people live in the shanties in the interior of Sikandarpur, and my visit there confirmed that their homes looked exactly like the rows of shacks I had visited often in Nathupur. What I had once seen, twenty years ago, as a four-acre pond, in the heart of Sikandarpur, where women were washing clothes and utensils, and the water was clear enough for children to swim and splash in, is now a dark green, greasy shrunken cesspool, perhaps less than a quarter acre in size. No sewage disposal arrangements exist; with the crush of thousands of new inhabitants sewage flows into this pond and it does what cesspools do best: breed mosquitoes and flies and every variety of intestinal vermin, and produces a most insalubrious environment.

What Prabhat has on his agenda, in collaboration with I Am Gurgaon, is to turn the cesspool back into a healthy pond where hundreds of birds flocked, fish fed on the mosquito larvae, and water lilies once grew. The villagers who own the land where the shanties and the multi-storey tenements rented to migrants are located cannot do anything about the unsanitary conditions—and during my visit in 2013, the MCG had done little to improve the situation. The village's natural drainage, in the form of channels and torrent beds, have been blocked, filled and paved over to construct the parts that the city needs to move its ever-growing vehicular traffic. Prabhat showed me the map of Sikandarpur on his computer and how its fields had now become part of its Metro station, almost obliterating the space where the fish and meat markets were formerly spread and where a small sliver of them still remains, and how the ecology of the entire area had been damaged by the thoughtless pouring of concrete to build the Metro station and its jumble of access roads. What takes one's breath away (actually it doesn't if you remember Nathupur's interior) is that this squalid village, so well hidden from the luxurious heights of the towers of Global Business Park which stands on its erstwhile fields, is the most expensive rental real estate in Gurgaon.

'Volunteer ladies' teach English to the villagers. Prabhat pointed to the rather quaint architecture of a building called City Court, with its clock tower: It was built by Kamaljit, thirty-five, who owned the land and is wealthy but not educated. He sells the water from his tube well to other residents. Modernity has taken its toll on the simple lives of farming families—they have money but they also have regrets: losing the way of life when they were the envied lot in their village—now they live in the shadow of a large corporate elite and resent the newcomers who regard them as crude country bumpkins. A six-lane highway is being built from Sikandarpur all the way to Shankar Chowk to NH-8 and will further fragment their village. This, they informed me, was a 'plan by DLF'. It does not care about what happens to their lives now that it has their lands.

I have already described the government school in the village of Nathupur (Chapter Six) to give a glimpse of what exists beyond and behind the skyscrapers, in the heart of the villages and in other city government schools. It is nothing short of scandalous to have this gaping chasm between the high standards of these private institutions and the public horror shows that pass for schools. Even low-ranking government officers eschew government-run schools when it comes to educating their own children, and that is an honest indictment of these institutions. The esteem for teachers in government schools is deservedly low and this has become a vicious cycle—they know they are despised and ill paid, so they are absentees and their students remain illiterate even in class six, which leads to further denigration of government schools and their teachers.

That said, it is not as if all is splendid in the private schools. There are some bad private schools too that have mushroomed near the villages absorbed by Gurgaon, that profess to be 'English Medium' or 'Convent Schools' where the standard of teaching is poor and the fees are high. In other words, education is in a state of crisis in Haryana and it will take thousands of people like Neelam Jolly, Kamal Capoor and Prabhat Agarwal to breathe fresh life and ideas into an outmoded and very poorly administered system. The alleged 'demographic dividend', which is a comforting way of thinking about the enormous Indian population, is a demographic liability in my view as an educator. Millions of the young children, even in our modern cities, are getting at best a totally inadequate education that will not be of much use to them in leading lives enriched by learning or prepare them to do anything other than low-paid, low-skilled jobs. It is a crisis that has a solution writ large in the dedication of the urban angels that run Vishwas, School No. 46 (formerly Happy School) and Aravalli Scholars and the models of learning they offer—but is the Haryana administration moved enough by these efforts to emulate them? It is the state of Haryana that has snoozed through the alarm bells that the Chautala scam rang nationwide. Putting him in jail was a good move, but rebuilding the schools he destroyed must follow.

A city that generates the ample revenues Gurgaon does could, if the government had any commitment to education, uplift all the schools with motivated educators, good libraries, and modern educational technology. The state needs to create a cadre of teachers— educated, selected and trained, much like IAS competitors, with salaries and perquisites to match, to draw some of our best minds into the imperative business of educating the generations to come. Otherwise the only things government schools will teach is how to spell 'doom' for a nation of hundreds of millions of bright, young children who cannot afford private schools. Privatizing education is not the answer, but pumping money into it and getting well-qualified teachers to run it is. In wealthy countries like the United States and those of the European Union, it is the government that provides excellent free education to every child until class twelve in fine government schools, run on the money obtained from property taxes—with draconian enforcement of truancy laws for students and competency standards for teachers. This is something to emulate and the Haryana state government is being sent a loud wake-up call. If we had a first-rate government school for every fast-food restaurant in the city, Gurgaon would be the shining new educational destination in the land.

Just as I thought I had plumbed the depths of the deficiencies of government schools and offered my solution, the front page of *The Times of India* of 12 July 2016 reported that government schools in Gurgaon were unpardonably understaffed—some fifty of them had only a single teacher on the payroll. The travesty this makes of education is difficult to describe, but there is small comfort in seeing that things have hit rock bottom—they cannot get any worse. I reckon that for every Prabhat Agarwal, Kamal Capoor and Neelam Jolly in Gurgaon, there seem to be a thousand unqualified and corrupt persons masquerading as teachers since the JBT scam who are not held to account. A shudder passed through my frame; teaching is a vocation, not a traded commodity, but not when a chief minister is the prime entrepreneur.

Before we begin to think of Gurgaon as an entirely dismal educational backwater we must remind ourselves that the literacy is at 83 per cent and thousands of educated, professional and middle-class migrants, who were mercifully educated elsewhere, have tipped the balance and fine private schools have grown in number to make Gurgaon a rather desirable place to get an education. The gist of many random conversations with dozens of well-to-do residents of Gurgaon with school-age children is this: They seem unanimous in their view that Gurgaon *is absolutely the best place to find a good school for their children.* This too is true. Delhi is tough, the schools are overcrowded, getting admission into a desirable school is next to impossible. The student–teacher ratios in Gurgaon are much better in comparison, it is far easier to let the children participate in extra-curricular activities. Many claimed they moved to Gurgaon once their children got admission in schools here.

Some of the most reputable schools in the country have their branches in Gurgaon. Foremost among these are The Shri Ram Schools (TSRS), established by the late Padma Shri Manju Bharatram, under the aegis of her family foundation that has supported higher education at the Lady Sri Ram College for Women and The Shri Ram College of Commerce in Delhi. She brought her sensitive and innovative perspectives first to primary education and founded a primary school in Vasant Vihar in Delhi in 1988. At its heels came the senior English-medium, co-educational senior school on Moulsari Avenue in Phase III of DLF in Gurgaon, a school that offered not only a CISC (Council for Indian School Certificate) or high school diploma, but also the coveted International Baccalaureate, a firm stepping stone into a good university anywhere in the world. It has students with special needs that are integrated into the classes and offers scholarships on merit. There is a quota for poorer students who cannot pay the fees. The success of this school has been so remarkable that Manju Bharatram then founded the Aravalli Shri Ram School in Phase IV in Gurgaon, which educates children from kindergarten to class twelve. The teachers I have spoken to at the two campuses in Gurgaon say that it was her peerless vision that made these schools so outstanding. Of course, the academic standard is arguably the best in the country, said Gita Chopra of the Aravalli campus, 'and there is a lot of emphasis on the positive sides of Indian culture, extra-curricular activities, and on teaching children the meaning and value of integrity'. These schools are consistently rated among the best in the country. What keeps their edge is the high quality of the teachers it hires and the administration's continual efforts to upgrade their pedagogic skills in special workshops, lectures from internationally renowned educators, and getting students and teachers to read as much as they can. I have met students of this school and found them excited by the books they read as they spoke enthusiastically of the DEAR period—when you simply **D**rop **E**verything **A**nd **R**ead. The teachers and students of The Sri Ram Schools have embraced this concept, originally borrowed from the New York schools. Unlike many of the borrowed ideas from the US, this one seemed well worth imitating. In an age when technology has reduced most teenagers to 'thumbs-only' action on their smartphones, 'it was a pleasant surprise to encounter pupils who looked forward to this period and read books they loved,' Lekha (Chotie) Gandhi, a retired librarian of the Aravalli Shri Ram School, told me. 'Our library is not only a place where books are checked out and in, as in most schools, but a very exciting place. It is about as much an interactive space as a library can be. The children have reading workshops. Authors are invited to introduce their works to the children to inculcate a love of reading from a very young age. This is in the primary section of the school.' So, the reputation for Gurgaon having so quickly become a place for excellent schools is well founded. Busloads of select students are driven from Delhi to Gurgaon to attend school and it is the millennial generation that speaks of it with fondness.

Both the rich and poor feel the same way about education: They univocally believe there's nothing more important than their children's education and they're prepared to make every sacrifice to give them that. (I wish the state government had receptive ears.) Checking with two sets of parents whose children were attending these top schools, I gleaned that the average annual expense of attending one of these schools easily added up to a total of three years of the average annual salary of a full-time maid in 2016. The monthly bus service and school meals alone cost as much as the monthly salary of my part-time cleaning woman. There is also a capitation fee—euphemistically called an 'entrance fee'—that tops the annual salary of a full-time maid, and there is a 'refundable deposit' of over twice that in many privately run schools. Yet, there is a scramble for seats in these institutions, and this clearly is a reflection on the pool of residents that have well-paying jobs in the city; and the inability of any of their servants to afford sending their children to such schools. There are also the aforementioned third-rate 'copy-cat' schools where the owners have taken the entrepreneurial opportunity to open the avidly sought-after schools with fancy names where the teaching is allegedly in English. Some of them are referred to by a teacher as 'tuition fee factories', where the owners collect the fees in cash and provide small, bare classrooms crammed with forty to fifty children, some seated on the ground, and a teacher leading a rote recital from a textbook, the 6 times table as the sole duty of her job in a kingdom of parrots. Other schools actually do a halfway better job but it is hard to know which is which. These absorb the huge demand of the lower-middle class for good schools without adhering to the standards of the known franchise and missionary schools. It falls to the lot of the children of the poor migrants to fill the seats in these institutions to get a dubious schooling at best. And they are hardly affordable.

On a visit to an English medium 'public school', in April 2018, I found the two teachers and the principal very well spoken and facilities adequate, although squeezed into a small plot on the edge of Nathupur. They charge Rs 23,000 annually for kindergarten goers, although this included a set of uniforms and class books and stationery; the cost increases every year as a child progresses to the twelfth class. These fees are an insurmountable barrier that perpetuates a permanent underclass that will never match its knowledge or skills with those who can afford them. One shrugs wearily and says: So, what's new? It is for the state government to take better care of its 'subject': education.

Hospitals, Clinics and Medical Tourism

Health services and an English education for their children are ranked as equals in the list of priorities for denizens of Gurgaon. Shortly after we moved to our house in November 1997, I remember our thirty-year-old cook lying unconscious on the floor. I panicked—he had served us our dinner an hour before and had retired very cheerful. I didn't know what was wrong, but he was breathing, so I calmed down and rang our trusted doctor and friend, Malkit Law, who luckily lives in DLF Phase I, and asked what we should do. It was late at night so she recommended we take him to a small clinic called Uma

Sanjivini, on the edge of the Phase II market square. I paid Rs 100 to get him admitted, but the sole doctor on duty was attending to an emergency, so the nurse—the only one on the premises—saw him, administered a glass of saline water which worked as a gentle emetic and Pran Singh (name changed) retched and vomited before he opened his bloodshot eyes. The nurse was very brave to handle the inebriated gent and walked him back to our car. I asked what I should do to help him and she said, rather coolly, 'Don't leave alcohol lying around the house. It is prohibition,' she added, 'so no alcohol in the market.' I came home to find that her guess was correct; our duty-free bottle of single malt whisky had been drained and had pickled Pran Singh's brains. Gurgaon was officially wet again on 1 April 1998. Now in 2017 we are living in a city that has 277 bars and dozens of liquor shops and country liquor thekas, and some of the latter are Government Approved Drinking Places, and booze is enriching the state government with the exorbitant GST (goods and services tax) they collect.

That night I had lain awake wondering what would happen if my husband, Philip, or I had a medical emergency in Gurgaon. Where on earth would we go? Well, twenty years on, that question is still valid because the choices have so proliferated that it is truly baffling. Will it be Max, or Medanta? Fortis or Apollo? Privat or St Stephen's? The Ayurvedic treatment place or the practitioner of homeopathy or acupuncture? There are at least a dozen large reputable hospitals, among the country's best, and now one chooses by speciality to match the ailment. It is also a city studded with clinics, including ones for infertility and abortions, pharmacies, doctors of all specializations some of them internationally famous, who have made Gurgaon their home, and it is on the map of the planet as a destination for medical tourism. I wouldn't have known what that phrase meant earlier, but today news about people travelling to Gurgaon from Colorado and Cincinnati and other cities in the United States to have affordable kidney and liver transplants or knee replacements or cardiac bypass surgery have created one more reason to travel to India.

My curiosity about this subject was piqued when I was on the subway in New York and sat next to a middle-aged man reading an Indian novel in English. He looked up and asked if I was Indian and I nodded. He told me that I came from a land of amazingly gifted doctors. He had needed a cardiac triple bypass as his only hope for life, and he didn't have medical insurance so he couldn't afford the surgery that would have cost him upwards of $250,000 in 2015. He became depressed and was preparing for that massive heart attack that would fell him, when a friend, who had just returned from a liver transplant in India, strongly recommended that he get in touch with a hospital in India and see what they could do. Within ten days of his inquiries he was in a city called 'Grrr-gown' (an expressive name, really), inside a very fancy hospital called Max. He had bought a medical package from an agent that included getting the visa, round-trip tickets to Delhi, and covered the hospital stay, diagnostic investigations, anaesthesia, the cost of the surgery and post-operative care, liability insurance, all prescribed medications, nursing, physiotherapy, rehabilitation *and*, if you please, a three-day vacation in a five-star hotel in Agra to see the Taj Mahal. Everything went smoothly—the 'doctor was a gem and the nurses kind and lovely', the room 'perfect, clean, cool, with big windows' and the experience was 'life-saving, the Taj Mahal was out of this world'. It all cost under $20,000, he said. 'I paid by a cheque to the company that made my arrangements and they were flawless. I haven't felt like this since I was forty and I still have my savings.' He was sixty-one years old with rosy cheeks and a broad smile.

Frankly, I was dazzled especially because this happened to him in Gurgaon of all places, and he could afford it. The travel agent had contacted the speciality hospital and the surgeon, and forwarded copies of the medical reports his doctors had provided. It was all professionally managed. Gurgaon has become even more sought after as a medical destination since Medanta Medicity joined the pool of possibilities.

Yes, the hospitals in Gurgaon are indubitably world-class in the quality of their services, accommodations, and emergency care, and they offer the gamut of health and healing procedures and processes. The surgical range here is jaw-dropping: from removing a tumour to complicated organ transplants or delicate laser eye surgery, or even the cosmetic nip and tuck to smooth wrinkles, is available, for a price to Indians, but very affordable for the medical tourist from the US where medical costs are astronomical and medical insurance prohibitive. Anything an American hospital can do we can do better (and cheaper), seems to be the sales pitch. What's more, these hospitals look like five-star hotels with the design, amenities, furnishings, and medical equipment that I have not seen even in hospitals in New York. Gleaming Italian marble, German bathroom fixtures, an uncommonly high standard of hygiene, banks of well-equipped ambulances, including the interiors of the three ambulance helicopters outfitted like operation theatres I saw at Medanta that looked like props in science fiction films.

There were 103 listed hospitals in Gurgaon in 2011; I am sure that this number has grown by 10 per cent every year. Every speciality has attracted finely trained talent: oncology, cardiology, pathology, orthopaedics, endocrinology, gastroenterology; the list is exhaustive, and there are dozens of dentists and eye clinics and ophthalmologists. The Shroff Eye Centre is reputed to be among the best in the country and I was personally treated by a marvellous retinologist, Dr Darius Shroff, who administered the periodic injections in my eyeball in a gentle and reassuring fashion taking the greatest care to protect me from infection. Some of the best pathology laboratories are also based in Gurgaon, including Quest, the one I use in New York, and facilities for MRIs and CT scans are readily available to those who can pay a fraction of what they cost in the US. There are other health facilities too to stay in better health—gyms, weight control centres, physiotherapists, and those who deal with the disturbances of the mind. And if you really want an esoteric experience, try a faith healer, a shaman, or a guru.

I asked Dr Naresh Trehan, chairman and heart surgeon at Medanta, about what persuaded him to build his hospital in Gurgaon.

His answers were frank and brief. He said that in India we tend to copy the West, particularly in medicine—we had totally lost our ability to do any original thinking and meaningful research in medicine. All our best hospitals aspire to replicate hospitals in the West. So, he, who had been part of a very innovative team doing 'frontier bypass cardiac surgery' at New York University Hospital, earning 'obscene amounts of money' in the 1980s, decided to return to India to run the Escorts Cardiac Hospital in Delhi. This hospital eventually exchanged hands and he didn't like the new management, so he decided to build his own holistic hospital. Escorts was only about cardiac care, and he wished to build a hospital that would be the best in the country in all departments. He also wanted laboratories and equipment which would enable the doctors to do original research and a teaching hospital where future generations of doctors would get the best possible training.

The confluence of his desire and the fact that the then chief minister Om Prakash Chautala (yes, of the teachers' scam fame) was his patient and urged him to do something in Gurgaon made him think seriously of the possibility. The 43 acres set aside in this city for a medical complex were to develop several hospitals on 3–4 acres each. Trehan said he made a bid for them all, at a discounted price, and now, this is the first phase. All possible medical departments with the best practitioners in the field have been recruited. Dr Ambrish Mithal is the head of endocrinology, he said, and arguably among the best in the world.

I asked about the teaching section and the geriatric care that was also part of the package he had promised Chautala and were not even on the drawing board. 'That will happen; at the moment we have 1,200 speciality patient rooms, and just managing these with all the staff and coordination necessary is what we are doing now.' Yes, it is fervently wished that one day Medanta would fulfil its promise to be a great teaching hospital … and even treat the poor for free—although these are pledges that seem to be pies in the sky.

The massive blot on this marvellously rosy picture is that 75 per cent of Indians have no medical insurance or private means to pay for their medical needs. It is probably a steeper proportion in Gurgaon because of the swell of poor migrants from the rest of the country and Bangladesh and Nepal. The crying need for a two-tier structure of fees and days of the week for pro bono treatment must be enforced in all the fancy new medical facilities that have profited much by receiving discounts in the price of land and other perks, and possibly, non-profit tax status. Luckily, we still have some large-hearted missionaries. The old St Stephen's Hospital in Delhi now has a branch in Phase III, and it is relatively an affordable place for the poor to take their ailments.

It is in the field of health care where the exclusiveness of the 'Gurgaon model' is manifestly and bitterly exposed. If the government was remiss in fulfilling their part of the partnership in the departments of roads, sanitation, water supply and education, in the hospital deals the shoe is on the other foot and this time the private sector hasn't matched its actions with its words. As a result, those who are betrayed are the poorest sections of a city; the voiceless who dare not complain but suffer their illnesses stoically or fatally. If anything is offered at a discount or free it is usually the better connected who can avail of this, the poor Bihari or Bengali relies on home treatments, the cheaper clinics that treat outpatients, and the odd quack operating in the villages. The irony is darker when one thinks that it is the very construction workers who have toiled to build these medical palaces who cannot afford their services. Long before the government rights this wrong there will have to be yet another band of urban angels who will find it in their plans to heal the sick and look after the dying.

While they have the potential of being urban angels, Resident Welfare Associations (RWAs) often fall short of their job description. The name should be self-explanatory and RWAs exist in all the major colonies and condominium complexes, and came into existence because of the Constitution (Seventy-fourth Amendment) Act that provided guidelines intended for a 'devolution of powers to increase citizen participation in urban local bodies (ULB) who would take care of problems affecting the everyday life of the residential areas.[4] They were supposed to function in collaboration with the ward committees of the municipal corporations, but since that was Gurgaon's weak point, no such collaboration has occurred or been very successful when it has. They get a qualified B-grade in Gurgaon because the purpose for which they came into existence has not exactly been upheld. Only the elite colonies seem to have got these associations. The informal housing areas have little or no representation or recourse and are completely at the mercy of the landlords, as we saw in the case of migrants in Nathupur in Chapter Six. The residents of a colony or condominium complex are de facto members of its RWA and have the vote, but in the Qutab Enclave RWAs a few retired officers of DLF seem to have retained power and entrenched themselves as the presidents, secretaries and treasurers. They keep a record of the residents—property owners or tenants—in a certain block in a colony or in a condominium building. They even publish periodic directories; keep their residents informed, through electronic mail, flyers, meetings and occasional gatherings at festivals, about the happenings that might affect their lives.

The RWAs are empowered to fight these everyday battles, about contracts breached by builders, or the long electricity power cuts and shoddy substations run by the agencies responsible for the distribution of electric power. However, many of the RWAs seem disinclined to take up cudgels against the poor upkeep by the builders in many residential complexes. Maintenance is a political football—kicked around by DLF that claims that the MCG is responsible, and the latter, quite rightly insists that they cannot do so until the builders hand over the charge to them officially and relinquish their grasp on the maintenance funds so that it can maintain public amenities and make sure that all complaints about its infrastructural defects and security issues, particularly the safety of women, are thoroughly addressed. The Ansals, Unitech, and other big realty fish are no better; ITC seems to be the only exception. The water supply situation in the builder colonies is also rocky, and this keeps residents anxious and angry. Security companies are hired and fired by the builders without any consultation with the residents about the quality of their services. They have also taken on onerous tasks that, in fact, should be the responsibility of the municipal government: garbage disposal, recycling and composting, as we have seen in Garden Estate. The latter works best because it is run by residents and their maintenance money is collected and spent by them; it is perhaps the model RWA in Gurgaon, and has set a standard that ought to be emulated by the others.

Socially, the RWAs reflect the values of the majority of stakeholders, and I was not surprised to find that class discrimination was common. They also frame a set of rules and regulations for servants, who are patently non-owners and have no rights even if they reside in servants' quarters in their employers' flats. The RWAs are the gatekeepers who are determined to keep 'undesirables' from entering their premises, as many critics point out. What I found undeniably ugly was the prohibitions created against the very people who serve the residents, cook their food, make their beds, mind their children, walk their dogs, drive their cars, and keep the homes swept and orderly. I have quizzed maids and chauffeurs in more than a dozen condominium complexes that have separate lifts for staff, including employees of the buildings, like cleaners and gardeners; and in some complexes, maids and other domestic help were not allowed even to sit on park benches while they watched over children at play. This mentality is widespread, and while caste distinctions among the wealthy are considered trivial, the class divide is a growing chasm that swallows up the social progress modernity is expected to bring.

What is even more shocking is the gender discrimination. Single women and men are presumed to be 'trouble makers' or sexually 'loose' and can be denied their rights to have visitors. It is often a huge impediment for a young, single woman to rent a flat in one of these condominiums as the landlords, in tandem with the RWAs, simply observe the unwritten rule to refuse to rent to single women who wish to live alone. And a single male tenant (it is always easier for men to be accepted as tenants) is not allowed to have a single woman (relative or friend) stay in his rented apartment even as a temporary guest. This kind of primitive and intrusive social vigilantism has only worsened as the numbers of the affluent have grown. Perhaps these RWAs reflect the ingrained values of the society at large that continue to be disappointingly hierarchical, biased against women and the class that services their needs. Despite the seventy-year-long conceit that it is the biggest democracy in the world, the educated and affluent residents of some of the most modern buildings in the world seem to reject the idea of equality and egalitarian behaviour. RWAs enforce a uniform code of hierarchical family values—the very values that have made so many of the younger generation wish to flee their families and seek to live alone and far away only to find themselves in enclaves that share their parents' ideology.

All RWAs, however, are not created equal and some are more proactive than the others. Some do very little and some, as has lately been alleged, are totally corrupted by the builders putting in their own employees to head these organizations and work only in their interests. So they range from the angelic to the darkly demonic. An example from each end of that spectrum will suggest how RWAs can become urban angels, as the Garden Estate RWA has shown the way.

Gurgaon's straddling giant, DLF, has lost its benign image in Gurgaon as it has grown to become a very powerful corporation that pays less and less heed to the clauses in its own contracts and the needs of those who have enriched it. It has been embroiled in lawsuits, such as the one that accuses it of collusion with businessman Robert Vadra, son-in-law of Rajiv and Sonia Gandhi, and enriching him without any investment or effort of his own and reinforcing the subtle advantage it has always had by its connections with the Gandhi family. Other legal actions have been brought on by buyers for breach of contract and, increasingly, for the illicit control of RWAs through its own employees, as ordinary property holders want better representation of their needs. A case in point concerns the residents of Carlton Estates who revolted against their own RWA, allegedly dominated by an ex-employee of the builder, in one of DLF's many upscale condominium complexes.[5] The residents complain that the RWA has acted arbitrarily on many occasions against their interests, and the estate manager refused to divulge the balance sheet of the RWA's annual accounts. The manager, they claim, acted arbitrarily, and in his latest action, he ordered a change of all the lifts in the complex long before there was any evident need to do so: he unilaterally bought the new lifts from a company of his choice without advertising in two newspapers to invite tenders for the project, in contravention of the rules of management. He has now billed the residents of 468 apartments to recover the Rs 2.5 crore that these new lifts cost, with a penalty of Rs 250 a month on every apartment until the sum is recovered. The residents are irate, they want the RWA to be disbanded, but so far, by 7 September 2017, they had not been able to do so.

In 2011, DLF lost its well-publicized cases that the buyers of Park Place and The Belaire fought against it and it was fined Rs 630 crore for duping its buyers. A few years later, it had to make an out-of-court settlement with the buyers of its highly touted Magnolia and Aralia buildings for breach of contract by building some sixteen extra floors than envisaged in the plans. Perhaps the residents of The Carlton Estates need to go the same route.

The happy ending to a similar fractious experience of buyers against their builder was at the tony World Spa Condominium in 2012. In this case, the RWA took over the complex from Unitech, the builder, who controlled the common areas, and set up their own maintenance agency to make a profit on the maintenance fees paid by the residents. They also delayed the delivery of residences by several years and never paid attention to the maintenance of the building, while keeping a grip on the maintenance fees. This galvanized the residents to fight and win—all with considerable economic clout, technical expertise, and high standards, to challenge the builder.

They formed an RWA that battled the builder professionally and successfully. Then they hired a well-vetted management agency that answers to the RWA, for the upkeep of the premises. The vice-president of the RWA, Gautam Gulati, a highly competent and technically experienced resident, whom I met in April 2013, explained to me how carefully the maintenance agency was chosen and how the residents now are far more involved in the upkeep of their common areas. The accounts are strictly audited and every penny is spent in the interests of those who live there. This RWA, much like the one at Garden Estate, is the angel of its own gated community and keeps things in tip-top condition, and a happier lot of residents is hard to find. But even the best RWA is jealous of its own bounds and their sights end at their own walled enclaves; and the areas that lie outside their purview and in the fifty-two villages that Gurgaon now has enveloped remain neglected and are abused by those uncivil members of society who dispose of their debris and garbage in untended areas.

There are many more angels needed and certainly those with an inclusive vision. For now, one is grateful for all those who have made a huge difference to the quality of life in the city. There is no doubt that Gurgaon needs an overarching visionary who can give its many varied and disconnected lobes a semblance of unity and trust, someone who can be depended on to demand and use its revenues to make the city as liveable as it ought to be.

Where is that angel?

Epilogue

So, at the end of this long narrative, Gurgaon is this crazy quilt in mid-process of being plumped and stitched with parts that glitter and others that are torn and ragged. It is a place with infinite potential and daring entrepreneurship, utterly exuberant with twenty-first century elan and aspiration, a glowing dot on the global scene but with shadows that are even sharper because of the fierce lights. It has slums that reek and gender inequalities that hark back to the savage twentieth century, inequalities that seem set in stone and the faint scent of the hope that material prosperity will bring with it social change. Both these aspects of the city have been described, parsed and analysed. The flood of 28-29 July 2016 and the humongous traffic jam that made the front pages of every national newspaper severely derided the very place we think of as Millennium City. Sociologist Sanjay Srivastava, resident of one of its gated apartment complexes, in an article on 20 August 2016 on Scroll.in considered Gurgaon as an example of how a city should *not* urbanize, laying the blame squarely on the private developers and an indulgent state that paid no heed to their rapacious deeds, illustrated by a photo collage from Twitter. Having examined the private–public partnership in some detail in this present work and the role of civil society in trying to keep both the state and private developers honest, I only half-agree. HUDA and Town and Country Planning Department have not yielded any authority or funds even to the elected MCG, and have a stranglehold on the External Development Fund, now amounting to tens of thousands of crores, to which private developers have been contributing regularly from the maintenance they collect from residents. An honest use of this money for the purpose for which it is collected would make Gurgaon problem-free and a city to behold. Its problems, no more acute than what we get in south Delhi, or Navi Mumbai, for example, have, as I have shown, a real chance of being dealt with entirely with its current resources held by the state. The builders let their greed dictate the corners they cut but there is also no denying that the state's response to the 28-29 July 2016 traffic jam produced a typical response from the government: they transferred the chief of police to a comparable post elsewhere in Haryana. Any urban expert or concerned resident would have suggested an unleashing of the PWD workforce to create drains, put in the long overdue sewerage mains, to do all that was left undone or forgotten, to prevent such a deluge in the future. The broken promises and damaged public–private partnerships that are at the bottom of the unstable foundations of a global city must be revisited, as SURGE is doing, and this time we need probity and determination and citizen participation to husband its considerable resources. And, I would add, most of the everyday traffic jams in any part of India, including Gurgaon, are caused by bad, impatient, selfish drivers—and when a monsoon downpour is added to the mix of overloaded streets, you can blame no one but the police for not enforcing the rules of the road when they are so recklessly broken every single day.

The gestures thus far, like the transfer of officials or changing the name of the city from Gurgaon to Gurugram (with no difference in their provenance or the meaning of the two names) are, in fact, the risible acts of governance that must be replaced with serious remedial actions. We need a sensible, substantive and sincerely effective single authority vested in an empowered MCG that elects councillors that are motivated by the wish to see Gurgaon blossom into a world-class city. Exceptions like the amazing Messrs Khullar and Rajpal notwithstanding, it cannot be vested in temporary government officials, commissioners or deputy commissioners, who are indifferent to the future of Gurgaon and are eyeing their next posting. And if they should act responsibly and get a few files moving from the 'in' box to the 'out' box, it might be only a matter of a couple of years when a successor, indebted to an opposing political party, undoes that action. The MCG must collaborate with the NGOs and urban angels that are the lifeblood of Gurgaon's civil society, and have brought the city many amenities that it would have lacked. It is time to recognize their work and to create a synergy between citizens and officialdom to fulfil the promise of Gurgaon. It is devoutly hoped that in the next few years all the efforts now underway to address the unfinished business of Gurgaon will be executed to bring about a colossal and tangible transformation in the quality of life in the city. The destiny of Gurgaon is in the hands of its inspired and energetic citizen leaders, increasingly more socially aware corporate leaders, and politicians and bureaucrats who have a mountain of unused resources, who can together shape the future of this young and vibrant city.

This is a historic opportunity to create, correct and retrofit the 'Gurgaon Model' that is inclusive, honest, efficient, and accountable, and that will become the blueprint for future cities in India. World-class cities are not built in a tearing rush or on plans drawn in the musty offices of town planners still joined at the hip to colonial policies, and of private builders, whose imperatives are neither functionality nor beauty but self-enrichment. Inarguably, the best global cities have emerged organically and slowly over centuries. The rush to judgement on Gurgaon is embarrassingly premature and ahistorical because the present-day city is fledgling and growing. It is worthwhile to remember that the adage 'Rome was not built in a day' was a French proverb coined in AD 1190, to upbraid the impatience of those who thought Paris was poorly developed and did not understand the fact that a vast and complicated project as a city takes a long time to consummate. Imperfect as it is now, should we reserve judgement for another decade?

Notes

One: The Obscure Millennia

1. The historical sections of every gazetteer of Gurgaon district appear to reiterate verbatim from the previous one. See, for example, *Punjab District Gazetteer, Volume IVA, Gurgaon District,* Lahore: Civil and Military Gazette Press, 1910, p. 19.
2. Shail Mayaram, *Resisting Regimes: Myth, Memory and the Shaping of a Muslim Identity,* Delhi: Oxford University Press, 1997, pp. 27–30.
3. My summary is based mostly on an engaging and meticulously researched account of Begum Samru and her doings in Michael H. Fisher, *The Inordinately Strange Life of Dyce Sombre,* New York: Columbia University Press, 2010, pp. 13–32.
4. I have a detailed discussion of colonial urbanization in my *The Making of Colonial Lucknow 1856-77,* Princeton: Princeton University Press, 1984; Princeton Heritage Library Collection, 2015.
5. Gazetteer 1910: p. 13.
6. Veena Talwar Oldenburg, *Dowry Murder: The Imperial Origins of a Cultural Crime,* New York; Oxford University Press, 2002, pp. 154–60.

I have discussed the serious ill effects on the canal colonies of East and West Punjab; this information is taken from there.

7. Clive Dewey, *Anglo-Indian Attitudes: The Mind of the Civil Service*, London: The Hambledon Press, 1993, pp. 63–67. I have seen the original sources but have abstracted my information from his summary.

8. *Gazetteer of Gurgaon District*, 1910, p. 101. The following information is extracted from that and the Gurgaon Settlement Report and Clive Dewey, *Anglo-Indian Attitudes: The Mind of the Civil Service*, London: The Hambledon Press, 1993, pp. 63–67.

9. A summary of the pertinent literature on colonial irrigations systems in the semi-arid areas of UP and Punjab is found in Rohan D'Souza's 'Water in British India: The Making of a Colonial Hydrology', in *History Compass*, Vol. 4, No. 4, 2006, pp. 621-28. I have also discussed some of these effects on Gurgaon District in Oldenburg, *Dowry Murder*, Chapter 4.

10. There is a vast literature on the Rebellion and Mutiny of 1857, so I will not elaborate on it here since it remains tangential to the path that Gurgaon village took on its journey to becoming a city.

11. For a more detailed discussion of the revenue system and its economic and gender consequences in Punjab in general and Gurgaon district in particular, please see Veena Talwar Oldenburg, *Dowry Murder*, Chapters 4 and 5. I am keeping this narrative closely trimmed to the effects on the Gurgaon region. This is a simplified and brief account.

12. For more detailed information see, *Gazetteer of Gurgaon District*, 1910, pp. 100–04.

13. Ibid.

Two: A New Wind (God) Stirs the Town

1. The K.P. Singh saga is retold in the next chapter. I have abstracted the convoluted tale of Maruti from several sources: 1. Uma Vasudevan's interview with Sanjay Gandhi in *Surge*, January–February 1976; 2. My interviews with now-retired Maruti Suzuki executives, especially Vijay Mathur, and Haryana cadre IAS officers, especially S. Yakoob Quraishi and Deepa Singh who served during this period; 3. Vinod Mehta's frankly courageous biography, *The Sanjay Story*, New Delhi:

HarperCollins, 2012, originally published by Jaico, 1978; 4. The officially commissioned inquiry by Justice Alak Chandra Gupta, *Report of the Commission of Inquiry on Maruti Affairs*. 2 Vols, New Delhi, 31 May 1979. This is the most rigorous and exhaustive account of the Maruti affair that I believe exists. A second volume containing Appendices, has the entire collection of the original documents and pertinent correspondence, minutes of meetings, etc., that were used to construct the report. All these sources are cited in the text, where necessary, in parentheses.

2. Mehta 2012: 45.
3. Ibid.: 65.
4. Gupta 1979: 4.
5. Ibid.: 16.
6. Reported to me in a joint interview on 8 January 2016 with two retired IAS officers of the Haryana cadre who served under Bansi Lal and worked closely with him. They wished to remain anonymous.
7. Gupta 1979: 26-27.
8. Ibid.: 31.
9. Ibid. 29.
10. Ibid.: 30.
11. Ibid.: 34.
12. Ibid.: 34.
13. Ibid.: 36.
14. Mehta 2012: 60–92.
15. Ibid.: 76–77.
16. Ibid.: 77.
17. Ibid.
18. Ibid.: 77–78.
19. Ibid.: 87.
20. Ibid.: 89.
21. For details see, *The Wire*, 19 March 2017.
22. A detailed documentary film of the unrest at the Maruti factory in Mansear is available at https://scroll.in/article/731388/a-new-documentary-brings-the-maruti-struggle-alive-through-the-stories-of-its-arrested-workers.

Three: Building Gurgaon: From Fallow Fields to Gold Mine

1. Shruti Rajagopalan and Alexander Tabarrok, 'Lessons from Gurgaon, India's Private City', George Mason University, Department of Economics, Working Paper, No. 14-32, 24 October 2014.
2. This section is drawn from various interviews with the living owners of the lands sold to builders. K.P. Singh's autobiography, as told at length by him to Ramesh Menon and Raman Swamy (*Whatever the Odds: The Incredible Story Behind DLF*). New Delhi: HarperCollins, 2011 is another rich source. Recognizing that many autobiographies include significant amounts of fiction too, I have taken care to verify the information offered in this book from newspaper accounts and interviews with knowledgeable associates of KPS who wished to remain anonymous.
3. Menon and Swamy, 2011: 186–87.
4. Names changed to respect their privacy. At their home in ITC's architecturally sophisticated gated complex, The Laburnum, on 17 May 2014.
5. Praveen Donthi, 'How A Group Of Home Buyers In Gurgaon Tamed DLF', *Caravan* magazine, January 2014.

Four: Glimpses of Grungy Gurgaon

1. *The Times of India,* Gurgaon City Section, 20 December 2015.
2. There are reports in the print media, and the incident was also covered by the TV channel NDTV among others. Private witnesses made videotapes of the incident with their cellphones and two of them were submitted as evidence to support Nisha Singh who arrived at the scene after the violence was in full force. A person who was standing beside her made a video of her appearance from start to the point when she was arrested. She is shown to be standing well behind even the phalanx of police who were beating up men, women, children and she took a video of the police brutality. Her phone was snatched by the police. See http://www.youtube.com/watch?v=pudaFiz_okc
3. John Harris, 'Antinomies of Empowerment: Observations on Civil Society, Politics and Urban Governance in India', *Economic and Political Weekly*, Vol. 42, No. 26, 2007.

4. Praveen Donthi, 'The Road to Gurgaon: How the brokers of land and power built the Millennium City', *Caravan* magazine, January 2014.

5. There is a huge amount literature on the various systems of municipal government, costs and benefits of having a 'strong mayor' system, but this is not the place to go into it. Unfortunately, most people here are comfortable with the idea that elected councillors should confine themselves to 'making policy' (if not passing laws), and allowing the 'professionals' (i.e., bureaucrats) to implement programmes and also set the rules of the programmes. That means that too many of the elite perceive the councillors' role of dealing with day-to-day problems as 'interfering' in administration. I can certainly understand Nisha Singh's frustration, as a knowledgeable 'doer' and councillor in a toothless MCG. On the other hand, Delhi hastily demolishes huge bastis and clears its streets of beggars when some big international sporting meet is imminent in the city; its governance is as flawed as the next city's and is definitely contributing to the gigantic urban crisis.

6. John Harris, 'Antinomies of Empowerment'. The author has written this influential piece on the emergence of the 'consumer citizen' and it should be widely read by those in power.

Five: The Cradle of Corporations

1. My perspective is historical and I have emphasized the collusion of the government and private industry as the key to understanding the development of Gurgaon. For a comparative economic analysis of these two cities see Bibek Debroy and Laveesh Bhandari, 'Gurgaon and Faridabad: An Exercise in Contrasts', Standford: CDDRL Working Paper No. 101, September 2009. Gurcharan Das's recent book, *India Grows at Night,* Gurgaon: Penguin, 2012, points to the failure of and absence of government regulations in Gurgaon that enabled it 'to grow at night when the government slept'.

2. Jack Welch with John A. Byrne, *Jack: Straight From the Gut*, New York: Warner Business Books, 2001; and K.P. Singh's previously cited *Whatever the Odds* written a decade later in 2011.

3. Interview with Pramod Bhasin, vice chairman emeritus of Genpact on 21 May 2013. What follows about Genpact, unless otherwise attributed, is abstracted from that interview which lasted three hours and seventeen

minutes and was done in his former office now occupied by N.V. Tyagarajan who is the current CEO of the company.

4. The information on Raman Roy was taken from the website: http://www. nasscom.in/raman-roy-chairman-md-quatrro-global-services-pvt-ltd (accessed on 10 June 2016)

5. Interview with Pramod Bhasin on 21 May 2013.

6. I have taken the liberty of conflating the responses of several call centre and BPO employees to create a sense of what I found after many separate casual interviews with several workers whom I met in restaurants from 2012 to 2017 in Cyber Hub at different points. Saumya Malhotra also contributed material gathered in the Beverly Park condominium.

7. Shilpi Arora, 'Bharat BPOs', cover story in *Friday Gurgaon*, 1–8 November 2012.

8. This discussion and what follows is taken from my *Dowry Murder: The Imperial Origins of a Cultural Crime*, New York: Oxford University Press, 2002, pp. 215–16, and from the pamphlet put out by the hospitality industry, 'The Indian Liquor Industry Prohibition Story: The Politics of Liquor', in 1998. The best article on the subject of prohibiton is David Hardiman's, 'From Custom to Crime: The Politics of Drinking in Colonial South Gujarat', in Ranajit Guha (ed.), *Subaltern Studies*, IV, Delhi: Oxford University Press, 1985, pp. 165–228. I have also conducted interviews with two former liquor vendors, who wished to remain anonymous since they are planning to bid again for the vends next year.

9. Ibid.

10. www.icmrindia.org/free%20resources/casestudies/The%20Indian%20 Liquor%20Industry%20Prohibition%20Story.htm

Six: Nathupur: The Village on Steroids

1. Ajay K. Mehra, 'Urban Villages of Delhi', in Evelin Hurst and Michael Mann (eds.), *Urbanization and Governance in India*, Delhi: Manohar, 2005, pp. 279–310.

2. To respect their privacy and their wishes, I have given pseudonyms and blurred identities of the Nathupur village residents I interviewed in depth. I met Manoj about twice a week or more, so I have not given dates of these casual encounters and the gist of what he said is also contracted

into a few pertinent sentences. Kohinoor and her family have their real names mentioned here.

3. The scholarly literature on urban villages and 'informal housing' in Gurgaon is scant at best. Mukta Naik, senior scholar at the Centre for Policy Research in Delhi, ably summarizes and gives us a very detailed picture of Nathupur's housing after detailed research in her very informative essay: 'Informal Renting Housing Typologies and Experiences of Low Income Migrant Renters in Gurgaon', *Environment and Urbanization, ASIA*, Vol 6 No. 2, September, 2015, pp. 154–75. This should be required reading for those who are interested or involved in governing Gurgaon (members of the MCG, HUDA and state bureaucracy) to apprise themselves of Gurgaon's dark and hidden recesses where the majority of its labouring classes dwell. She also has a first-rate blog called 'Ramblingthecity' which would be of interest to Gurgaon residents.

Seven: Destination: Bourgeois Lifestyle

1. Sanjay Srivastava, *Entangled Urbanism*, New Delhi: Oxford University Press, 2017.
2. Aditya Arya and Indivar Kamtekar, *History in the Making: The Visual Archives of Kulwant Roy*, Noida: HarperCollins, 2010.
3. All this and more detailed information of this wonderful resource is available on the AIIS website.
4. Heritage Museum of Transport Website, http://www. heritagetransportmuseum.org/

Eight: Gurgaon's Increasingly Civil Society

1. I have used first names of persons after the first mention. This is with the approval of the people concerned. Pradip Krishen introduced me to Atal and Swanzal and Latika via e-mail in 2013 and he shared my concept and outline of this book with them which was indeed an enormous help in getting me connected with knowledgeable citizen activists in Gurgaon.
2. My account is a composite of the information gleaned from interviews with the I Am Gurgaon team, and Pradip Krishen, Vijay Dhasmana

and the article by Shirin Mann, 'One with the City', in *Friday Gurgaon*, 14 October 2011. My husband Philip Oldenburg and I have also walked in the park regularly in the mornings for many years even before it officially became a park and observed the changes as a native forest was replanted.

3. The national news media had a field day with this story. Shouting matches on NDTV and other news channels were heard being broadcast in prime time. All the national dailies, especially *The Indian Express*, *The Hindu* and *The Times of India*, which I read in detail, had in-depth reportage of the scam with details of Om Prakash Chautala's crime-ridden career. *The Indian Express* of 22 January 2013 has as full an account by Mukesh Bhardwaj reporting from Chandigarh, the state capital. I have summarized my extensive reading of the subject here.

4. A thorough study and critique of seventeen RWAs in seven cities was undertaken by *Participatory Research in Asia* or PRIA. Available at https://www.slideshare.net/PRIAIndia/resident-welfare-associations-in-india-a-promise-belied-pria-publication and published as an occasional paper entitled 'Resident Welfare Associations in India: A Promise Belied?' in January 2015. It is a detailed piece of research on a very large sample of RWAs and should be read by those who are interested in the functioning of these bodies in a wider context.

5. For a detailed report by Ravi Kavuur, see https://www.socialpost.news/national/look-how-dlf-and-rwa-are-cheating-their-residents/

Index

295

Acknowledgements

When I began envisioning the writing of a holistic account of Gurgaon, all the way from its rustic origins through two lacklustre millennia until it became a forgettable district HQ, to the last three decades of development when it morphed into an unruly and audacious city, there were not many who cheered me on.

The naysayers (chiefly my colleagues and friends from Delhi and Lucknow) were hard to overcome. In their view, Gurgaon was clearly neither an exciting topic or place—it was just an extended fringe of Delhi with little to recommend it. They perversely braced my conviction that Gurgaon had many stories to be told and a new generation of listeners, not jaded by sojourns in famous old cities, existed and were curious about this new world they'd come to inhabit.

By the end of the first decade of the new millennium, a very arresting urban drama was playing out on an ever-enlarging stage of Gurgaon and its surrounding villages, and it came to embrace the title, Millennium City. In 1984, my spouse and I had already laid claim to a tiny plot of land in an up and coming colony, Qutab Enclave, intermittently lived through two decades of enormous changes, had dug up information about Gurgaon and its villages in an archival molehill in London and in Patiala, and were sitting on a stack of historical notes.

Real estate brokers would periodically ring or send postcards asking if I wanted to sell the plot, and I noticed in the rising prices they offered each year for the next decade, that something serious was stirring there, out in the boondocks. The inducement that our plot in Gurgaon in 1992 would buy a capacious marble and glass flat in a south Delhi colony was not acceptable because the sellers demanded more than 40 per cent of the value in cash (read 'black money') and would only give a dubious document as a putative title to the new property; and we were determined not to encourage this dishonest practice. This was also the germ from which this book grew.

By 2010, the imperative to write a history of Gurgaon was fully grown. I sketched a book outline in 2011 and I am grateful that my friend and chairperson, Cynthia Whittaker, in the history department at Baruch College of the City University of New York took it up with the powers-that-be in academia and soon, in 2012-13, I had an academic year's paid leave to explore this.

Stanley Buder, my urban history colleague and friend, who gave me backstories of various New York neighbourhoods, encouraged me to tackle the project. I sent a detailed outline of this book's chapters, already vetted by my scholar-spouse, Philip, to my friend Pradip Krishen who was exploring the arboreal landscape of Delhi, for comment. He thought this was a worthwhile project and sent this on to socially aware residents of Gurgaon whom he had recently met. Two of them were the architects Atal Kapur and Swanzal Kak Kapur, and the third was Latika Thukral, a former banker who, with Swanzal, co-founded the NGO I Am Gurgaon. We finally met in February 2013 and they enthusiastically endorsed my project, and assured me that such a volume was desperately needed; there was no other. Atal and Swanzal promised any help I would need with maps, dealings with government departments for plans and projects underway, and speak about their involvement—and struggle—to create the Aravalli Biodiversity Park. I am thankful that they were always happy to hear me out and give me advice, even when Atal was battling a lethal cancer. He tragically passed away in 2015.

Latika, with her boundless energy and zeal for the project, gave unstintingly and generously of her time and shared her various invaluable connections in the rapidly growing corporate world and some important community leaders of the civil society in Gurgaon. For a total of thirteen months between 2013–16, she made appointments for me to meet CEOs of several companies, and often even accompanied me for the interviews in a city of unchartered and unmarked streets. Without her help the chapter on Gurgaon's corporations would have lacked depth. Whenever I drove by myself, I often called her—lost and bewildered on the tangle of new roads and buildings—my inner compass jammed and mental landmarks wiped out. I sent her every chapter of the book as I wrote it and she was encouraging and supportive in every way. I thank her from the bottom of my heart for her invaluable help and friendship and I hope she will not think of it as wasted time when this book actually appears.

What enabled the writing of this book was my timely selection for the Nehru-Fulbright Senior Fellowship for Academic and Professional Excellence—Research, 2015-16. This gave me leave without pay and funds to live nine months in Gurgaon with single-minded focus. Adam Grotsky, the director of Fulbright, with his encouragement and hospitality and the obliging and stupendous staff at Fulbright House eased the journey tremendously. I was determined to finish the book before my term ended in August 2016. And this I did. For all this, I offer my boundless gratitude.

I was now contemplating to send off the manuscript to a reputable publishing house that did trade books. A pivotal person in my search was Arvind Hoon, the gifted photographer—a few of his photographs appear among the insert pages of this book—who happens to be my cousin's son. He arranged an immediate phone conversation with Ananth Padmanabhan, CEO at HarperCollins India. A brief and productive chat followed and by February 2017, the book was under contract under the aegis of publisher Krishan Chopra. After a brief lull, in March 2018, Arcopol Chaudhuri was appointed as the copy editor and things got moving again. He was accompanied by S.K. Ray Chaudhuri, the proofreader, and together, they did a careful job of ensuring the text was fit to publish.

As is his wont, my spouse, Philip Oldenburg, read every chapter and gave valuable editorial and substantive suggestions. He also peppered my inbox with emails attaching newspaper reports on happeneings in Gurgaon, many that I would have otherwise missed. Philip even dug up some valuable old documents about the Maruti saga of the 1970s from his personal collection on political events of import, which helped me flesh out the seminal chapter on the industrial origins of Gurgaon. Philip took up the cudgels once more when the typeset proofs arrived and did the final copyediting that I could not have done with macular degeneration making reading a great challenge. My gratitude and love is boundless.

Aman Nath of Neemrana Hotels provided me the irrefutable proof of my argument that Gurgaon was planned as a colony rather than as a city by DLF. I am grateful for his friendship and the trouble he took to dig this up from his archive and it is now the first image in the photo insert section in this book.

Sunil Sethi, with his astonishing mental rolodex, linked me to several key people who have enriched this text.

Golak, friend, artist, architect and fine chef, produced suggestive drawings which now adorn the beginnings of all the chapters and add to the playfulness of the contents of this book.

Vijay Dhasmana made the Aravalli Biodiversity Park a destination for nature lovers and contributed the photographs of the park that are reproduced in this volume.

Aditya Arya made it possible to have fourteen artistic photographs that capture the city being built up until 2013. These originally belong to an exhibition he curated called 'Millennium Dreams' in 2013 where I first met the dazzling young photographers that made Gurgaon their subject under the aegis of the Neel Dongre Awards for Excellence in Photography. I am especially thankful that Vaibhav Bhardwaj, Manoj Bharti Gupta, Arvind Hoon, Saumya Khandelwal, Natisha Mallick, Ajay Sood and Monica Tiwari roamed the city with cameras fired by their interesting perspectives and fertile imaginations to give us a pictorial feast.

Sanjay Srivastava's enlightening and provocative articles on Gurgaon stimulated lively conversations on our shared interests.

Atul Sobti, the editor and underwriter of *Friday Gurgaon* graciously supplied me with back issues of his very interesting weekly paper. My deepest regret is that *Friday Gurgaon* did not become *the* city paper which Gurgaon still desperately needs.

On the domestic front, my housekeeper Kohinoor not only kept our home clean but also accompanied me on my research forays in the innards of Nathupur.

Our daytime guard Mintoo Kumar and his nose for crime kept me informed and regaled with the quotidian skirmishes of life in the service class of Gurgaon.

Ramesh Paneru, our part-time cook kept me out of the kitchen and at my computer; his tasty meals made this possible. He would often bring along his two-year-old, Arjun, who provided some necessary laughs and pranks that revived my spirits.

To all of them, I'm thankful and grateful for their support.